UNITED NATIONS UNIVERSITY
STUDIES ON PEACE AND REGIONAL SECURITY

AFRICA

PERSPECTIVES ON PEACE & DEVELOPMENT

UNITED NATIONS UNIVERSITY
STUDIES ON PEACE AND REGIONAL SECURITY

The United Nations University project on Peace and Regional Security was a special study carried out under the programme area on Peace and Global Transformation. Focusing on the Third World and Europe, the project attempted to analyse the trade-offs between the conflicting conditions in these regions of vulnerability and security and competition and solidarity. Five regional seminars were held in Africa, Asia, Europe, Latin America, and Oceania and the Pacific on themes related to conflicts over natural resources and security and human rights in determining global, regional, and national development. The results of these studies are part of the United Nations University's contribution to the United Nations International Year of Peace.

Project Co-ordinator: Janusz W. Golebiowski

UNITED NATIONS UNIVERSITY
STUDIES ON PEACE AND REGIONAL SECURITY

AFRICA
PERSPECTIVES ON PEACE
& DEVELOPMENT

EDITED BY EMMANUEL HANSEN

The United Nations University

Zed Books Ltd.
London and New Jersey

Africa: Perspectives on Peace and Development was first
published in 1987 by:

Zed Books Ltd., 57 Caledonian Road, London N1 9BU,
United Kingdom and 171 First Avenue, Atlantic Highlands,
New Jersey 07716, USA

and

The United Nations University, Toho Seimei Building,
15-1 Shibuya 2-chome, Shibuya-ku, Tokyo 150, Japan.

Cover design by Adrian Yeeles
Printed by Biddles of Guildford

British Library Cataloguing in Publication Data

Africa : perspectives on peace and
development.—(The United Nations
University studies in peace and regional
security).
1. Peace—Study and teaching—Africa
2. Peace—Research—Africa
I. Hansen, Emmanuel II. Series
327.1′72′096   JX1904.5

ISBN 0-86232-702-4
ISBN 0-86232-703-2 Pbk

Contents

Tables

Preface

Peace and security are matters of life and death for the whole of humanity. The increasing danger of a nuclear holocaust is making the peoples of the world more and more conscious of the fact that peace and security cannot be left to the initiatives of the nuclear superpowers. This growing worldwide concern has been intensified by the fact that in a world where a "nuclear peace" prevailed, a great number of "conventional" local conflicts were devastating many of the world regions especially in the *periphery* of the world system, that is, the *Third World*. It was thus made more and more apparent that the different world regions had themselves to find the ways and means to guarantee their own peace and security, beyond the crisis management intervention of external powers within the framework of the nuclear balance of terror.

Such measures would have to be devised with a better knowledge of regional realities, not only military but also political, economic and socio-cultural. Such measures should also take full consideration of the specific values and interests of the nations and peoples concerned. This is why the UN University organized a series of regional seminars on peace and security in different world regions, in San Jose for Latin America (November 1984), Addis Ababa for Africa (January 1985), Tashkent for Asia (April 1985), Tatsmandorf, Austria, for Europe (May 1985) and Auckland, New Zealand, for the South Pacific (March 1986).

Each seminar called upon about twenty researchers of each region to prepare papers and revise them on the basis of the seminar discussions. The six volumes of this series have come from this process of regional dialogues. In view of the above-mentioned necessity to adopt a multidisciplinary approach to the complex regional realities, the problematic of regional peace and security has been approached from different angles: the impact of the global political and economic context on the regional conflict patterns, the interaction between conflict and maldevelopment, the process of militarization versus democratization, the issues of cultural identity, national integrity and security, etc. etc.

In different regions, different conflict configurations, as well as political, economic and socio-cultural background factors, had to be taken into consideration, so that the themes selected by each regional team of experts varied. The present series is composed of six books whose common features are twofold: they represent regional researchers' positions on their own regions' peace and security and they relate peace and security issues to broader regional realities. Thus the series presents a bottom-up perspective to international peace and security.

Made as a contribution of the UN University to the UN International Year of Peace, the series of regional seminars is expected to encourage the development of research on regional peace and security. The readers of this book are invited to consult also the others in this series. The comparison of the different regional realities is expected to provide readers food for thought in reflecting on their own regions in a comparative perspective. We hope that they will find in this comparison a new insight in approaching the global peace and security issues of today.

Kinhide Mushakoji
Vice-Rector,
The United Nations University.

The Editor of this volume, Dr Emmanuel Hansen, organised the African regional seminar on Peace and Regional Security in the framework of the United Nations University Programme on Peace and Global Transformation and its Programme on African Regional Perspectives, with the support of the Third World Forum.

1. Introduction

by Emmanuel Hansen

Concept of the Peace Problematic

Some people are apt to be startled or at the least raise eyebrows at the mention of an African perspective on peace. Peace, it is claimed, is a universal desideratum. This is not a contestable position. How then can we begin to particularize it by talking of an African perspective? How legitimate is it to talk of European peace or Asian peace? To conceptualize peace in this narrow way is manifestly absurd. In addition to the theoretical problems it raises it would seem to have undesirable consequences for peace scholarship as well as for the quest for peace and the peace movement. It compartmentalizes peace studies into narrow, chauvinistic and national or local concerns and fragments the peace initiative at a time when the need for unity is greater than ever. Although the state systems of most countries of the world claim that peace is desirable, the concept of peace, the obstacles to peace, what peace actually is and how it can be realized are issues on which there is no agreement. What is designated here as the African perspective is the consensus of a majority of African scholars on the peace problematic.

To recognize that there are or could be different perspectives on the peace question is not to indulge in irresponsible relativism or to take refuge in philosophical anarchism of the type 'all systems are fine; it all depends on your point of view'. While we seek to understand other perspectives which may be different from ours, we do not hold the position that all perspectives are equally defensible. The perspective which a group brings to the peace problematic depends on its history and material conditions as well as the position of the group within the power structure of the national or international system. If, as we have argued, certain perspectives are less defensible than others, then the question arises as to what yardstick we use to decide which positions are defensible and which are not. This should not be a difficult issue. For us the perspective on the peace problematic which we can defend and justify is that which makes it possible for the majority of the people on this planet to enjoy physical security, a modicum of material prosperity, the satisfaction of the basic needs of human existence, emotional well-being, political efficacy and psychic harmony. This we believe will enable the mass of men and women in the world to develop their potentialities and consequently

1

themselves as full and autonomous human-beings; it will enable them to develop not as means to other ends but as ends in themselves. Willy Brandt captured the essence of this when he declared in a recent lecture that

> the vast majority of those who carry responsibility for their people and nations ... are full of goodwill and ... intend to solve the problems and let our world reach a state of security and well being. A state in which according to the capabilities of all its members mankind could overcome oppressive misery and develop its immense resources.[1]

We are aware that many people or nations will not find it difficult to accept this general statement. The problem arises when we seek to attach definite meanings to these terms and when we seek to put these ideals into practice. We shall come to this later on. But we need to stress that it is this collective consensus shared by the large community of African scholars on the peace problematic that we call the African perspective. If we have taken so much space to establish and clarify this point, it is because of two things. We recognize that the peace problematic is not unproblematic even at the conceptual level; and we need to emphasize the difference between our own perspective and what I would call, for the want of a better term, the 'establishment perspective'.

Any African scholar who has attended any large gathering of peace workers, peace researchers and peace activists or followed the activities of these people will appreciate the distinction we are trying to make and will no doubt not fail to notice certain differences in people's perceptions.[2] It is important to notice these differences, not for the purpose of scoring political or intellectual points, but to lay the basis for a meaningful intellectual confrontation and a common struggle for world peace. We find that in certain crucial matters such as the concept of peace, the nature of the peace problematic and the ways to seek peace our position tends to crystallize around certain ideas and themes and differs from mainstream European thought or the views held by the leaders of European states. Nowhere was this more amply demonstrated than at the recent seminar of African scholars called by the UN University to discuss peace, development and regional security in Africa as part of a series of regional seminars (its contribution to the United Nations International Year of Peace). The seminar was attended by a representative group of African scholars. It is therefore right and proper to call the ideas which crystallized at the seminar the African perspective. The papers which make up the volume were all, with the exception of one, presented and discussed at the seminar. The present effort is limited to attempting a synthesis which captures the essence of the peace and development problematic as perceived and conceptualized by this representative community of African scholars who gathered in Addis Ababa for the seminar in January 1985.

We stated at the beginning that peace is regarded as a universal desideratum. Even people who wage wars claim they do so to maintain the peace. It was not only the ancient Romans who saw things in this way. It might have been hoped that over the years humanity would have made some progress towards the goal of peace. But it is not so. To declare or accept that peace is a universal desideratum does make it unproblematic. On the contrary it is clear that if everyone is for peace then different people will have different perceptions of what it is and what its purpose is. We can then legitimately ask the question, what kind of peace? What kind of peace was Reagan defending when he justified his invasion of the tiny island of Grenada in 1984? Or when he sent his war planes to attack Libya in April 1986? It is comforting to note that not all Americans went along with his reasoning. But it is also frightening to recall the number who swung to his support and supported the invasion in the name of God and country. What kind of peace was Reagan after? Was it the peace of the strong and the powerful or of the rich, high and mighty to do as they please, unrestrained by law, custom, conscience or international morality? Was it the peace of a superpower to do as and what it pleases, to pursue its own interests without regard to the interests, security and concern of other nations which appear to be weak? It is clear that for Reagan peace means keeping the 'communists' out of areas of US interests; he is prepared to do anything, including using armed force, to accomplish this irrespective of what the people of the areas may feel.

In this connection, even Botha, the leading white supremacist and leader of apartheid South Africa, says he is for peace. We believe him. But what does he mean by peace? For him peace means the acceptance of the current status quo. For Botha peace in South Africa can only be maintained if blacks and white are rigidly segregated in all aspects of their lives and if blacks occupy subordinate positions in all walks of life. Anything else would create friction which would lead to conflict. He does not seem to recognize or admit that the present structure is the basis of much tension and conflict not only in South Africa itself but in the whole sub-region. Looked at it in this way it is clear that the sort of peace which Botha wants is not the same as that demanded by the majority of the people of South Africa. Nor can we say that Botha's perspective on peace is as defensible as that of the mass of the population in South Africa. Botha says he wants peace; but he wants peace only to continue to oppress the blacks of South Africa. Most people want peace so that they can develop their potentialities fully as human-beings and attain psychic well-being. Botha's 'peace' is dialectically contradictory to the people's peace.

The example of South Africa is one of the more grotesque; but it illustrates the point we wish to make. The question of peace cannot be separated from the question of the struggle for social and democratic rights and for human dignity. In other words the peace problematic is not unrelated to the issue of extant social and political conditions and the distribution of power. The consequence of this for policy options will become clear as we go on. But this point relates to two central issues of the peace problematic to which we need to address ourselves: peace for whom and peace for what? It is only by probing such issues that we can get to the heart of the matter and set out the conditions which would be necessary for a lasting and meaningful peace. Any peace problematic which does not respond to this is not facing the reality of the situation.

It is easily conceded that wars are fought not only for the defence of a given territory but also for the maintenance of a certain moral and social order. But it is right and proper to ask what values and ideals the social order we claim to be fighting for upholds and maintains.

The peace question has to be seen in two aspects: peace should be conceptualized and perceived not only in the negative sense of minimizing or resolving conflict but also in the positive sense of creating material conditions which provide for the mass of the people a certain minimum condition of security, economic welfare, political efficacy and psychic well-being.[3] The two positions are intimately related not only for the purpose of analysis or as an intellectual exercise but as the only meaningful and fruitful way to face the peace problematic and define the practical conditions for societal peace and development. For us in Africa the minimalist condition of peace conceptualized as merely the removal, resolution or as it is sometimes less defensibly called, management of conflict, which leaves the social and material conditions which cause tension and lead to conflict intact, is unacceptable. It is unacceptable at both the national and the international level. It is this thinking which makes us say that, important though the anti-apartheid struggle is (and its removal would remove a major cause of conflict not only in South Africa itself but in the Southern Africa sub-region as a whole), its removal will meet only the minimum conditions for the promotion of peace in the sub-region. For a durable and lasting peace it will be necessary to develop mechanisms to ensure that the broad mass of the people achieve a measure of material and psychic well-being and control over the political processes which guide and order their lives. From this point of view it should be obvious why we in Africa perceive programmes of food security as more relevant to our immediate peace problematic than the star wars programme of President Reagan.

This brings us to a separate but related question. This year (1985) Europe has been celebrating forty years of peace. This, indeed, is a noble and commendable achievement and justly deserves to be celebrated. Such a long period of uninterrupted peace in one area of the globe noted for violent conflicts, and which has the greatest concentration of the most deadly instruments of destruction, is a rare occurrence in recorded history. But two observations need to be made. In nearly all the celebrations, the accompanying symbols and fanfare were symbols and accoutrements of war, not of peace. The imagery invoked was that of strength, not peace. There is a thinking among the European states and among certain people who hold what I call the establishment view of peace that peace is the result of strength. This is based on the Hobbesian concept of man as a naturally selfish and aggressive animal to be restrained only by the fear of death and terror. For some this is the only realistic view. It is a sad commentary on our evolution that although in science and technology we have devised techniques for solving problems which would have amazed Hobbes and those of his time, in the field of political and social relations we have not gone beyond his basic postulates. It could be argued that the focus on war which characterized the celebration of peace was meant to bring home to the present generation, especially those too young to know or remember, the full horrors of war and to allow those old enough to remember it to relive the horrifying experience. It was, however, strength, especially the strength of armaments, which was displayed and which was centre-stage.

This was underscored by statements made by some of the European leaders. Particularly instructive was that of Geoffrey Howe, the British Foreign Secretary, who declared that it was nuclear weapons which had kept the peace of Europe for forty years. President Reagan echoed the same sentiment. His insensitivity was amply demonstrated by his insistence on visiting Nazi war graves, an event which brought a justifiably sharp rebuke from Israel. To celebrate the peace of Europe by paying homage to the most dangerous protagonists of war the world has ever seen was an astonishing thing for a world leader with claims to desire world peace. If we have belaboured this point, it is to demonstrate an important flaw in what I call the establishment perspective on the peace problematic which sees minimalist conflict management as a sufficient condition, or the only sufficient condition, for peace. For Reagan it would appear that there is really no difference between the perpetrators of the most hideous crime against humanity and its victims. Both need to be remembered equally. Not even the most fervent advocates of the pluralist theory who make a fetish of maintaining a balance would defend such a position.

Three things follow from this viewpoint. In the first place, for Europe world peace is European peace. It is true that to have succeeded in maintaining peace in Europe is an important achievement. But commendable as this is, Europe is not the world: to be completely oblivious of the wars and conflicts, limited though they may have been in the rest of the world, for the mere reason that their existence did not disturb the peace of Europe, is to display an arrogance and insensitivity of the kind which can only undermine peace and collective security. At the moment there are many areas of conflict in Africa, Latin America, Asia and the Middle East. But these obviously did not enter into the calculations of the people who celebrated forty years of world peace because they do not seriously affect the peace of Europe. This leads us to accept the position advanced in two of the contributions in this volume to the effect that Europe and the United States export their conflicts to the Third World. This helps them to maintain some measure of limited domestic stability. If this is the case it is not surprising that the world powers show such astonishing insensitivity to conflict in the non-European and 'peripheral' areas of the world.

In addition to this concept of world peace as the peace of Europe, there is also a tendency, particularly among the nation states of Europe and United States, to make the minimalist concept of peace the maximalist position. It is interesting to note that not only the extant state systems but even certain well-meaning individuals and organizations concerned with peace conceptualize the peace problematic in this way.[4] The third aspect of the peace problematic which is closely identified with the European state system and also, we must regretfully say, with some peace groups and peace activists, is the concept

5

peace as nuclear peace. There is a certain thinking in the state systems of Europe and America and among the world powers generally that this is the kind of peace worth campaigning for. This is the kind of peace which world leaders such as Reagan and Gorbachev have in mind when they meet to talk about the arms race. It is a concept that sees nuclear weapons as the only threat to peace. It is a concept which regards peace as a balance of terror. To do this is to base the peace of the world on fear and mutual suspicion instead of mutual trust and cooperation. This, as we have already had occasion to point out, is no improvement on the Hobbesian position. The kind of approach which has characterized peace research in Europe and the United States is an illustration not only of the dominance of this perspective but of its persistence.[5] Although much work in peace research has now shifted from its earlier preoccupation with the arms conflict between East and West and has begun to tackle issues like the North-South relationship, the problem of creating stable political orders and the question of food security, this is more of a continental European viewpoint than a British or North American one.

Not only do the states of Europe and America entertain this concept of peace as the right and correct position; they insist on imposing this definition on the rest of us. We are not saying that the dangers of nuclear war should be underestimated. For the first time in history humanity has developed instruments of violence which have the potential to destroy our species several times over. But to regard this as the only problem is to seriously misrepresent the issue. From our point of view it is not so much nuclear weapons which pose a threat but the social systems which bring nuclear weapons into being and the kinds of struggle for control of resources which make nuclear weapons necessary. We appreciate that it is easier to get agreement on limiting nuclear weapons or to seek their abolition than to obtain a consensus on appropriate social and political systems; but this is a position which, if adopted, still leaves the victims of oppression where they are. We support, and we shall continue to support, efforts to destroy, limit and abolish the use of nuclear weapons. But we are also painfully aware that before nuclear weapons were invented we were dominated by Europeans through slavery, colonialism and now neo-colonialism. For us this is a painful reality. If all the nuclear weapons in the world were destroyed we would still be dominated until the social system which oppresses us and which gave rise to the creation of nuclear weapons were eliminated. So long as people are oppressed the basis of serious conflict exists.

It is this which makes us say that a perspective on the peace problematic which addresses itself only to the technical question of the instruments of violence without looking at the deeper structural issues such as the system of power, both at national and international levels, is not likely to achieve much. This is why we say that for us the destruction of nuclear weapons is only a minimalist condition for the attainment of peace. It is this establishment conception of peace which the African position rejects: a conception which sees peace as the peace of Europe, or merely as the absence or management of conflict or as nuclear peace unrelated to extant social and material conditions. The African perspective sees peace and development as intimately related: it sees peace not only as the resolution of conflict but as the transformation of extant social systems at both national and international levels. It is a concept which relates peace to the physical, social and existential needs of people.

To sum up: we stress that the position we take on the peace issue is to articulate, defend and make practical a peace problematic other than the one defined by the superpowers or controlled by the transnational corporations. It is a concept of peace which, though arising out of our particular historical circumstances, responds to the needs not just of our own people but of the mass of humanity. We need to strive for a peace which not only entails the peaceful resolution of conflicts or the removal of major conflict in the main theatres of Europe, but also ensures peace in all areas of the globe and responds to the developmental needs of people at both the national and international levels. We are not claiming that we hold a monopoly of these views. We are only saying that this perspective, which represents a consensus of the views of African scholars, underlies the papers presented in this volume. We are aware that certain individuals and certain peace organizations also hold such a position. What is remarkable in the African situation is that many of the participants at the seminar did not perceive or define themselves as peace researchers, nor did they formulate their intellectual concerns within the established frameworks and paradigms of peace research; but once confronted with the problem, they responded in a way that put them on the progressive side of peace research and peace initiative. For most African scholars there is no difference between the peace problematic and the development problematic. We are aware that even within the peace movement there are many individuals and peace organizations whose concept of peace is very close to that which we have characterized as the establishment perspective and which we insist should be rejected if the world is to attain any meaningful and lasting peace. To say this is not to condemn such peace movements but to state a historical fact. The perspective on peace we have outlined here informs our intellectual posture and political behaviour and is the concept of peace which we seek to put into practice; it is the concept of peace which informs the chapters and individual contributions which form this volume. The logical implications, as we shall see shortly, are clear.

Social and Political Context of the Peace Problematic: The Global Crisis

We are seeking to elucidate a peace perspective which, as we have seen above, runs counter to the position articulated and defended by the state systems of Europe and the United States and world powers generally. This in itself poses problems; not only do we not get support; we encounter serious opposition. What is more important is that we are seeking to put these ideals into practice at a moment in world history which is characterized by a severe crisis of global capitalism. This affects us in three ways. It reduces our capacity to confront the peace problematic; it enables the Western capitalist countries to increase their pressure on us and it weakens the determination and capacity of certain progressive countries to assist us.

In Africa the crisis has several features. At the physical level it is characterized by poor economic performance. Although it has now become customary for our leaders to blame this on the global crisis—and we should neither forget nor underestimate the impact of this on our economies—it should be noted that our problems predated the current crisis of global capitalism. The economic conditions in many African countries started to deteriorate in the 1970s and the present trends show even greater rates of decline. Although GDP grew at an average rate of 3.6% in the 1970s it has since fallen.[6] With population growing at the rate of 3% per year it was estimated that income per head in 1983 had fallen to about 4% below its 1970 figure.

Nowhere has the poor performance of our economies been more amply demonstrated than in the agricultural sector. Agricultural output has continued to fall. The drought of the last few years has not made things any better. Originally confined to the Sahelian areas it has now spread to many areas in Eastern, Western, Central and Southern Africa. It is now estimated that 36 countries are affected. The human dimensions of this are incalculable. In Ethiopia about a million people are reported to have died, and many more have perished in Burkina Faso, Sudan, Niger, Mali and Senegal. The drought has aggravated an already bad food and agricultural situation. The African region now produces only about 20% of its cereal requirements.[7] Per capita grain production in the 24 countries affected by the drought has been falling on average 20% per year since 1970. It is estimated that if this trend continues per capita production in 1988 will be the same as in the drought-stricken year of 1984, even if 1988 has normal weather.[8] It is true that the picture is not uniformly bad. Certain countries are worse off than others; but even the so-called 'strong economies' such as the Ivory Coast, Kenya and Malawi, often lauded by the World Bank, the IMF and donor agencies, are not doing so well.[9] Not only has agricultural production been declining, there is even a danger of a crisis of the entire agrarian system. To make matters worse there has been a virtual collapse of commmodity prices. In addition to declining exports the terms of trade have not been in favour of the primary producer. It has been estimated that between 1980 and 1982 the prices of non-oil commodities fell by 27% in current dollar terms.[10] This represented a loss of income of 1.2% of GDP for sub-Saharan African countries.

It is not only in agriculture that the story is bad. Industry has also been an abysmal failure. Much industrial capacity now lies idle and many of the early import-substitution industrialization efforts have foundered. The situation in West Africa is particularly grave. Here manufacturing declined by 6.8% in 1983; in East and Southern Africa it declined by 1.9%, and in sub-Saharan Africa as a whole it fell by 3.3% in the same year.[11] Relative to world manufacturing output Africa had a share of manufacturing value added of only 0.9% in 1980 and it does not look as if the figure is going to increase in the near future. [12] If these statistics tell a depressing story the human dimension is even worse. It is banal to say that something needs to be done to reverse this trend. It is estimated that child mortality in sub-Saharan Africa, which was 50% higher than the average for developing countries as a whole in the 1950s is now almost double the average. [13] In spite of massive imports in food and food aid it is estimated that about 20% of Africa's population eats less than the minimum needed to sustain good health. [14] With projected GDP of 2.8% per year and a population growth of 3.5% per year we should expect, all things being equal, a fall in per capita GDP of 0.7%. A recent World Bank report concludes, 'On this basis, real African incomes in 1995 will be so low that between 65 and 80% of the people will be living below the poverty line, compared with roughly 60% today.' [15] The situation is deteriorating.

Another aspect of Africa's current economic problem is what is commonly called the debt crisis. This has now emerged as one of the most serious burdens on Africa. Even the continent's 'strong economies' are not free from this. Even countries such as the Ivory Coast and Nigeria which benefited from the commodity price boom of the 1970s are facing serious problems in meeting their debt obligations. Africa is rapidly replicating the Latin American experience. Debt service repayments are due to rise sharply in the future thus making the situation even more grave. The World Bank report for 1984 comments,

> On the existing public and publicly guaranteed medium and long-term debt alone, they are due to rise from $4.1 billion in 1981 and $5. billion in 1982 to $9. billion in 1984, and an average of $11.6 billion a year in 1985-87. [16]

Africa's external medium- and long-term borrowings increased from $12.7 billion in 1972 to $99.7 billion in 1983, representing an average growth rate of 21.47% per year for the period. If we were to add undisbursed credits, short-term credits and 'military aid' (these figures exclude Libya and the lusophone countries of Africa) the figure would be even larger. [17] Such large external borrowings attract debt services which put a severe strain on the continent's economy. Nominal interest payments by African countries increased from $0.2 billion in 1972 to $4.9 billion in 1983, a rate of 33.41%. [18] Many of the new loans have merely gone into servicing debts and not into new investments or the rehabilitation of the economy. To fully appreciate the adverse effects of the debt crisis on the African economies it is necessary to quote *in extenso*.

> Another adverse impact of the debt crisis in Africa is the fact that when a debtor country accumulates arrears and/or announces intention to reschedule its debt, the flow of new resources declines due to erosion of the country's creditworthiness. The erosion in creditworthiness also leads to higher costs of borrowing, both explicit and implicit. Higher implicit costs are reflected, for example in higher margins on imports and in more stringent conditions for import payments. The decline in new inflows, particularly private inflows, has forced many debtor African countries to adopt contractionary measures in order

to generate surpluses to meet debt-service payments. These measures...have not only reduced economic activity but have also resulted in quite heavy social costs. [19]

These statistics tell a depressing story, but it is the unquantifiable human dimension which tells an even sadder one. Development economists argue endlessly about the causes of these problems—are they the consequence of internal policy failures or are they generated by the world economy? The mass of the people in Africa only know the effects as they impinge on their material and social lives. Although we made some impressive improvements in the period immediately following independence, particularly in the areas of education, sanitation and public health and transport and communication, on the whole, as the above statistics show, the performance of the post-colonial economies leave a lot to be desired.

We have also faced serious problems at the social and political level. At the present moment serious conflicts affect many of the sub-regions of the continent: Southern Africa, the Horn, Sudan and Chad, Eastern Africa, and the Western Sahara to mention only the most prominent ones. In addition to these sub-regional conflicts there are other no less serious conflicts at national and local levels. The sources of these conflicts are many. They can be manifested as ethnic or religious, the result of the claims of particular groups, or of conflict among the various fractions of the petty bourgeoisie which control the post-colonial state. Conflicts can arise in the process of nation-building itself. It is tricky to harmonize particular interests and claims with the urgent and persistent tasks of nation-building and we cannot always be sure that the necessary tensions can be handled in such a way that conflict can be avoided or minimized. In many countries in Africa we have not been able to work out effective and regular patterns of political succession and competing claimants often have recourse to the gun—with tragic consequences. This has undermined political stability and caused untold human suffering.

One effect of such an unsettled state of affairs is the rise of refugees. Africa now has an estimated five million. Twenty years ago there were less than half a million. One in every 200 Africans is a refugee. [20] (These figures do not include economic refugees or those who have been displaced within the borders of their own countries.) The depressing conditions of refugee existence, as well as its humiliation and demoralization, are too well-known to need repeating. In political terms the contemporary history of our continent has been marked by a steep increase in the rise of authoritarianism (not that it is a new phenomenon). This has been with us since the colonial period; but we have improved upon it instead of working for its elimination. Leaders who have come to power decrying the authoritarian rule of their predecessors have all too easily succumbed themselves. Of the 51 independent African countries nearly half of them are currently under military rule or have had at least one military government. Now a new brand of military regime is emerging on the political scene, practising a mixture of authoritarian populism and absolutism. The net effect is to push off the agenda the programmes for democratic rights and the aspirations of the mass of the people for democratic control of the political processes which order and guide their lives. We as intellectuals can argue and disagree among ourselves as to the cause and dimensions of these social and political pathologies; but we cannot deny their existence or the fact that they do not contribute to the improvement of the material conditions of the lives of our people. The only proof that we as intellectuals can offer of our commitment to the mass of the people is to come out with solutions. This implies taking a position dictated by praxis.

We have here outlined the nature of the African crisis and its manifestations. At the economic level we have drought and famine, the near collapse of the agrarian system and low productivity of both agricultural and industrial goods. The crisis has been intensified by the collapse of commodity prices and an increasing debt burden. At the social and political level it is characterized by conflicts and a rise in authoritarianism and military dictatorships and refugees. We argued that the global crisis enables Western capitalist countries to put more pressure on us and reduces the capacity of progressive countries to assist us. We shall now turn our attention to these questions.

One of the basic features of the global crisis in the West has been the problem of capital accumulation. Western governments have responded to the crisis with a combination of austerity measures, including the abandonment of welfare and the deliberate creation of unemployment. This is meant to increase the capital-labour ratio and consequently increase profits. The response from labour to these measures has been an intensification of the class struggle which has attracted further repression from states bent on reducing and disciplining labour. On the external level the Western capitalist countries have sought to deal with the developing countries in virtually the same way as they have tried to deal with labour. They have sought to do this through political repression and an increase in appropriation in order to discipline the workers of the developing countries. It is this which underlies their response to the demands made by the Third World for the creation of a New International Economic Order or the North-South dialogue or the demands which Third World countries have been making at various meetings of UNCTAD. These requests, minimal though they are, have all been ignored.[21] It would seem that both East and West share a basic consensus that the present international economic and power arrangements which militate so much against our development efforts, should be maintained. It is this which leads some to the conclusion that it would appear that the most relevant divide in the world today is not the so-called conflict between East and West but the contradiction between the North collectively and the South collectively. Of course, no one would be naive enough to deny the reality of the East-West confrontation; but it would appear that both the East and the West are agreed about the nature of the conflict and that in this consensus the collective interests of Africa tend to be sacrificed.

The IMF and the World Bank have been operating—in the words of Lenin—as 'learned salesmen' of the metropolitan bourgeoisie and gendarmes of finance capital in the attempt to solve the problem of the crisis of accumulation at the centre. The effect of this is, in the words of Samir Amin, to increase the 'compradorization' of Africa even further. The IMF adjustment plan, which is resented almost uniformly by every African country, is the overseas version of the monetarist policies now being pursued with vigour in Britain under the leadership of the Conservative government. In Europe and the United States we see the same trend in the rise of the New Right. Its main purpose at the centre is to subordinate labour more effectively to the rule of capital and thereby increase the rate of appropriation. In Africa the goal is the same. An IMF plan often demands massive retrenchment of labour, euphemistically called labour redeployment; trade liberalization with consequent denationalization of local capital; massive devaluation of local currencies (which could be defended on the grounds of bringing overvalued local currencies down to their realistic value but has had the net effect of drastically reducing the purchasing power of the mass of the people) and support for authoritarian means of implementing such measures, often excused by pointing out the need for decisive and strong governments—with all that that means for civil and democratic rights.

Political violence against individuals and groups which a few years ago would have caused uproar in both Africa and the international press now passes hardly noticed. There would seem to be a conspiracy between the metropolitan bourgeoisie and our local rulers to increase the pressure on the mass of the people. And in the name of what do the metropolitan bourgeoisie do this? In the name of capital. We have to admit that not all the countries at the centre have been operating in this way. There have been progressive European countries, in Scandinavia in particular, and individuals and organizations committed to our cause which have helped us in the past and still show some willingness to help. But the global crisis of capitalism is beginning to undermine both their capacity and their determination to offer us material support in a way which will lead to a real break through in our struggle. This is the national and international political framework in which we are operating and in which we are seeking to respond to the peace problematic. This is the framework which circumscribes our actions and establishes the parameters within which we operate and pursue our objectives. It is important to understand this if we are to understand the nature of the peace problematic in Africa and our perspective on it.

Issues of the Peace Problematic: Conflict

The basic starting point for the study of peace is conflict. We argued above that the resolution of conflict is only a minimalist condition for the achievement of peace. The first real condition is to understand the nature and character of conflict in Africa. This implies two things: an identification of the salient issues and adoption of the appropriate methods. On the question of issues some of the important ones to consider might be: the causes of conflict, the nature and dynamics of conflict, the patterns of conflict, the effect of conflict, the involvement of external powers in Africa's conflict, the style and nature of this involvement and what it entails for the peace and security not only of the country or countries directly involved but for the peace and security of the sub-region. Other issues could be: problems of conflict resolution, the mechanisms for peaceful resolution of conflict, the conditions for peaceful resolution and the effects of conflict on the developmental goals of the country and the sub-region and region as a whole. There are several patterns of conflict in Africa. Thus, we have conflicts of secession, ethnic nationalism or self-determination. Space does not permit a detailed discussion of all forms of conflict here. Suffice it to say that the form is often only the outward manifestation of other deep-seated issues. It has often turned out that a conflict apparently caused by ethnic or racial divisions has been nothing more than a conflict between competing elites for the control of state power and consequent access to certain material resources.[22] It is to the credit of the present generation of African writers that they have grasped this.[23]

Another feature of conflict in Africa is its sheer prevalence. We have already detailed the many instances of current conflicts in Africa both at territorial and inter-territorial levels. Since independence there is hardly any African country which has not experienced a major conflict of one kind or another. The geopolitics of the region mean that conflicts in one area easily spill into another, with the danger that they may engulf the whole sub-region. Thus the conflict in the Sudan spilled over into Ethiopia and Uganda while the conflict in Zaire involved Angola, Burundi and and Uganda. We have already seen how the conflict in South Africa tends to engulf the whole sub-region. In 1979 incidents in Amin's Uganda led to an open military conflict with Tanzania and for a while threatened the security of the whole sub-region.

Another important feature of the conflicts in Africa is the extent to which outside forces play a central role in maintaining them. It is doubtful whether the conflict in the Chad would have continued till now but for outside intervention. The same can be said of the conflict in the Horn of Africa and that of the Western Sahara. External intervention escalates conflicts and leads to arms transfers which in the last few years have considerably increased. In addition to the transfer of arms there have also been bilateral external agreements between African countries and certain metropolitan countries. The military pacts between France and many of her former colonies are well-known.[24] What may not be so well-known is the extent to which both the US and the Soviet Union are involved militarily in Africa. The US, for instance, concluded a mutual defence agreement with Ethiopia in 1975 (although this was abrogated in 1978 during the time of Ethiopia's conflict with Somalia), with Ghana in 1972, Kenya in 1980, Liberia in 1972 and Zaire in 1972. The Soviet Union also has had treaties of friendship and cooperation with Angola since 1976, Mozambique since 1977 and Ethiopia since 1978 (ratified in 1979). The Soviet Union has also concluded treaties of friendship and cooperation with Congo (1981), Egypt (1971) and Somalia (1974). Guinea-Bissau, Mali, Mozambique, Nigeria, Somalia and Uganda have all received Soviet military assistance under additional military cooperation agreements.[25]

These bilateral agreements provide access to naval and air facilities for the external power. The consequence of this is the possibility of drawing Africa into external conflicts. This not only endangers security in Africa but produces an atmosphere in which peaceful settlement of disputes becomes more difficult.

Another feature of the African conflicts is their intractability. The conflict in the Southern Sudan has been going on since 1957 (close to three decades) and that in Uganda has lasted for almost two decades. Although mechanisms for peaceful settlement of disputes exist in the form of the mediation and reconciliation committees of the Organization of African Unity (OAU), they have not been successful. The OAU was unable to stop the Nigerian civil war; it was unable to stop the war between Uganda and Tanzania and has been so far unable to stop the conflict in the Chad, or in the Western Sahara or between Ethiopia and Eritrea. We have already shown how these conflicts lead to such a displacement of people that Africa now has one of the fastest growing refugee populations in the world.

Two main approaches to the study of conflict in Africa can be discerned. One is the modernization paradigm which tends to see conflict as endogenously generated; this looks for explanation to such factors as the conflict between primordial loyalties and the strains of the modernization process. The other I shall call, for want of a better term, the structural approach; this uses the economic and political linkage between African countries and metropolitan countries as a wider canvas against which to work out issues of conflict. This latter approach does not claim that external factors *cause* conflict in Africa; but they do lay down the parameters within which conflict occurs and they sometimes fuel them. It would therefore be futile to attempt to work out lasting mechanisms for conflict resolution without taking external factors into consideration.

At the present moment Southern Africa is the most serious area of conflict in the continent. It poses the gravest intellectual and political challenge to the African leadership. The chances of the conflict escalating into a major war with superpower involvement in the sub-region are ever-present. South Africa is in a state of undeclared war against her neighbouring African states. Although South Africa claims that its action against the neighbouring states is a response to guerrilla attacks on its own territory and is merely meant to attack and destroy guerrilla bases, and is thus part of its internal security operations, it is clear that it perceives the existence of neighbouring independent black states as a major threat to its system of apartheid; that is the major reason for the attacks. They are meant to deny the African states bordering on South African territory a chance to develop self-sustaining economies independent of South Africa. South Africa wants to reduce the black states around it to the status of entirely and totally dependent bantustans which are in no position to offer any assistance, material or moral, to the liberation struggle in South Africa. This is the idea behind the Nkomati Accords with Mozambique and the Lusaka Agreement with Angola both signed in 1984. This is the main cause of the conflict in Southern Africa. It is therefore clear that the conflict cannot be meaningfully resolved without changes in South Africa itself.

14

In the last few years the conflict in South Africa has escalated to a level where many people are predicting a major flare up in the area if there are no substantial changes in the apartheid system. It is clear that apartheid is no longer useful to capital, especially finance capital. South Africa is becoming ungovernable and capital needs stable conditions for its reproduction. The social conditions in South Africa are now becoming an obstacle to further accumulation. So apartheid must go. It is not surprising that it has been the representatives of industrial and financial capital who have been in the forefront of the demands to the government to seek some form of accommodation with the liberation movements. In 1985 a group of South African industrialists and financial leaders went to Lusaka to talk to the leaders of the African National Congress, an action which drew open rebuke from Botha, the apartheid prime minister of South Africa. When we connect this with the increasing loss of confidence shown in South Africa by the international business community then we know that the time for change has come. The critical question is, what kind of change?

There has been talk of talks about talks; it is clear that some feelers have been put out to try and find a way out of what looks like becoming an ugly situation. The West's main interests in South Africa are economic and strategic. It is therefore clear that any settlement will have to take this into account. It will also have to be based on the emergence of a black government moderate enough to calm the fears and maintain the privileges of the white minority, at least in the short term, but militant enough to command legitimacy and keep the lid on the aspirations of the black population. This is possible but not easy in the current situation. To this extent the recent statement by Botha that he would be prepared to hold discussions with the ANC if it renounced violence and terrorism and cut off its links with the South African Communist Party and the Soviet Union is significant. There is one sense in which South Africa is uniquely different from all other ex-colonies. This is not because it has been independent for a long time, as is sometimes asserted; it is because of the importance of its strategic position to the NATO defence system and its possession of nuclear weapons. These two factors introduce an entirely new element into the situation.

It is because South Africa occupies an important place in the Western defence system that the West has allowed it, and even helped it, to develop nuclear weapons. In fact it is claimed by certain strategic analysts that South Africa's possession of nuclear weapons is less for the internal suppression of its black population than as part of the Western defence system against confrontation with the East. Seen from this point of view we can appreciate South Africa's constant appeal to the West not to abandon it. From this point of view we can also appreciate the West's dilemma over South Africa. In the event of black majority rule how can the West be sure of maintaining its strategic interests in South Africa?

There are only two ways to achieve this. The West would have to promote a black leadership which would be so compromising that it could be entirely depended on, in the event of a confrontation, to allow the free use of its nuclear power and territory in the pursuit of NATO interests. This would present two problems. Considering the polarization in South Africa, is such 'moderate' black leadership likely? What legitimacy would such a leadership have? The second strategy would be to integrate South Africa further into the Western economic and strategic defence system before majority rule; any succeeding African government, moderate or militant, would then find itself so circumscribed that the imperatives of *Realpolitik* and political survival would dictate its operating within the general framework of the Western defence system. But this would not be easy to achieve and would probably founder on the legitimacy issue. Can a black leadership in South Africa, no matter how reactionary, be depended upon to use nuclear weapons on behalf of the West in the event of an East–West confrontation? Another option would be to dismantle the nuclear weapons in the event of majority rule if a satisfactory compromise which would ensure the West's strategic interests could not be reached. But this would deprive the West of a vital strategic base. This is the heart of the problem in South Africa. Whatever option emerges will depend on the nature of the struggle and the extent to which an accommodation can be worked out between the dominant forces in the conflict. What will be the impact of these arrangements on the peace and regional security of the area? Should the West succeed in working out a formula which would maintain its strategic and defence interests in South Africa, it would continue to threaten the peace and security of the whole sub-region.

Peace and Development

We have argued that for us peace and development are inextricably intertwined. Removal of conflict, as we have argued, is only the minimalist condition for the attainment of peace. For a lasting and reliable peace to be attained, it is important to fashion economic systems which can generate sustained economic growth, guarantee for the mass of the population a certain minimum of material existence or basic needs. This would not in itself remove all conflict but it would eliminate some of the causes of tension which lead to conflict. It is not by accident that at a time of economic depression there has been an increase in inter-personal and inter-group social conflict. This has been made more likely by Africa's poor development record.

At the risk of oversimplification to the point of caricature, let me say that African developmental paradigms in the last two decades have been characterized by three main trends: African capitalism, populist socialism or welfarism and Marxism. We should immediately qualify this by saying that all typologies—and these are no exception—simplify a complicated reality. And some African countries have been ecletic in their developmental choices. We should also judge development paradigms not only in terms of what a country has actually been able to achieve but in terms of its aspirations. (This however is not to validate arbitrary self-identification.) We would venture to make a few cautious remarks about the criteria for identification. Is the state the main allocator of value or is allocation left to the free play of market forces? Considering the dominant role which the state plays in nearly all African countries it will be necessary to consider this further. Does the state appropriate on behalf of itself, in the form of the creation of state capital, or does it appropriate on behalf of private capital, local or foreign? Is the basic form of social organization of labour planned, cooperatized or collectivized? Are there plans to achieve this or is it considered desirable that capital should primarily be in private hands? What is the attitude of the state towards the welfare of the people? Does it attempt to be the main provider of the basic welfare of the mass of the people or is it the ideological postulate of the state that this should be the main responsibility of private individuals?

On the basis of these questions it is possible to outline Africa's three main developmental paradigms. The Ivory Coast, Nigeria, Kenya and Malawi typify African capitalism. In these countries there has been a strong ideological preference on the part of the petty bourgeoisie which control the apparatus of state power to rely on the market mechanism as the main allocator of value and a tendency for the state to appropriate on behalf of private capital (either domestic or foreign).[26] The second tendency is what I would call welfare socialism or welfarism. Tanzania typifies this position perhaps more than any other country. Here the state is the major allocator of value and surplus is appropriated on behalf of the state. The social organization of labour is based on parastatals or peasant collectives and individual peasant holdings.[27] The third paradigm is the Marxist state which shares some characteristics of the populist socialist state. Perhaps the main difference between this and the populist state is the role of the party as an elite group of dedicated cadres and a formal proclamation of state adherence to Marxism–Leninism as an official ideology. Angola, Mozambique and Ethiopia typify this pattern.[28]

It is important to stress that these basic developmental paradigms should be separated from the specific policy options chosen as a means of achieving developmental goals. Julius Nyerere's recent remarks on nationalization, for example, should not be taken to infer that the entire populist socialist development model was wrong but only that certain policy options chosen to achieve it were neither well thought out nor well implemented. Nor should we regard some of the recent shifts in policy in Mozambique on state farms and agricultural production as evidence of the abandonment of Marxism–Leninism. In our view they are an attempt to shift policy in another direction in order to realize more effectively the objectives of the developmental model. One aspect which must be stressed is the dominant and interventionist role played by the state in all models of African development. In addition to these general development paradigms there have been some specific strategies which have been pursued by nearly all African countries in an attempt to escape the legacy of underdevelopment; import-substitution industrialization is one of these. With the benefit of hindsight it has become fashionable to castigate these policies; but they have been the main article of faith proclaimed by development economists as the sure way for African countries to escape from the legacy of underdevelopment and embark on industrialization. Another strategy is the continuation of the colonial policy of primary product promotion; a third which is now being vigorously advocated by finance capital in the form of the World Bank and the IMF is export-led industrialization. This is designed to increase the export of primary products as a way of building up surpluses which can then be used to modernize and industrialize agriculture, so preparing the base for further industrialization. Without getting into a long discussion on this it has to be said that there is only a very limited market for the expansion of primary products for export—as Nkrumah was to realize in 1965 when Ghana produced twice the amount of cocoa it produced in 1955 but earned only half the 1955 value. There may be likely benefits when only a few countries embark on this policy; but were all African countries to adopt it it would become self-defeating.

The African development experience for the last two decades has been a major disappointment, whatever the developmental options. The hopes of the early 1960s have not been fulfilled and disillusionment seems to have set in. This has led to a sobering reappraisal which has resulted in many debates. These have led to the emergence of two main schools of thought. The modernization school, relying on the historical framework of the development of capitalism in the West, puts forward a model in which through the process of diffusion of innovation and the provision of certain inputs like capital, managerial training, change of attitudes and the removal of archaic and outmoded processes, development is seen as a linear progression from the present underdevelopment of Africa to a replica of Europe. The basic assumption here is that the transition *is* replicable. If that is true then all that is required is the realization of its potential. According to this model African capitalism is not only possible, but desirable; it is the one sure road to success. Rostow, Hagen and others have produced the intellectual basis of this position.[29] Its defenders point to the record of impressive growth rates particularly in the agriculture of the Ivory Coast. As Crawford Young has ably noted, the disasters of Zaire, a country which has also followed this road, or Nigeria, which in spite of its enormous oil revenues seems to be in no better position than some others less well endowed, are hardly mentioned.[30] The modernization school concedes that colonialism had some very unsavoury aspects and cannot in all respects be defended on moral grounds; but it argues that on political and economic grounds it is defensible. Colonial capitalism turned stagnant and archaic African societies into rudimentary forms of the modern economy characterized by the cash nexus. It enabled Africans to enter into the cash economy and therefore begin to accumulate a surplus. What needs to be done is to work out a system to continue this process and remove the obstacles which colonialism put in the way of African accumulation. Posed in this way the theory finds it possible to condemn colonialism without condemning capitalism. This has provided a much needed and convenient intellectual umbrella for liberals of all shades.

For some time the modernization paradigm dominated the intellectual landscape until it was decisively demolished by Andre Gunder Frank in his now famous essay *Sociology of Underdevelopment and Underdevelopment of*

Sociology.[31] In a subsequent work in which he acknowledged his intellectual debt to Paul Baran, he argued that, far from having no developmental function in Latin America, capitalism had been responsible for its current underdevelopment.[32] This argument had an immediate impact in intellectual and political circles and was applied to Africa. One of the most important and influential works on this subject was Walter Rodney's *How Europe Underdeveloped Africa*.[33] This provided an intellectual and political justification for the countries which had made a policy choice against capitalism. If it is argued that capitalism has underdeveloped Africa then it stands to reason that a minimum condition for development is disengagement from capitalism and the creation of an alternative system: socialism is seen on both ethical and economic grounds as the most viable choice for African countries. Julius Nyerere's speech 'The Rational Choice', which he gave to a gathering of intellectuals and leaders of the Sudanese Socialist Party Union in 1973 in Khartoum, is one of the most eloquent statements on the issue.[34] Those who take this position also counter the argument about the impressive growth rates of countries like the Ivory Coast and Malawi with the claim that such growth rates have been obtained by depriving the mass of the people of welfare services; in any case the growth is temporary. But as we have pointed out, in neither case have the results been impressive. Of late the modernization theory has been resuscitated, strangely enough by certain Marxists who claim that capitalism has not underdeveloped the developing countries. On the contrary, it can and does develop underdeveloped countries. This position was first and vigorously put forward by Bill Warren in his *Imperialism: Pioneer of Capitalism*[35] in which the essentials of the modernization theory are presented in Marxist terms. He uses selective examples from South-East Asia to try and demonstrate his case. In Africa Goran Hyden has been perhaps the most foremost defender of this position. His work *Beyond Ujamaa in Tanzania* is a serious indictment of Tanzania's development strategy which he regards as premature and wrong. His subsequent work states the same position.[36] At present there is no dominant paradigm and development theory is in a state of limbo. What is important is to develop a holistic approach to the problem which will combine useful insights from different paradigms— always bearing in mind the need to regard the peace and development problematics as inseparable.

Peace and Development: The African Perspective: A Challenge to Europe

If we are right in what we have been saying so far on the concept of peace, the intricate relationshp between peace and development, and the need not only to understand and study the peace problematic but to put it into practice, and the recognition that peace in one corner of the world is related to peace in another corner of the world, the next question becomes, what is Europe's response to the peace and development problematic of Africa? It would be presumptuous for us to tell Europe and the United States what they should do. But we have the right to state what we expect if our assumption of a common humanity and destiny and universal desire for the collective peace and development of the world is correct. We ask for a greater degree of commitment and support for the demands of the Third World—particularly in the form of the creation of a New International Economic Order. Limited though the proposals are, they are steps in the right direction. The Third World has also made demands for a change in the international power system. We have lately seen the emergence of what we might call the New Right. The leading figures of this are President Reagan, Mrs Thatcher and Chancellor Kohl. Their attitudes towards Africa and the Third World are marked by contemptuous arrogance and belligerence. This does not augur well for the prospects for world peace. These leaders have been in the forefront of the drive to intensify the compradorization of Africa and the Third World. These trends must be reversed and the strong support for the collective efforts of Africa and the Third World contained in the *Brandt Report*[37] is the minimum we should expect from Europe and the United States.

We have argued that of all the areas of conflict in Africa, South Africa poses the most serious threat not only to the peace of the area but to the continent as a whole and consequently to the world. South Africa has been engaged in a protracted struggle to destabilize the economies and governments of its neighbours, particularly Angola, Mozambique and now even Botswana. This is for no other reason than that South Africa cannot tolerate the existence of an African state close to its border which is sufficiently independent-minded, economically successful and nationalistic to provide inspiration and moral and material support to the liberation struggle in South Africa and Namibia. South Africa has extensive military, political and economic links with the Western countries and the United States. We would like progressive opinion to be brought to bear on South Africa to abandon its path of destruction and violence.

Africa has been heartened by the kind of public response which was aroused in Europe in response to the famine appeal. Millions of pounds were collected for the victims. While we are grateful for such a show of humanity we would like to see an equal importance attached to efforts by people in these areas to create self-sustaining economies to improve the quality of their lives and become independent; the next time such disasters occur they will then be in a better position to withstand them without international charity.

We have seen how the current crisis in Africa is making even feeble attempts at democratic government a thing of the past. United States and Western governments have been supporting unashamedly authoritarian governments so long as their so-called leaders offer protection and security for capital. If we regard democratic structures as desirable in themselves and as instrumental for achieving peace and stability then we would expect Europe to support the initiatives, few and limited though they are at the moment, to create democratic structures which will make it possible for the mass of the people to have meaningful control over the political processes which control and guide their lives. This is the only way in which we can ensure peace and development in Africa. If Europe and United States are truly interested in peace these are minimum conditions which could be met without any difficulty.

Notes

1. Willy Brandt, *Peace and Development*, Third World Lectures, Third World Foundation, Monograph 14, 1985, p.1.

2. Nigel Young has analysed the various trends and tendencies within the peace movement. See his *An Infantile Disorder?*, Routledge and Kegan Paul, London, 1977.

3. Johan Galtung was the first to conceptualize the peace problematic in terms of negative and positive peace. See his 'Violence, Peace and Peace Research', *Journal of Peace Research*, vol.6, no.3, 1969. For an interesting discussion of these two conceptual approaches see Bjorn Hettne, *Approaches to the Study of Peace and Development*, European Association of Development Research and Training Institutes (EADI) Working Paper, no.6, 1984.

4. Nigel Young, 1977.

5. Marek Thee has discussed various trends and tendencies in peace research. See his 'Scope and Priorities in Peace Research', *Bulletin of Peace Proposals*, vol.14, no.2, 1983; also 'Extension of the Arms Race into Outer Space, and Countervailing Strategies', Discussion Paper Prepared for the Round Table on the Role of Scientists in Preventing the Arms Race in Outer Space, Prague, 4-6 October 1985.

6. The World Bank, *Toward Sustained Development in Sub-Saharan Africa*, Washington, 1984, p.1.

7. Ibid. .

8. Ibid.

9. Ibid., p.8.

10. Ibid.

11. Economic Commission for Africa *Survey of Economic and Social Conditions in Africa, 1982-1983*, E/ECA/CM.10/4, Addis Ababa, 1984, p.48.

12. Economic Commission for Africa *ECA and Africa's Development, 1983-2000*. Addis Adaba, 1983, p.11.

13. The World Bank, 1984, p.9.

14. Ibid.

15. Ibid.

16. Ibid.

17. African Development Bank (Abidjan) *Economic Report on Africa*, 1985. A Report of the African Development Bank (Abidjan) and the Economic Commission for Africa (Addis Ababa), 31 March, 1985, p.29.

18. Ibid., p.44.

19. Ibid., p.45.

20. The World Bank, p.9. For the literature on the refugee situation in Africa see R. Chambers, 'Rural Refugees in Africa: What the eye does not see', Paper presented at the African Studies Association of the United Kingdom Symposium on Refugees, London, 13-14 September 1979; H.C. Brooks and El-Ayouty (eds), *Refugees South of the Sahara: An African Dilemma*, Negro Universities Press, Westport, Connecticut, 1976; E. Chartrand, 'The AOU and African Refugees,

World Affairs, vol.29, No.137; R. Mathews 'Refugees and Stability in Africa', *International Organization*, vol.26, no.1, 1972; G. Melander and P. Nobel (eds), *African Refugees and the Law*, Scandinavian Institute of African Studies, Uppsala, 1978; Gaim Kibreab, *Reflections on the African Refugee Problem: A Critical Analysis of Some Basic Assumptions*, Research Report No.67, Scandinavian Institute of African Studies, Uppsala, 1983.

21. For a critical review of this see Andre Gunder Frank, *Crisis. In the Third World*, Heinemann, London, 1981; William D. Graf, 'Anti-Brandt: A Critique of Northwestern Prescriptions for World Order', *Socialist Register*, 1981.

22. Several writers have demonstrated this particularly with regard to Nigeria: Okwudiba Nnoli, *Ethnic Politics in Nigeria*, Nigeria Fourth Dimension Publishers, Enugu, 1978: Richard Sklar, 'Nigerian Political Parties, Political Science and National Integration: A Radical Approach', *Journal of Modern African Studies*, vol.5, no.1, 1967; Mahmood Mamdani, *Politics and Class Formation in Uganda*, Monthly Review Press, New York, 1976.

23. Ngugi Wa Thiongo, *Petals of Blood*, Heinemann, London, 1977; Chukwuemeka Ike, *The Naked Gods*, Fontana, London, 1970.

24. Robin Luckham, 'French Militarism in Africa', *Review of African Political Economy*, no.24, 1982.

25. Military Balance, 1984-5, Institute of Strategic Studies, London; for Western and Eastern military presence in Africa see Christopher Coker, *Nato, the Warsaw Pact and Africa*, Macmillan, London, 1985.

26. For an analysis of the economic performance of countries under this designation see Colin Leys, *Underdevelopment in Kenya*, Heinemann, London, 1985; Henrik Secher Marcussen and Jens Erik Torp, *The Internationalization of Capital*, Zed Press, London, 1982.

27. Andrew Coulson, *Tanzania: A Political Economy*, Oxford University Press, London, 1982; Issa Shivji, *Class Struggles in Tanzania*, Tanzania Publishing House, Dar-es-salaam, 1975; Goran Hyden, *Beyond Ujamaa in Tanzania*, Heinemann, London, 1980 and *No Short Cuts to Progress*, Heinemann, London, 1983.

28. David and Marina Ottaway, *Africommunism*, Africana Publishing Company, New York, 1981; Joseph Hanlon, *Mozambique: The Revolution Under Fire*, Zed Press, London, 1984. Some would prefer to call these countries states of 'socialist orientation'.

29. See W.W. Rostow, *The Stages of Economic Growth: A Non-Communist Manifesto*, Cambridge University Press, Cambridge 1960; E.E. Hagen, 'How Economic Growth Begins: A Theory of Social Change', *Journal of Social Issues*, vol.19, no.1, 1963, pp.20—34; E.E. Hagen, *On the Theory of Social Change*, Dorsey Press, Homewood, Illinois, 1962; D. McClelland, *The Achieving Society*, van Nostrand, Princeton, 1961.

30. Crawford Young, *Ideology and Development in Africa*, Yale University Press, 1982.

31. Andre Gunder Frank, *Latin America: Underdevelopment or Revolution*, Monthly Review Press, New York, 1970.

32. Andre Gunder Frank, *Capitalism and Underdevelopment in Latin America*, Penguin, Harmondsworth, 1969.

33. Walter Rodney, *How Europe Underdeveloped Africa*, Dar-es-salaam, Tanzania Publishing House, 1972.

34. Julius Nyerere, 'The Rational Choice' in Julius Nyerere *Freedom and Development*, Oxford University Press, London, 1974.

35. Bill Warren, *Imperialism: Pioneer of Capitalism*, London NLR, 1980.
36. G. Hyden, *op cit*.
37. *North-South: A Programme for Survival*, Report of The Independent Commission and International Development Issues under the chairmanship of Willy Brandt, Pan Books, London 1980.

Part 1: Africa and the World Crisis

2. The Crisis: The Third World, North–South and East–West

Samir Amin

For more than ten years the world economic system has been undergoing a structural crisis. The depth of this crisis—far more than a conjunctural recession in a period of expansion—has led some to revive the theory of long cycles or Kondratieff cycles, and so on. The crisis is worldwide and marked by the collapse of growth; a marked collapse of productive investment; a notable fall in profitability (but very unequally distributed among sectors and enterprises) and a tendency for the acceleration of inflation (stagflation).

It is a crisis of the capitalist system since the world system is largely ordered by the fundamental laws of this mode of production. The crisis also touches the countries in the East (commonly called socialist, with all the reservations attached to this designation) in so far as they participate in the world system by commercial and technological exchanges, capital loans and so on. But these latter countries are also suffering from another crisis which is peculiar to them: the difficulty of proceeding from extensive accumulation to intensive accumulation. This crisis has, of course, obvious political aspects. The countries of the Third World which make up the periphery of the world capitalist system are also victims of the crisis.

My object here is certainly not to propose a new theory of capitalist expansion (for this refer to the *Dynamics of Global Crisis*). But a few points are worth making. It is not so much the periods of long depressions which are to be explained but, on the contrary, the periods of long expansion. The latter are closely associated with the reconstructions and recoveries which follow long periods of war, with technological revolutions and epoch-making colonial expansions. According to one Marxist interpretation—which we agree with and which, I believe, is that of Paul Sweezy and Harry Magdoff[1]—the capitalist mode of production has a profound inherent tendency towards stagnation; this is an expression of its tendency to develop the forces of production beyond effective consumption demand. There is nothing mysterious in the current crisis following upon the long post-war expansion period.

The capitalist economic system has always been worldwide in the sense that it is not merely a collection of national systems. It has always been made up of centres and peripheries in which class structures and functions are complementary. It has been so since its mercantilist origins and not only since the end of the 19th Century as Lenin's *Imperialism, the Highest Stage of*

Capitalism, tends to imply. Marx perhaps underestimated this worldwide and unequal character of capitalist expansion.[2] Now, this worldwide character produces political effects which pose crucial questions. What transformations are on the historical agenda? What is really at stake in the actual conflicts which determine the general movement? Who are the agents of these transformations?

To these key questions we can sketch contrasting answers. According to the orthodox Marxist vision the essential conflict opposes socialism (working classes and not necessarily countries of the East, as the Zdanovian[3] theory claims) to capitalism. Other conflicts (North–South, inter-imperialist) are secondary. This vision is ideological; it is not empirically confirmed. Do the working classes in the most advanced countries struggle for socialism? And what socialism? In the framework of what type of world system? Then there is that vision, wrongly characterized in the West as Third Worldism. In that vision, rightly, the worldwide character of capitalist expansion compels the capitalism/socialism question to be posed in an indirect manner. The major conflicts currently at the forefront of the historical stage (what is actually at stake in these struggles) results from the contradiction between the pressures for globalization (or transnationalization) imposed by the predominance of capital and the aspirations of working classes, peoples and nations for some autonomous space. The fiercest of these conflicts (Russia in 1917, China, Viet Nam, Cuba) have led to a break with globalization which has been associated with profound social transformations and with national construction. First proposed by Lenin, the concept of the weakest link has been associated with the strategy of an alleged construction of socialism starting with ruptures in the peripheries of the system. All the questions posed by this strategy obviously remain open: what can or could this revolutionary break really lead to? (See my Expansion or Crisis of Capitalism.)[4]

In any case, the reality of globalization implies 1) that any crisis of the capitalist system will be a crisis of the international division of labour, thus, especially, a North–South crisis; 2) that the alternatives of the day will be trans-nationalization *or* autonomous development and not (directly) socialism *or* capitalism; 3) that there are several different active social forces other than simply the working class (such as peasants etc...and nations as such) which intervene in the course of history.

Our thesis is that this conflict is particularly relevant to the current period. Up to the end of the 19th Century, there was no major contradiction between the emergence of a new bourgeoisie as a ruling national class and its participation in the capitalist international division of labour. Since then this contradiction has appeared. In other words, integration into the world system has been a growing obstacle to the emergence of new centres. The bourgeoisie in the South are caught between their nationalist desires and their submission to compradorization. Periods of crisis (as presently) are periods of recompradorization in the South, and therefore, of revolts or potential revolutions against it. Contradictions in the construction of national autonomy are by no means limited to the peripheries. In the centre itself the weakest capitalisms are equally threatened.

The evolution of capitalism in the centre defies the orthodox (and simplified) theory of class struggles. Working classes have abandoned the idea of a classless society and rallied to strategies for the amelioration of their position within society as a result of centre–periphery polarization. Therefore the economic struggle of these working classes in the centre can bring the capitalist system into question again only if it dares to go so far as to bring into question the world system. As to the new middle classes, whose growth is so closely tied to the dominant position of the centres in the world system, they are well aware of their privileges (including *vis-à-vis* local working classes) expediently justified in terms of the legacy of education.

The question of socialism is therefore posed in the centre in new terms, different from those imagined in the 19th Century. Inter-class movements in favour of a new model of development (feminism, the Greens) bear witness to this. These movements can potentially pose anew the question of a popular North–South alliance since they again bring into question the very content of development on the national and global levels.

The current crisis, like its predecessors, is seen in the ungovernability of the system. This occurs on three levels: 1) the periphery's resistance to the exigencies of the logic of transnationalization; 2) the resistance of working classes in the centre (their economic strength in the workplace and their refusal of Fordism) and the resistance of peoples in the centre to the predominant lifestyle (inter-class movements); 3) the conflict between the strategies of global capital and the national policies of the state. In the absence of a hegemony (that of the United States is in decline) ensuring the functions of a global state, the national states have less and less of a hold over the strategies of capital.

Hence the logic of capital's response to the crisis, necessarily from the right, comprises a triple offensive. This includes the overcoming of the South by compradorization (witness the end of the North–South dialogue and the emergence of a Northern bloc confronting the South, as at the Sixth UN Conference on Trade and Development (UNCTAD) in Belgrade in June 1983; the undermining of the worker's movement in the centre by unemployment, and of the inter-class movement by inflation (winning over the middle classes to the right); and the submission to the American counter-offensive which seeks to re-establish the hegemony of the United States and the consequent instrumentalization of the IMF, which is the embryo of a supranational state.

The offensive against the South must, in our opinion, be placed at the centre of an analysis of the conflicts brought about by the crisis. The relatively favourable conditions which arose out of capitalism's worldwide expansion from 1945 to 1970 have occasionally allowed the Third World bourgeoisie to force some concessions from the imperialist system. The radical wing of this bourgeoisie (often operating from state positions), emerging from a strong national and popular liberation movement, has frequently established and legitimized its national leadership by social reforms (especially agrarian), development 'of a public sector and institution of an accelerated industrialization policy. A Soviet alliance has at times extended the margin of manoeuvre for these new bourgeoisies. However, these national policies (Nasser provided perhaps the best model) depended upon class structures, internal alliances and ideologies that precluded consideration of breaking out (or delinking) from the international division of labour (they only sought accelerated import-substitution industrialization, thereby guaranteeing greater consumption for the privileged classes). Nor did they consider a popular strategy (an industrialization supporting the priority of agricultural development, which requires town–country relations based upon mutual support and not exploitation. Such a strategy would have implied a worker and peasant alliance as the basis of the political system).

The crisis reveals the fragility of these national bourgeois development attempts in economic terms (deficits, external debt) and in political terms (disaffection of popular support). The current period of crisis thus creates favourable conditions for destroying the impossible aspirations of the bourgeoisie in the South and forces them to capitulate. All means are deployed to this end: financial (through the IMF and the Club of Ten), economic (rejection of the New International Economic Order's claims) and even military (Zionist expansion, destabilizing South African interventions). The West *en bloc* has so far followed the United States in these pressures, notwithstanding some verbal disclaimers here and there.

The success of this global offensive against the South would lead to the recompradorization of bourgeoisies in the South and would continue their further growth within the strict logic of monopoly capital's strategies for trans-nationalization. This vast ebb and flow of the South's national projects testifies, in our opinion, to the pertinence of the kernel of Leninist and Maoist theses: national liberation is indeed always on the agenda and cannot be accomplished by the bourgeoisie in the periphery; popular alliances (worker and peasant) are here the sole means of surmounting the social contradictions increasingly sharpened by capitalism's development. National and popular objectives imply 'delinking', therefore, such a revolution can initiate a long transition, which could eventually lead to socialism. Hence, we can say that this revolution has a socialist dimension. As long as there are no visible prospects for the initiation of socialist changes in the developed centres, this becomes the most important aspect of the problematic of socialism. In our opinion the historical limits of Leninism and Maoism are not situated within the logical structure of these theses. Rather, they are situated elsewhere: in the realms of state-party-masses relationships and in their extension to the problematic of plan-market-social management-democracy.

In the current crisis it is absolutely out of the question for bourgeoisies in the South to take up the initiative in a new radical way. Moreover, in the preceding period of expansion Southern bourgeoisies used the autonomous space open to them to attempt to insert themselves further into the world system, though sometimes to the detriment of their weakest partners. Examples of this include local expansionisms and intra-Third World wars (even though partially caught up in conflicts between the superpowers); attempts at insertion into the global financial system such as OPEC; and attempts to accelerate dependent industrialization (the newly industrialized countries). All this is consistent with the bourgeois class nature of the ruling elite in these countries.

Hard pressed in the crisis, the powers in the South have only verbal responses—such as the intensification of South-South relations— which are difficult to put into practice given the particular states in question. Alternatively, they believe themselves able to call upon the USSR; although this call may be largely ineffective. The offensive aiming at recompradorization is thus destined to secure only a short-term advantage. But a response, primarily in the form of a violent popular rejection, also becomes more likely (as proved by such varied events as have occurred in Nicaragua, El Salvador, Ethiopia, Ghana—and so on). These events, beyond their variety, are reflections of the blind alley of peripheral capitalism. Whether this 'populist' response, which is mobilized around ideologies of rejection (Islam, for example) will go further, and allow for the emergence of a new national popular state is an open question. This response will depend, in part at least, upon the response given to another important question: can external forces (a leftist Europe for example) break with the offensive against the South, play the role of non-alignment (thus of real and equal opposition to the two superpowers), and support the national and popular outcome in the South?

Is the working class of developed capitalist countries condemned to defeat, that is, to accepting restructuring according to the exigencies of capital's profitability? This outcome appears inevitable if we accept the sacrosanct international competitiveness as the criterion of last resort for immediate choices. To avoid bowing to the exigencies of capital's strategy, we must base an alternative strategy on the following two complementary options: opting for another development path as formulated, although embryonically, by diverse inter-class movements such as the Greens Movement in Germany, by discourse about expansion of the non-commodity sector and so on; and opting to support a popular national project in the South as formulated, for example, by the Greek Pasok. (The present Socialist Party that Papandreou has put together.) The progressive emergence of such an alternative development path could engender the extension of social property (the programme of Swedish social democracy). Of course, this evolution remains yet to be invented and must find its own solutions to the real questions which it poses, especially with regard to relations between the state and democratic socialization. Obviously, the beginning of such an evolution implies the abandonment of neo-Keynesian illusions, just as it implies a counter-offensive against the ideology of the right currently in vogue.

Defeat is equally inevitable if we accept the Atlanticist rallying calls which imply subordinating North-South relations and intra-West relations to East-West relations. Is the USSR really today's primary menace? Why does it not use its supposed military superiority to attack the West instead of waiting to lose that superiority? Is this not simply a propaganda campaign aimed at making the re-establishment of United States hegemony acceptable? The Atlanticist rallying call undermines the possibility of any revision of North-South relations, as shown by Europe's astonishing retreat on the question of

Palestine and Africa (support for Zaire and South Africa and so on).

The offensive against the East also conceals an offensive against the South and against the working classes in the West in order to re-establish American hegemony. Certainly, the East is not incapable of becoming potentially expansionist, or even of choosing the path of adventure in order to surmount its deep internal crisis. That crisis will not be surmounted by a progressive integration of the East into the world system. Such a choice would carry the threat of losing control by a too extensive integration. The East will thus pull back each time it feels itself threatened. Such is the lesson of the failure of Khruschev's illusions, followed by the return of Brezhnev. How peoples in the East might surmount this impasse is not our question here. The question to debate is thus neither the nature of the USSR, nor its prospects. The issue is rather the empirical question of tactical equilibrium on the military plane. *The current offensive against the East is partly a mask for Reagan's offensive against peoples of the Third World and workers in the West*. The idea that by ceding to American demands we could negotiate better economic concessions has proved a delusion. The opposite has occurred: Atlanticist rallying has reduced the space of economic autonomy.

Thus, three alternative scenarios for East-West relations present themselves. First, there is the Atlanticist rallying of Europe, accepting the aggressive policy of the US, which could well start a war in Europe. These trends are more pragmatic and less ideologically prejudiced towards the USSR. Secondly, there is the possibility of a Europe-United States divergence on East-West relations. Wallerstein envisages here the possible consolidation of a Paris-Bonn-Moscow axis, against a Washington-Tokyo-Peking axis.[5] This is a possibility which was raised some years ago; its possibility was highlighted by the Soviet gas affair. [Massive imports of Soviet gas by Western Europe against the wishes of the Americans]. This may even be the most probable option if certain trends on the right prevail in Europe. These trends are more pragmatic and less ideologically prejudiced towards the USSR than certain views of the European left, which display such ideological prejudice, and could fall into Reagan's trap i.e., in the name of anti-communism to accept American hegemony. In any case, in this perspective, North-South relations are seen from a strictly imperialist point of view, in which Europe-USA competition is maximized (the Gaullist vision). By contrast, the Atlanticist currents—of right and left—envisage a sharing of the tasks between the USA and Europe (especially in Africa). Thirdly, there is the possibility of a leftist or alternative European politics which would be simultaneously anti-hegemonist, non-Atlanticist and Third Worldist. The third possibility is, in fact, a genuine non-alignment.

This option would reduce the risks of war, and would reinforce autonomy of workers in the West and of peoples in the South. It might also open the door to some kind of reformist transformation in the East, which is closed off in the other scenarios. But this choice is obviously excluded in the foreseeable future. Europe does not appear ready to consider it. The European left does not always understand that we cannot have the privileges of imperialist domination and at the same time refuse to carry out the restructuring which its expansion imposes. From 1960 to 1970 China was counting on such developments on the left, both in Europe and in the Third World. If these developments had occurred that would have been the most effective trend in the interests of peoples and in the advancement toward socialism. Isolated in its struggle 'against the two hegemonies', it then relinquished active non-alignment. The responsibility of Europe, and of its left, which in the end preferred to rally with Reagan's Atlanticism is a heavy one.

Notes

1. Paul Sweezy, *The Theory of Capitalist Development*, Monthly Review Press, New York, 1942; Henry Magdoff, *Imperialism*, Monthly Review Press, New York 1978. See also various articles in Samir Amin et al, *Dynamics of Global Crisis*, Monthly Review Press, New York, 1982.

2. See *La Deconnexion*, La Dicouverte, Paris, 1985.

3. Zdanov was associated with the chauvinistic nationalism which arose in the Soviet Union in 1935 during the time of Stalin and which sought to present the Soviet Union and Eastern Europe collectively as the proletariat of Europe and to denigrate the scientific and cultural achievements of the West while exaggerating those of the Soviet Union. Editor.

4. *Third World Quarterly*, Vol.5, No.2, April 1983.

5. See Immanuel Wallerstein, 'European Unity and its Implication for the Interstate System'. Paper presented for United Nations University Seminar on 'Europe's Role in Other Regions' Peace and Security', Schlaining Castle, Austria, 2-4 May 1985.

3. Africa within the Context of Global Superpower Struggle

Yash Tandon

It is the contention of this paper that the broad parameters of conflict in Africa—both inter-state and intra-state—are defined primarily by the global superpower struggle as it manifests itself in Africa. It follows that the primary cause of threat to peace in Africa stems from this superpower rivalry for hegemony, and that all other causes, though important, are secondary. It is further argued that in general the African appreciation of the dynamics of the international system has deteriorated over the last twenty years since most states became independent and that correspondingly the capacity of these states to influence not only events in the international system but also the situation within their own countries has rapidly declined. Let us take this second point first.

Before independence the struggle of the African peoples was limited to clearly defined goals. Though the details of the strategy and tactics of achieving these goals differed from one country to another (compare Algeria with Nigeria for example), the objective was in general clear enough; to secure political independence from colonial rule. While the main strength of the struggle came from the people of Africa themselves the international system was an important source of material and diplomatic support in the cause of political independence for Africa. Neither the USA nor the USSR had a particular interest in preserving European colonialism in Africa; it was only with the demise of European colonialism that they could begin to stake their own imperialist claims to Africa.

Independence has changed this. African countries have achieved their political independence; but the end of direct European political control has created a power vacuum. At the same time the global superpower struggle has intensified and Africa has become, mainly because of the strategic materials it possesses, a major theatre of superpower rivalry.

The situation is further complicated by the fact that whereas in the pre-independence period objectives (of national struggle) were clearly defined, that is now no longer the case. Most African countries would in general subscribe to the view that they are now struggling for economic independence; but economic independence is a much less easily definable objective than political independence. To the extent that the objectives of the struggle are less clear than before, an ideological vacuum is now added to the power vacuum. Ideas of African socialism and African capitalism have created confusion rather than clarity.

Both the power vacuum and the ideological vacuum are related to the particular kind of class politics that have emerged in Africa since independence. While the working classes were a significant force in many countries during the struggle for political independence, in no country did they actually lead the struggle or take over state power. The struggle was led mainly by nationalist elements from the other classes of the population, with the petty bourgeois elite providing the ideological leadership and the peasantry providing the main force. Post-independence politics in Africa have generally deteriorated into intra-class rivalry within the petty bourgeoisie who were the ideological banner-holders in the struggle for independence but now see one another as the enemy. Instead of uniting people under a single banner, as during the independence struggle, the post-independence leadership have, almost everywhere in Africa, managed to divide the people. Some of these leaders may be nationalistic in their own petty bourgeois fashion, but many of them are unashamed agents of imperialism. The result is that the African people are divided not only along narrow ethnic, racial, regional and religious lines in pursuit of petty interests of their own; they are further divided in the interest of conflicting imperialist powers, including the superpowers, as well as their former European colonial masters.

It is in the light of this compounded power and ideological vacuum on top of the essentially petty bourgeois politics of intra-class struggle in Africa that we must analyse how Africa is conditioned and influenced by the global power struggle.

How the Global Superpower Struggle Constrains Africa

One remarkable aspect of petty bourgeois politics in Africa is that most African leaders think they have more power than is really the case. This is not without an element of irony. While the serious economic crisis facing Africa over the last decade has made Africans a little more aware of their helplessness in the face of economic forces beyond their control, many of the leaders in Africa nurse the illusion that they can change the situation either through moral exhortations (many liberal and humanitarian leaders fall into this category) or through the exercise of personal will (a view held by many African dictators).

It is doubly ironical that this illusion is further encouraged by none other than the World Bank. This global agent of imperialism, in its three separate reports on Africa in recent years, has squarely placed the blame of the present economic crisis in Africa on the structural and policy defects of the African countries themselves.[1] Implicit in this analysis is the idea that if African governments were to pursue correct economic strategies in their countries and to put right the structural defects in their systems, they would be able to overcome the present crisis. Those who subscribe to the conspiracy theory

35

would argue that this is a deliberate attempt on the part of the World Bank to mislead African leaders about the strength and source of their power.

In fact the power of African governments to influence not only the international system but also their own domestic environment is circumscribed by the global superpower struggle. We shall analyse the local situation later. First let us examine how the global superpower struggle sets the parameters within which African states can act independently.

The critics could argue that not even the superpowers can act independently of each other; independence is a fantasy in a world in which all countries are interdependent. We do not wish to get bogged down in a linguistic philosophical trap. It is enough for our purposes to comment that within the international system some states are more independent than others. There is a qualitative difference between the independence of the superpowers and that of Third World countries, including Africa.

We do not need to prove the obvious point about Africa's powerlessness to influence the international system. How can we begin to measure the influence of African states on the arms race between the superpowers? Even if we grant Africa some moral authority to speak on this issue in international fora such as the United Nations or international peace conferences, how much influence is Africa likely to have? Perhaps to phrase the question in this way is already to prejudice the answer against Africa. At any rate, at this global level, Africans, like their brothers and sisters in Asia and Latin America, can only speak as consumers of international peace and not as its producers. Their voice is the voice of humanity crying out for survival and, at this general level, it has a certain moral weight. But the two chief producers of peace, or rather of war, at the international level are caught up in an antagonistic contradiction which Africans are powerless to resolve. When this contradiction manifests itself within Africa itself, for example in Southern Africa, it is still the case that the broad parameters of conflict are defined by the superpowers rather than by independent African states. We shall return to this point a little later.

Let us take another example at the international level. Africa is amongst the world's largest producers of copper. One of the major uses of copper is for the production of electric and telecommunications cables. These cables are an important element in the industrialization of developed countries. But the market and price of copper are controlled by the developed user countries. Of course, this is common knowledge. But let us look a little more into the future and examine how the advancement of science and technology affects the copper industry. Already in the field of telecommunications, for example, technology has advanced far enough to displace copper with optical fibres made out of glass which can carry communications impulses a thousand times more efficiently than copper cables. Optical fibres are also easier to instal and maintain. In the next twenty years they will probably dominate the field of telecommunications. Africa has no control over the forces of science and technology which are threatening the export base of many of its commodities. At the same time as the World Bank is haranguing African states to improve their export performance the rug is being pulled from under their feet by the development of science and technology. The main research in science and technology is carried out in the USA and the USSR and countries like Japan. Between them these countries have monopolized most scientific research, and the competition between them defines the development of the productive forces in Africa.

Let us take another example—Grenada. Here was a country which, under the New Jewel Movement of Maurice Bishop, was seeking to consolidate its national independence, and had, by all objective accounts, the backing of its people. To be sure, it had invited the Cubans to come and build an airport as well as to serve as doctors, engineers and so on. But it was enough for the Americans to perceive this country as a threat to American security (because the US administration tends to see a Soviet missile lurking behind every Cuban presence) for the United States to destroy whatever independence that country had. Now, as a result, Grenada is in the vortex of superpower struggle. What is true of Grenada is true of El Salvador, Afghanistan, the Philippines, and potentially true of all—without exception—countries in the Third World. The helplessness of Africa is obvious.

Let us now turn to the less obvious: the case of Southern Africa. How does the superpower struggle for global hegemony circumscribe the ability of African countries to independently influence the situation? Many commentators underscore superpower involvement in Southern Africa, but more often than not this is done as a mere platitude. In most cases the analysis then advances by putting the superpower rivalry in the region on the sidelines and vilifying the South African regime for its abysmal human rights record, or saying how strong and powerful it is. Apart from the obligatory reference to superpower involvement, no serious effort is made to analyse exactly how the superpower conflict determines the development of the situation. We shall qualify this point later; but it is important to note that it is not just church people and humanitarian commentators who obscure the global aspects of the conflict. Most African leaders also maintain this dualism which enables them to separate the South African regime from United States imperialism and even leads them to approach the United States to do something for them in South Africa. Another example of this dualism is the Southern African Development Coordination Conference (SADCC) whose *raison d'etre* is to delink independent Southern African states from Southern Africa. But this delinking is supposed to be achieved with the assistance of imperialist capital, although this same capital sustains the South African regime and profits by the exploitation of the people there.[2]

The most powerful forces at work in Southern Africa are first, the working masses of which the industrial and mining workers, especially in South Africa but also in Zimbabwe, Zambia and other SADCC countries, constitute the core of a revolutionary force, backed by the peasant mass and second, international monopoly capital which organizes production in Southern Africa, tying it up with international capitalism at the global level through a network of finance, credit, marketing, management and technology. The third force is the Soviet Union which has made considerable headway in the last decade in Africa and which threatens to subvert the genuinely revolutionary movement of the masses to serve its own interest in its global struggle with the United States. Then we have the South African English and Boer bourgeoisie who have secured the ownership of a certain amount of landed and other productive assets and who want to salvage whatever control they can in the face of a threat by the superpowers, much as Ian Smith and his petty tobacco and manufacturing based bourgeoisie tried to do in the 1960s and 1970s. Lastly there is a miniscule African petty bourgeoisie with self-delusions of power and bearing the ideology of petty nationalism, they would like either to replace or to share with the English and Boer national bourgeoisie whatever economic assets the latter have been able to accumulate.

The view of Southern Africa that comes through the writings and speeches of most African leaders who hold state power in Africa, not excluding the resolutions passed at the OAU, is one that essentially emanates from the contradiction between the last two forces. It is the Botha regime that invariably gets singled out as the enemy of the people of South Africa and, in so far as it threatens to destabilize the neighbouring independent states, as the enemy of the people of Southern Africa generally. The more class-oriented analysts talk not about Botha as the enemy but the national bourgeoisie, or even more narrowly the Boer bourgeoisie, as the enemy, divorced from imperialism. [3]

If references are made in their analyses to imperialism, of both the Eastern and Western variety, these are purely incidental and suppose these forces to be external to Southern Africa. The global superpower struggle is thus seen not as something which is part and parcel of the very movement of contradictory forces within Southern Africa but as something outside to which an appeal can be made for assistance. Because of this dualism which enables the leaders to talk about superpower conflict in *general* terms while denying that the struggle is already manifested *concretely* in Southern Africa, it is possible for left-wingers among them to seek material help and weapons from the Soviet Union and for right-wingers to seek to influence the United States to talk sense to Botha on their behalf. Some of them can even perform the conjuring trick of asking both the United States and the Soviet Union at the same time to assist Africa to get rid of this evil of apartheid.

Yet it is not possible to understand any major event in Southern Africa without relating it to the contradiction between imperialism on the one hand and the struggling masses on the other. This contradiction, in its turn, influences and is influenced by the superpower struggle in this part of the world, and this, too, cannot be ignored in analysing any major event in Southern Africa. In order to illustrate this point let us look at some of the major events that have taken place in Southern Africa in recent years.

Let us, to start with, take the movement for apparent social reform inaugurated by the South African government in recent years. Few knowledgable people in Africa are taken in by this reform movement; most see it for the sham it is. But this is not the point at issue in the present discussion. The point at issue is, who instigated it and whose interests is it supposed to serve? We would contend that it is US imperialism (with British imperialism playing the second fiddle) which is in the final analysis, behind this reform movement, and is its chief beneficiary.

Despite periodic congressional disapproval of the system of apartheid in South Africa, racism as an ideology advances the interests of British and American dominated international finance capital in South Africa by providing access to cheap labour and sources of strategic raw materials and keeping the Soviets out of South Africa. As long as the resistance against apartheid had not acquired a revolutionary momentum and as long as the Soviet threat was not immediate, imperialism was prepared to tolerate apartheid. The separation of races in buses and public parks did not hurt imperialist interests; on the contrary, it helped to nurse the petty racial bigotry of the white community whose support in South Africa was necessary to ensure access to cheap and. disciplined labour and to keep the Soviets out.

But, when the rising revolutionary tide in South Africa made it necessary for imperialism to placate black South Africans, petty apartheid began to be dismantled. The section of the white population which was most infuriated by this was not that which had its economic and social future secured by imperialism, but the weaker bourgeoisie and the white working classes for whom apartheid was a way of life and a means of securing economic and social status. They grouped themselves around the camp of the *Verkrampte* and accused the reformist government of action disloyal to their forefathers and to the history of their struggle in the Boer Wars.

The United States government has presented this reform to African governments as evidence of the real possibility that the South African system of apartheid can change through gradual evolution. In fact, it is a reform instigated by American and British imperialism to pacify those elements in the revolutionary movement which are moderate and open to cooption into the system. It serves the interests of Anglo-American imperialism to prolong the day of reckoning in South Africa for as long as possible. If it ever becomes necessary to jettison apartheid in order to safeguard immediate imperialist interests against possible encroachment by the Soviet Union, then the promoters of petty bourgeois apartheid within South Africa need be under no illusion that they will be able to defend it. They will meet the same fate as Ian Smith in Rhodesia. The parameters of reform in South Africa are set by US and British imperialism in the context of superpower rivalry in this area.

Let us take another example: the controversial Nkomati Accords signed by Mozambique and South Africa in early 1984. The agreement has been viewed, especially in left-wing circles in Southern Africa, as a victory for the Botha regime and a capitulation by the FRELIMO government. We take the view that Nkomati represents not a defeat but a victory for the people of Mozambique. However, the point at issue here is whether Nkomati can be understood in isolation from superpower struggle in Southern Africa.

Most analysts have explained Nkomati in terms of the trilateral relations between South Africa, the FRELIMO government in conflict with the Movement of National Resistance (MNR) and the African National Congress (ANC) of South Africa. This is, however, an incomplete formulation. What is missing are the two major contradictions in the region: that between imperialism and the people of Southern Africa (of which the ANC is an *important* element but only an element) and the contradiction between the superpowers. When these contradictions are taken into account, the picture becomes more complete and complex. In fact, we argue that Nkomati has to be understood *primarily* in terms of these two major contradictions (of which that between imperialism and the people of Southern Africa is the principal one) and that the trilateral relations mentioned are *secondary*.

Viewed from this perspective the contradiction between the ruling FRELIMO Party and those people of Mozambique who are opposed to the ruling party is essentially subsidiary. To understand why and how these differences have arisen amongst the people of Mozambique it is necessary to go back to the origins and history of FRELIMO and the MNR, which is only one aspect of opposition to FRELIMO. One theory has it that its birth was encouraged by the Smith government in Rhodesia as a counter to FRELIMO's assistance to Zimbabwe's National Liberation Movement.[4] There is also evidence that the MNR has received, and continues to receive, substantial material support from the South African government and the white ex-Mozambican settlers who now reside in South Africa and Portugal. MNR uses terrorism against the people of Mozambique, but it also feeds on the discontent of the rural people. But it is difficult to imagine that the MNR would have developed as it has without at least the tacit approval, and even support, of the United States government. Direct evidence may be difficult to come by, but we know from the evidence given about Angola by the CIA operative, John Stockwell, that major South African initiatives in Southern Africa did and do have the backing of the American Administration.[5]

The MNR must therefore be seen not just as an instrument used by South Africa to destabilize Mozambique. We would contend that it is first and foremost an instrument in the hands of American imperialism to weaken the revolutionary movement in Southern Africa (just as UNITA is in Angola) and to reduce the prospects of Soviet entry into this region.

It is important that we bear in mind these two aspects of the MNR. Primarily it is an instrument for American imperialism in its struggle against both the people of Mozambique and against the Soviet Union. But, secondly, there is an element in the MNR which feeds on rural discontent in Mozambique and capitalizes on a secondary contradiction among the people themselves. (Parenthetically we might add that the same applies to the case of UNITA in Angola. There is no doubt that UNITA gets support from imperialism. At the same time, however, it does have some kind of a popular base in one region in Angola.)

Turning to the other side of the equation, the African National Congress is a major movement of the people of South Africa and the only one recognized by the FRELIMO and given facilities in Mozambique. But it has also received considerable material and diplomatic support from the Soviet Union.

The American and British governments must certainly recognize that they have to come to terms with the South African liberation movement sooner or later, but if the victory of the liberation movement brings with it victory for the Soviet Union as well, then this will be totally unacceptable to them. They will therefore try either to separate the ANC from the Soviet Union or, failing that, to neutralize the ANC. Once again we might add parentheticaly that the same equation applies to Angola and Namibia as well. If the presence of Cuban troops in Angola has become a major issue in resolving both the Angolan and Namibian situations, then it is primarily not because of the insistence of the government of South Africa; it is an issue raised by South Africa on behalf of American imperialism. Can there be a better proof of how the superpower global struggle defines the parameters of struggle in Southern Africa than the fact that there has been a virtual standstill in the progress for Namibian independence mainly because of the Cuban issue?

Thus, we would view Nkomati in the framework of superpower conflict in Southern Africa. It is to the credit of FRELIMO that instead of soliciting further military intervention from the Soviet Union to counter the threat of the MNR it has chosen to talk to the South African government. The alternative of Soviet intrusion would have intensified superpower involvement in Southern Africa and further compounded the problem. If Nkomati in the long run enables FRELIMO to neutralize the MNR and to resolve the secondary contradictions with its people through political means, then it will have justified itself.[6]

To conclude this section it is necessary to re-iterate that African countries in the post-independence era are working in an international environment different from what they were when they were struggling for political independence. Then too, of course, the superpowers provided the global context in which decolonization took place. But neither of them had a strong vested interest in preserving the European colonial system. Where decolonization proved to be a messy affair, as in the former Belgian Congo (now Zaire) and the threat of Soviet intervention became a real possibility, the United States intervened, using the agency of the United Nations, to keep the Soviets out and to put in power a government which would guarantee the protection of American interests. Once the colonial powers had left and a number of revolutionary movements in Africa turned to the Soviet Union for assistance superpower rivalry on the continent became more intense and dangerous.

In this situation the options open to independent African states to influence the international system became even more circumscribed than before. Independence created more the illusion of power than its reality. Independent African states thought they had room to manoeuvre and advance their own interests within the arena of superpower conflict. After twenty years it is now beginning to dawn on them, as on their brothers and sisters in Palestine, that their interests take secondary place to those of the superpowers. We have tried to demonstrate that the options available to independent African states are narrow and that their ability to influence the international system is severely constrained by superpower rivalry in the region.

If Africa's ability to manoeuvre within the context of an African problem is limited, then its ability to influence events outside Africa is even more so.

African states can join the international chorus of moral exhortations for a new international economic order, for better prices for petroleum or against the injustices committed in El Salvador and the Philippines or against the denial of the right to self-determination in Afghanistan, Kampuchea, and Grenada, or against the spiralling arms race, but they can do very little to alter the balance of power. This is not to dismiss altogether the importance of the collective moral strength of the leaders of Africa but to indicate the limits of such moral pressures when superpower interests are at stake.

The Domestic Politics of African States and the Superpowers

There is a tendency not only among the bourgeois social scientists but also in certain Marxist circles to regard independence as a fundamental break with the past. Independence, of course, has been a significant victory won by the people through enormous sacrifices, but it is a victory only at the political level. But, for some analysts the acquiring of a national flag and a national currency is tantamount to acquiring national economic independence. Suddenly, at independence, the African governments which have taken over power are supposed to have acquired a control over their own destinies and to be fully responsible for their actions. We have stated earlier that even the World Bank subscribes to this view and takes African governments to task for their acts of commission and omission.

Many people, including those who use the term, do not take the reality of neo-colonialism seriously. Institutions such as the World Bank and the International Monetary Fund may be excused for never wanting to use this term in their official reports on Africa; but every act of theirs is, in fact, neo-colonial. This Neo-colonialism is a fact of post-independence life in Africa.

None the less, it is easier to conceptualize the economic aspects of neo-colonialism than the political. Over the last twenty years a massive amount of literature has accumulated documenting the economic subservience of Third World countries to economic forces over which they have little or no control. Africa has generally fared the worst.

However, when it comes to analysing the political aspects of neo-colonialism, confusion reigns. Even some Marxists separate the politics of neo-colonialism from its economics; while much is made of the economic dependency of African countries on imperialism, the politics of Africa are analysed primarily in terms of the struggle between classes within each African state.[7] One consequence of this dualism is that the politics of internal class struggle are viewed in abstraction from the politics of imperialism. The national struggle is understood by these analysts primarily as struggle between the various internal classes rather than as a struggle for national liberation from the domination of imperialism. The analysis of these Marxists does not really differ from that of bourgeois social scientists who replace class analysis by analysis based on ethnicity, race and religion.

In contradiction to this view, we hold that the primary determinants of politics in the neo-colonies are the politics of imperialism and the politics of national struggle against imperialism. All other politics, including working-class politics and the intra-class politics of the petty bourgeoisie, are secondary to and conditioned by the politics of imperialism and those of national liberation. To be sure, the internal class struggles appear to loom large in the post-independence period because the internal classes now have access to the media, to parliament (where it exists) to the state bureaucracy, the military and military toys, and, of course, international fora such as the United Nations and the Non-aligned Movement. These are used to create an illusion of power and independence and lead to the separation of internal politics from international politics.

We are living through an era in which the exploited and oppressed peoples of the world are struggling for socialism and national liberation. Even large Third World countries such as India and Brazil cannot be said to have achieved national liberation. In the context of this struggle for national independence, governments can come and go and appear to swing from one extreme to another; but the essential character of politics does not change. Thus Somalia, for example, was yesterday an ally of the Soviet Union and today is an ally of the United States, the same is true of Ethiopia, vice versa. Egypt under Nasser was pro-Soviet, but Sadat swung the country to the side of the United States. He ousted the Soviet ambassador from Cairo only for him to be invited back by his successor, Mubarak. Some leaders have themselves swung from one side to the other. Milton Obote of Uganda was at one time a socialist but when he regained power following the defeat of Idi Amin, he became a 'capitalist' banner-holder of the IMF.

The point of the above argument is not to discuss the merits of the various policies pursued by African governments, but to make the general point that underlying all these changes in policies and personalities there lies a fundamental contradiction between imperialism and the peoples of Africa. While governments in Africa oscillate between the two superpowers they get the illusion of power and independence; but it is the independence of a worker moving from one factory to another. Nothing fundamental changes.

The achievement of national liberation from imperialism is not a one-off business. It is a long, dynamic process. As the revolutionary classes acquire consciousness of their exploitation and oppression and a clearer understanding of who their real enemies are, and as they are more or less able to organize themselves, they are better able to fight against imperialism.

Let us take one or two examples. Ghana in 1957 was the first black African country to achieve political independence. Its first leader, Kwame Nkrumah, was a radical spokesman for Pan-Africanism and for continental liberation from imperialism. He did well as long as the price of cocoa was high in the world market and his attempt to mobilize the people of Ghana was backed by the availability of essential commodities that people could buy in the shops. Widespread discontent arose, however, when cocoa prices deflated, external debt soared and the ideology of socialism, which Nkrumah advocated, became an empty slogan against the background of high black market prices of soap,

43

salt and other essentials. The military government that ousted him in 1966, at the direct instigation of imperialism, thought it could perform better. But it had as little control over the price of cocoa as Nkrumah did and as the country continued to buckle under the weight of soaring inflation and external indebtedness the people thought that the problem lay with the military and that the answer was a return to civilian rule. The civilians led by Dr Busia came back to power under the banner of democracy in 1969; but they had as little success as the preceding regimes and were overthrown in a second army coup in 1972. The National Redemption Council, later succeeded by the Supreme Military Council, ruled for seven years, but unending economic crisis fuelled discontent against them. In 1979 the civilians came back to power under Dr Limann. They were in turn ousted in a third military coup in 1982 led by Flight-Lieutenant Jerry Rawlings. Rawlings has promised to remove corruption and to restore the power of the people with a radical programme of economic and social transformation. Barely two years after his rule, however, the people are now again taking to the streets and the trade unions are calling into question the government's stabilization programmes carried out on the advice of the International Monetary Fund.

This sketch of the last 27 years of post-independence Ghana demonstrates the point that the struggle of the peoples of Africa is slow and arduous. It does not mean that no progress is being made; but the progress is not as readily visible as we might expect after over a generation of independence. The most obvious fact in the history of post-independence Ghana is the rapidly changing personnel in the seat of political power. The most enduring reality in this history has been the continued domination of imperialism over the people of Ghana.

Uganda is a country with a similar history. Its first leader, at independence, was Milton Obote, a friend and admirer of Nkrumah. He thought he could resolve political problems with his internal enemies by military means and at the same time challenge imperialism on ideological and Pan-African issues. In 1971 he was ousted from power by a military coup aided by Israel and British imperialism. The succeeding eight years of rule by the dictator Idi Amin were noted more for brutality and human carnage than for the support the regime received from British imperialism, although the country flirted for a time with Soviet social imperialism. Amin's removal from power, mainly as a result of armed intervention by Tanzania, led to a short-lived democratic regime. This regime was toppled by yet another military coup. The military then installed Milton Obote in power again by a rigged election legitimized by a British-inspired Commonwealth observer group. In return for services rendered Obote disowned his previous commitment to socialism and surrendered himself heart and mind to British imperialism, the European Economic Community and the International Monetary Fund.

Like the history of Ghana, the history of Uganda is a story of changing personnel at the helm of state power who, with varying ideological rhetorics, continued to serve the interests of imperialism. This, again, does not mean that the people of Uganda have taken all this lying down. They have fought, and are still fighting, against all forms of imperialist domination, including the negation of democratic freedom and the violation of their human rights. The broad framework of this struggle, however, is defined by the politics of national liberation from imperialism.

As a final example we take the case of Tanzania, one of the few countries in Africa that has enjoyed a relatively stable rule under the same person since independence in 1961. In 1967 President Nyerere declared a radical programme of socialism inspired not by Marxism–Leninism but by a native brand called *ujaama*. The *ujaama* experiment excited social democratic and humanitarian circles in Europe and America more than it excited the peasants and workers of Tanzania. After a decade of experiment the lower classes of Tanzania were in a worse economic plight than before. The government had nationalized some of the commanding heights of the economy. This gave the state a stake in the economy but did not weaken the hold of imperialism. In a revealing testimony to neo-colonialism President Nyerere said this in an address he gave to the convocation at the University of Ibadan in 1976:

> (T)here is no such thing as a national economy at all! Instead, there exist various economic activities which are owned by people outside its jurisdiction, which are directed at external needs, and which are run in the interests of external economic powers. Furthermore, the Government's ability to secure positive action in these fields...depends entirely upon its ability to convince the effective decision makers that their own interests will be served by what the Government wishes to have done. [8]

Now, 23 years after independence, Tanzania has been forced to accept the humiliating conditions imposed on it by the International Monetary Fund in order to receive the capital that it so badly needs to revitalize an economy which is all but shattered. Nyerere, it must be added, made a courageous effort to resist the pressures from the IMF, but finally had to admit that he really had very little room to manoeuvre.

These three rather sketchy case studies bring out the more enduring aspect of African history. As Mwalimu Nyerere said in his speech quoted above, the economies of African countries are not really national economies at all. They are part of the international economy over which imperialism has total control. That is the enduring part of the African scene. Imperialism and the revolutionary movement of peasants and workers basically determine the parameters of economics and politics in Africa.

Shifting internal and external alliances and counter-alliances are the result of two factors. At the international level they are the product of the superpower conflict between the USA and the USSR to secure economic and/or political leverage in Africa against the background of an ideological and power vacuum in Africa. At the local level, the dynamics of superpower conflict manifest themselves through intra-class struggle amongst the petty bourgeoisie who everywhere in Africa hold the seat of government and use their position to advance the interests of one or the other imperialist country. When pressed from below by the peasants and workers, who are getting increasingly impoverished, the petty bourgeois nationalist leadership do from time to time raise their voice against imperialism; but they mainly end up shunting between the two superpowers looking for non-existent room for manoeuvre.

The fact that it is American and Western imperialism which is generally the dominant imperialist force in Africa is of course a product of history. But this domination is being increasingly challenged by the coming of Soviet social imperialism. In 1961, when the Soviet Union wanted to assist Patrice Lumumba in his struggle against Belgian imperialism, it could not even land a plane in Leopoldville. Now, twenty years later, the Soviet Union can not only land a plane in many airports in Africa; its naval vessels are now able to regularly visit some of the most strategic ports in Africa and it can use Cuban troops to influence political events where the people have risen up to challenge Western imperialism.

Thus the situation has radically changed over the last twenty years. Apart from the persistence of imperialist control over Africa, we now have a tangible Soviet presence in Africa. Although the Soviets are not calling the major shots in Africa yet, they are beginning to influence the dynamics of change and consequently the nature of inter- and intra-state politics of African countries. We shall now consider how this is beginning to affect the prospects for peace and development in Africa.

Peace and Development in Africa

Bourgeois scholars of the African scene, when analysing the prospects for peace and development in Africa, tend to emphasize the internal conflicts between and within states. Often the only homage paid to the international dimension is a passing reference to the residual aspects of colonial rule in Africa. Due recognition is thus made of the fact that colonial boundaries were arbitrarily drawn by the colonial powers, for these often cut across tribal communities. But having glanced cursorily at the past, scholars quickly get down to analysing the present in terms of either such mundane sociological factors as tribalism and religion or in terms of personality. In their view threats to peace and security in Africa arise either from wicked and corrupt leadership or because a wrong ideology has taken hold of a misguided leadership or because conflict is endemic in a tribal society.

It would be futile to deny that all these factors have a certain role to play in the generation and exacerbation of conflicts in Africa. No one would deny, for example, that the scale of the atrocities carried out in Uganda during the period of Idi Amin had something to do with the dictator's idiosyncratic personality. Similarly, it would not be correct to assert that tribal differences played no role in the Nigerian civil war or the civil war in Chad.

But if tribalism is so important, how do we explain the fact that in some countries it leads to conflict and in other countries it does not? Is the tribal factor any less potent in Kenya than in Uganda? Why should Uganda be torn apart tribally while Kenya seems to have been able to hold together since the two countries achieved their independence in the early 1960s? Why should tribalism be a source of conflict at a certain period in a country but not at another? Why should tribalism generate a violent confrontation between the Ibos and the rest of the people in Nigeria during 1966-9 and not before or after?

We do not intend to discuss this at any length except to say that the explanations cannot lie in tribalism itself. There must be some other factors besides, for if tribalism was the source of all internal strife in Africa, as some bourgeois scholars contend, then there should be a continuous war of all tribes against all other tribes all the time.

The thesis we would advance is rather that the existing contradictions amongst the people in Africa are manipulated by larger interests and that the source of conflict in Africa has other roots; these differences are, however, exploitable material for these larger interests to feed on. In the process, conflicts in Africa do at times become violent, though no more than conflicts in other parts of the Third World.

We would contend, for example, that the source of conflict in South Africa is not primarily racial, although undoubtedly it has some racial aspects. It serves certain interests in South Africa better to present the conflict in racial terms. These interests include imperialism, which wants to mask the exploitative relations it feeds on in South Africa—the real source of conflict—by presenting race as the real problem. This also serves the interests of certain classes within the liberation movements who want to remove the racial manifestation of the conflict so that they can assume power and take over the economy in order that they, rather than the whites, can profit from the exploitation of the people. It is to the credit of the major liberation movements in South Africa—including the ANC, the PAC and the recently created UDF—that although they accept that racism is an aspect of the situation, which indeed it is, they regard it as a secondary factor and argue that essentially it is a question of national liberation in which, in general, the concerned whites and the coloureds have as much of a role to play as the blacks.

If we take all the other major events which have disrupted or are disrupting the peace and security of the peoples of Africa—such as the Nigerian civil war, the civil war in Chad, the Morocco-Sahrawi Republic conflict, the problems in Southern Sudan, the problems on the Zaire-Angola border, the Ethiopia-Somalia connflict, the conflict between MPLA and UNITA in Angola and so on—we would contend that although tribe, religion, race and internal class divisions do fuel the fire, the origin of the conflict lies in the larger struggle between imperialism and the desire of the peoples of Africa for national liberation. In some of these conflicts the United States and the Soviet Union are directly involved. In some, however, the prevailing configuration of forces allows a minor Western imperialist country to take the direct role instead of the United States; for example, France in Chad and in Zaire and Britain in Rhodesia and Uganda. Similarly, the Soviet Union may not itself be directly involved in certain situations, allowing its interests to be advanced rather by its allies or dependants such as Cuba in Angola, Libya in Chad and North Korea in Uganda.

One question comes to the fore as a result of this analysis. If, as we say, tribal or racial differences are not the generic factors that cause the disruption of peace in Africa and are manipulated by external forces, then why is it that African leaders allow themselves to be so manipulated?

Our answer is that both because of the class character in the leadership in Africa and because of historical and contemporary circumstances, African leaders have very few options. There is no country in Africa in which the working classes have assumed state power, that would presume a proletarian revolution. Despite the rhetoric of many leaders professing socialism, most of them are actually scared of allowing the initiative to pass into the hands of the working classes. They would rather socialist changes were introduced from the top by using state power than from the bottom by the people themselves, for in the latter case the leadership would become dispensable. The petty bourgeois leadership can neither be consistent democrats nor steadfast revolutionaries. The real weakness of their situation is that they are themselves victims of circumstances over which they have little control. They have inherited an economic system managed by imperialism and a political structure fashioned out for them by the departing colonial powers. Even radical leaders such as Nkrumah, Sekou Toure, Nyerere, Samora Machel and Mugabe have discovered that the economic and political structures left behind by the existing colonial powers have heavily circumscribed their freedom to create their own policies.

In this situation what impact does the superpower conflict have on the prospect of peace and development in Africa? All we can say is that in the short to medium run, Africa is likely to go through a series of political convulsions in which the issues are likely to become increasingly polarized between the options offered to Africa by the United States on the one hand and the Soviet Union on the other.

This is not to say that within the next one, two or ten years African states will fall into line behind one or other superpower. The process of polarization will not only be slow but will also be less definite and more complex than that. We have already alluded to the shifting character of alliances in Africa. That pattern is likely to continue. Furthermore, the degree to which each superpower pursues its interests in Africa aggressively or delicately will depend on, among other factors, whether the hawks or the doves are in power in the United States and the Soviet Union, the extent of their stakes in a particular situation and the general international climate.

For the present the Reagan administration in the United States is pursuing its policies rather aggressively. This aggression has expressed itself in a violent form in places like Grenada, Nicaragua, Libya and El Salvador where the United States sees the revolutionary movement of the people as being closely linked with possible provocation by the Soviet Union. Of course, the present aggressiveness of the United States must not be personalized in the character of Reagan. We have in the past seen some of the most serious problems to international security posed by more liberal-looking American presidents such as John Kennedy for example.

In Africa the United States would seem to be the more aggressive superpower, whether it is acting direclty or through its local agents. The Soviet approach to Africa, for the time being, is more tentative. This has partly to do with the fact that the Soviet Union has a certain historical and institutional disadvantage in Africa. But it has also to do with the fact that its possible allies in Africa are, for the moment, weak and divided. None the less, as we stated earlier, the Soviet Union has made considerable inroads in Africa. The Soviet posture could, in time, become as aggressive as that of the United States.

The logic of superpower struggle is such that, as in the arms race, the increasing power of one superpower pushes the other to try to match it. Each believes that only by retaining its own hegemony can international peace be secured. There is, however, in Africa a third factor besides the two superpowers; the masses of the peoples of Africa themselves, whose revolutionary consciousness and organization is daily improving. As this happens, the United States feels increasingly insecure and therefore becomes increasingly aggressive. At the same time, this revolutionary consciousness opens the door to Soviet entry. Even a moderate African leader like Bishop Desmond Tutu, the winner of the Nobel Peace Prize in 1984, can make a statement to the effect that South Africans would prefer the Soviet Union to the continuation of the present situation.[9] It is the logic of the superpower conflict that potentially polarizes every conflict in Africa.

The dynamics of peace in Africa are thus three-sided, with the revolutionary force in Africa constituting the third element. The trilateral relationships work themselves out in three sets of dialectical relations in which each relationship influences and is influenced by the other two.

We stated earlier that in the short and medium run Africa is likely to undergo a convulsive period of conflict because there is no solid social force in Africa that can stabilize the situation. Against the overbearing might of the superpowers, the weaknesses of the petty bourgeois regimes are glaringly evident. How long will this last? When will peace come to Africa?

If humanity can save itself from a nuclear war which would, in all likelihood, put an end to the civilization we know, the only way in which a certain level of peace and stability can be created in Africa is if the superpowers keep out of the continent or are kept out. Africa could develop with great speed and relative stability if the superpowers, and the other lesser imperialist powers, were to withdraw and restrict themselves to providing the material and technical assistance necessary for Africa's development. The sudden expression of collective effort by all the imperialist powers, including the Soviet Union, to dispatch food and transport equipment to the drought-stricken areas of Ethiopia is a rare example of what is possible. We know, however, that such cooperation between the superpowers is the exception rather than the rule in the conduct of their relations in Africa. We must therefore leave out any possibility of peace in Africa through the superpowers voluntarily agreeing to withdraw. Having said this, it must be added, however, that if it is possible to create a nuclear free zone in Africa, for example, in the Indian Ocean, or the West Coast of Africa, within the larger context of arms control agreement between the superpowers, then it is a cause that Africans must not give up in despair.

If the superpowers do not voluntarily withdraw from Africa the only alternative is to keep them out. Is this possible? Is there a power strong enough in Africa to hold the superpowers at bay? Kwame Nkrumah used to talk about the creation of an African High Command which, under the umbrella of a Pan-African organization like the OAU, would militarily intervene in a conflict situation in Africa and isolate it from superpower involvement.

The OAU does not exactly measure up to Nkrumah's vision. It is important, none the less, to assess the extent to which it has succeeded in isolating African conflicts from the direct intervention of superpowers. This could be the subject of an entirely different paper, but we offer a tentative evaluation. In our view, the OAU has found it difficult to prevent superpower intervention, directly or through their agents, in situations, such as the civil war in (ex Belgian) Congo in the 1960s, the Nigerian civil war and the whole of Southern Africa, where the superpowers have high stakes. In these situations the OAU has found itself either displaced by another agency, such as by the United Nations in the Congo, or reduced to a peripheral role, as in Nigeria and in Southern Africa. On the question of Namibia, for example, the front line states under Nyerere's leadership did at a certain time maintain a certain amount of initiative. But as soon as matters became crucial this initiative was taken out of their hands, first by the four power contact group and then the United States.

This is not to discredit the role of the OAU but to put on record the severe limitations under which it functions. To come back to Nkrumah's High Command; is it really a feasible proposition? In our view it is neither feasible nor desirable. Given the character of most regimes in Africa, internally weak and susceptible to manipulation by the superpowers, such a command force, instead of insulating Africa from conflict could become a millstone around the neck of revolutionary forces in Africa.

If the superpowers will not withdraw from Africa on their own and if there is no force presently existing which can keep conflict in Africa insulated from superpower involvement, is the situation hopeless? That depends on the manner and pace at which the working classes in Africa are able to organize themselves to fight imperialism. If Latin America and South-East Asia have anything to teach us it is that the revolutionary march of the exploited and oppressed peoples is inexorable. If countries such as Nicaragua, El Salvador, the Philippines, Viet Nam and Kampuchea appear at the moment to be threatened by the counter-revolutionary forces unleashed by imperialism, they also demonstrate that the revolutionary will of the people is irrepressible, though they also show that imperialism is not likely to be defeated in a swift battle or two. Both these lessons, the indomitable will of the people, and the fact that imperialism will not yield easily, indicate that Africa has still a long way to go, but the African peoples will inexorably travel the path to victory.

Conclusions

The last sentence may sound like a visionary cry in the wilderness. The objective of this paper was to draw attention to both the hard realities of the present day African situation and the aspects in the current situation which hold the seeds of change. All we can say for the present moment is that Africa faces a troublesome future. The configuration of internal and international forces does not augur well. The present weakness of African leadership, arising partly from its class character but mainly out of the circumstances in which leaders find themselves, combined with the ideological and power vacuum created by the end of direct political control of the former colonial powers, has created the ideal background for superpower intervention into conflict situations in Africa. These conflicts in Africa are not, as many bourgeois and some left-wing scholars tend to argue, products primarily of the internal tribal, racial, class, and regional factors, though these do indeed contribute to the conflicts. They are *primarily* caused by the justifiable attempts on the part of the people of Africa to liberate themselves from this domination.

Against this background the superpower struggle for global hegemony looms large, its logic tends potentially towards the polarization of every major conflict situation in Africa, as indeed in other parts of the Third World. The present weakness of Africa, at the economic and political levels, makes the continent vulnerable to this kind of polarization inherent in the global struggle for hegemony between the two superpowers.

But the situation itself contains its own remedy. A power will arise from the social bowels of Africa, led by the working masses, which will stand up to the superpowers and call a halt to the continuing pillage and immerization of the peoples of Africa. The seeds of that development have already germinated, as events in South Africa in recent years amply demonstrate.

Notes

1. The most famous of these is the report the World Bank brought out in 1982 analysing the situation in Africa. The report, *Accelerated Development in Sub-Saharan Africa: An Agenda for Action* (or more commonly, the Berg Report, after its chairman), while drawing attention to 'external constraints', put the blame for lack of development in the 1970s in Africa on what it called the 'domestic policy inadequacies' of African governments.

2. The inaugural meeting of SADCC was held in Lusaka on 1 April 1980, when a declaration entitled 'Southern Africa: Toward Economic Liberation' was signed. After stating that the main objective of SADCC is to liberate the economies of SADCC countries from the domination of South Africa, the declaration goes on to invite 'all concerned to assist us in this high endeavour'. Of the total of US$276m that was pledged at the Maputo SADCC Conference in November 1980, the largest contribution ($150m) came from the EEC and the United Nations and the rest from Scandinavian and Benelux countries. The only East European country to

have indicated concern was the GDR which pledged an unspecified sum.

3. Here we would specifically identify a certain school of South African writers represented, among others, by Dan O'Meara, R. Davies and D. Innes who, over the last few years, have produced a number of papers and books concentrating on internal classes in South Africa without showing concretely how these are linked with imperialism, as if the problem in South Africa were purely or even primarily internal. See Robert Davies and Dan O'Meara 'The State of Analysis of the Southern African Region: Issues Raised by South African Strategy', *Review of African Political Economy* No.29, 1984; Duncan Innes and Martin Plaut, 'Class Struggle and the State', *Review of African Political Economy* No.11, 1978; Robert Davies and Dan O'Meara, 'The Workers' Struggle in South Africa: A Comment', *Review of African Political Economy* No.30, 1984: Robert Davies, David Kaplan, Mike Morris, Dan O'Meara, 'Class Struggle and the Periodisation of the State in South Africa', *Review of African Political Economy* No.7, 1979.

4. This theory is put forward in a revealing book written by the wife of a former member of the Rhodesian Central Intelligence Organization. See Barbara Cole, *The Elite*, (publisher not known). Reported in *The Herald* (Harare), 16 November 1984.

5. See John Stockwell, *In Search of Enemies*, Future Publications, London, 1979.

6. We have analysed some of the major implications of the Nkomati Agreement on the region in 'SADCC and the Preferential Trade Area (PTA): Points of Convergence and Divergence'.

7. Most analysts belonging to the so-called centre-periphery school indulge in this kind of dualism. For example, see Issa G. Shivji, *Class Struggles in Tanzania* (Tanzania Publishing House, 1975), and M. Mamdani, *Politics and Class Formation in Uganda*, Monthly Review Press, New York, 1976.

8. Parts of Nyerere's speech were reproduced under the title 'Process of Liberation', in *New Outlook*, Dar es Salaam, no.5, 1977, p.5.

9. See *The Herald*, Harare, 14 November 1984.

Part 2: Conflict and Instability

4. The National Question and the Crisis of Instability in Africa

Nzongola-Ntalaja

The seating of the Sahrawi Arab Democratic Republic (SADR) as a sovereign nation at the 21st summit of the Organization of African Unity (OAU) in November 1984 in Addis Ababa was a triumph for the people of the Western Sahara and their right to national self-determination and independence. It was also a triumph for the OAU principle of the non-inviolability of colonial frontiers. According to this principle, the political map of Africa should correspond to the map that resulted from the partition of Africa one hundred years ago, save for territorial adjustments to which the people concerned have agreed democratically. [1]

In defending this principle in the face of the often-repeated and accurate charge that the imperialists had divided Africa without regard to ethnic or cultural boundaries, Africa has not only opted for political realism but also recognized that the inherited boundaries have within them the necessary conditions of modern nationhood. Since any attempt to remake the map of Africa in accordance with pre-colonial boundaries is doomed to failure the principle of the non-inviolability of colonial frontiers has been given preference over the idea of territorial reconstruction based on historical claims, whether credible or dubious, such as the ideas of Greater Morocco, Greater Somalia and others.

In spite of the near unanimity of this principle, the problem of the political map of Africa has not been settled to everybody's satisfaction. Such a situation is not peculiar to Africa, as the existence of autonomist and separatist movements in Asia, Europe and North America demonstrates. [2] What is particular to Africa is the destabilizing threat that the problem poses for peace, development and the social order as well as for regional stability in a continent of economically underdeveloped and militarily weak countries. Such a threat carries with it the danger of foreign involvement as each of the contending forces seeks to obtain external military assistance. For these reasons, the national question remains a salient factor of regional instability and civil strife in Africa. It is central to the conflicts in the Horn of Africa and the Western Sahara and a contributing factor to the civil war in Chad and to the crisis of instability in several other countries.

This paper is a modest attempt to examine the nature of the national question and its relationship to the crisis of instability in Africa. It seeks to highlight the conditions under which the national question arises as a critical issue in a country's politics and to identify the lessons, if any, that Africa may draw from its recent history for ways of resolving the issue. After a brief discussion of what constitutes the national question, the paper examines the problem historically by looking at a number of related issues, including the impact of colonialism on the national question, the objective conditions for the rise of dissident nationalism in post-colonial Africa and the relationship between the national question and the class struggle in Africa.

The National Question

Any scientific analysis of the national question must begin with a theoretical discussion of the following problematic: what is a nation? Are there nations in Africa? Are African countries nations? These and related questions are still a subject of intense debate in the world today. In the Western news media, for example, the popular image of Africa is that of countries rent by ancient tribal enmities that complicate and retard the development of national consciousness. These media tend to explain all African political crises in terms of tribalism, an attachment to tribe or ethnic group which remains a more relevant unit of identification than the country as a whole.

This image of Africa was given scientific respectability in the early 1960s by anthropologist Clifford Geertz's thesis that primordial sentiments were the most relevant factor of social reality in the newly independent countries.[3] It was enthusiastically applied to Africa by modernization theorists like David Apter and Aristide Zolberg.[4] This thesis has been revised under a new label by Goran Hyden, who refers to primordial ties of solidarity as 'the economy of affection'.[5]

By granting an *a priori* determinism to blood, kinship, religion and other primordial ties, loyalties and affinities, this thesis obscures the interplay of class, economic and geopolitical factors which weigh heavily on contemporary African politics. Its defenders are also guilty of a serious methodological flaw. They insist, on the one hand, that Africa is a unique or special case to be analysed differently from other parts of the world. And yet, on the other hand, they maintain an evolutionist perspective, according to which Africa will some day look like the West. The flaw resides in the fact that, contrary to the purported uniqueness of Africa and the need to analyse it with original theories and concepts, it is the same old modernization theory with its dichotomous vision of tradition and modernity that is being applied to Africa.

According to this vision, whose ablest representative today is Goran Hyden, Africa will in due time evolve from tribal to non-tribal society, from mechanic to organic solidarity, from an ascriptive-oriented behaviour to an achievement-oriented one and from the economy of affection to a legal–rational economic order. There are no short cuts to development. The only development strategy necessary for effecting a successful transition, and the one Hyden proposes, is to strengthen an indigenous capitalist bourgeoisie unfettered by state regulations and left free to wage a deadly battle against pre-capitalist structures and mentalities. Peasant power, interests and autonomy must be sacrificed for the sake of national development. The modern nation is born through the passing away of the traditional society.[6]

It may come as a surprise to some that this way of looking at the national question is close to that of dogmatic Marxism. Like modernization theorists, dogmatic Marxists assume that the nation is a social phenomenon produced by the development of capitalism. Their understanding of the national question is primarily, if not exclusively, based on their reading of Joseph Stalin's classic, *Marxism and the National Question*, in which he defines the nation as '*a historically constituted, stable community of people formed on the basis of a common language, territory, economic life, and psychological make-up manifested in a common culture*'.[7] For Stalin, such a community requires for its viability an integrated home market and, consequently, belongs to the epoch of rising capitalism.

The four characteristic features delineated by Stalin are not to be used mechanically as a checklist against which nationhood is to be gauged.[8] They have to be seen as necessary rather than sufficient conditions for nationhood. For they can also be found in social formations based on pre-capitalist modes of production. What is sufficient to make a nation, Stalin's followers argue, is the 'particular historic practice that produces those features as a unity— the formation of distinct capitalist social formations'.[9] Why, it may be asked is capitalism the only mode of production capable of grafting these features onto a socio-historical entity to produce a nation? Is it impossible to achieve the centralization of economic organization and political authority essential to nationhood under other modes of production? Stalin's followers have no satisfactory answers to these questions other than appealing to European history, which is their point of reference.

Nicos Poulantzas and Samir Amin have made extremely pertinent critiques of this orthodox theory of the nation.[10] Poulantzas castigates the profoundly empiricist and positivist conception of the constituent elements of a nation in this theory and raises doubts about the usefulness of the central argument that the nation is a creation of merchant capital.

> The generalization of commercial exchange cannot explain the creation of the modern nation: if it reveals the necessity of the unification of the so-called internal market and the elimination of obstacles to the circulation of goods and of capital, *it does not in any way explain why this unification takes place precisely at the level of the nation*.[11]

According to Samir Amin, the orthodox theory confuses the existence of nations with one of its historical expressions, namely, the emergence of nation states in Europe in connection with the development of capitalism.[12] It is inadequate for a full understanding of the phenomenon of nationhood in other parts of the world because it assumes that nations cannot exist in the absence of capitalist development.

According to these assumptions, nations would only exist at the centre of the world capitalist system, in the areas where the bourgeois revolution has established the national power of the local bourgeoisie. Elsewhere nations would not actually exist, at least not in a finished form. What then are we to say of the social realities of the precapitalist world, where an old statist tradition blends into a cultural and linguistic reality? Thousand year old Egypt has always been united on the level of language, culture and—except during some brief periods of decadence—on the level of political power as well. Whilst it is not a bourgeois nation, it is certainly something more than an incongruous and unorganized conglomerate of peoples. Furthermore, even those regions which were not organized into unified and centralized states, and which were not united culturally and linguistically, have increasingly become so following upon their integration into the international capitalist system as colonies or as dominated semi-dependent countries. Even if this unification has not been the work of a national bourgeoisie it is nonetheless an important social fact. [13]

As a social phenomenon, the nation is not necessarily or exclusively a product of the capitalist mode of production. It may appear at every stage of history as a particular unit of reproduction of social relations in class societies based on modes of production which require a centralization of economic organization and political authority. Such a centralization is best achieved through state power. This is why there is a dialectical relationship between state and nation in the modern world. The nation either emerges to coincide with an existing state or consolidates itself as a modern nation by creating its own state. [14]

The relationship between the two is mediated through two matrices which constitute the material framework of institutions and social practices: the spatial matrix of territory and geographical contiguity and the temporal matrix of a shared historical and cultural tradition. [15] Both matrices are necessary conditions of the existence of a nation as well as factors that the state and/or the social class playing the unifying role of political and economic centralization can manipulate to promote among the people a greater sense of collective identification with the nation as a socio-historical entity larger and more meaningful than their locality or regional groupings. Such a promotion is the work of all institutions belonging to or subject to the influence of the state system, including educational, cultural and religious organizations.

The phenomenon of nationhood is both reversible and variable in its intensity. The level of nationhood may be more or less intense depending on the development of the productive forces and the impact of the state's role in the material organization of time and space on the constituent elements of the nation. With more resources and well equipped armies, bureaucracies, prisons, schools and other institutions with which to fashion the nation, advanced capitalism does have better conditions for sustaining a stronger or more intense level of nationhood than pre-capitalist and underdeveloped societies. Samir Amin's proposition that 'the phenomenon of nationhood is a reversible process', whereby a nation may develop and grow stronger or 'regress into a formless conglomeration of more or less related ethnic groups', is particularly applicable to these societies. [16]

The Formation of Nations in Africa

These reflections allow us to place the national question as it relates to Africa in its proper perspective. There were nations at different levels of intensity in pre-colonial Africa, corresponding to social formations made up of closely related lineages or other kinship groups unified by a core cultural tradition and a relatively durable politico-administrative structure. These formations were held together by ruling classes based on tribute collection and which succeeded in promoting the growth of long distance trade, protecting markets and trade routes and ensuring the centralization and redistribution of the surplus. The myths of origin, the ideologies of kingship and the oral histories of migrations and conquests were instrumental in creating for these ruling classes a cultural tradition that served to cement a national identity and to help galvanize political loyalty and support among their peoples. The national fact was so real for some of these societies that even after their disintegration as a result of external conquest and colonial rule serious attempts were to be made to revive them in the post-colonial period.

It must be emphasized, however, that not all pre-colonial states corresponded to or overlapped with nations. In Central Africa, for example, there were trade and conquest states that did not exhibit nationality characteristics as developed over two or more centuries in those entities like the Kongo, Kuba, Luba and Lunda kingdoms which emerged as relatively viable nations.[17] Unlike these nations, the trade and conquest states were heterogeneous entities lacking a distinctive cultural tradition linking the state to a people with deep historical roots in the territory. These states included Queen Nzinga's Kingdom of Matamba, the Imbangala Kingdom of Kasanje, the expansionist Lunda Kingdom of Kazembe and the Nyamwezi/Yeke Kingdom of Garenganze.[18]

With the colonial conquest and occupation, the potential of African social formations to develop viable nations was greatly diminished. Those nations which existed at the time of the conquest lost their vitality, if not their very existence, as nations. The intensity of nationhood depended on the structure of the colonial state: stronger where the latter corresponded to a historical state— as in Burundi, Egypt, Lesotho, Libya, Madagascar, Morocco, Rwanda, Swaziland, Tunisia, and Zanzibar— and weaker where it incorporated different nationalities and groups.

In the latter case, the traditional rulers were to serve as subordinate agents of local colonial administration as well as representatives of their subjects *vis-à-vis* the colonial state. Whether the method of colonial rule was said to be direct or indirect, they performed their administrative tasks in a more satisfactory manner than they were ever able to defend the interests of their people.[19] These tasks were chiefly extractive and regulatory in nature: revenue collection, labour recruitment, conscription, forced labour on public projects, compulsory cultivation of certain export crops, law and order and the enforcement of public health and other state regulations. Alienated from their traditional rulers, ordinary people had to seek a new leadership in their struggle against colonialism. They found it in the new African petty bourgeoisie, the class that was to become the standard-bearer of modern African nationalism.

The impact of colonialism on the national question was thus a complex one. On the one hand, the imposition of colonial rule resulted in the fading away of a large number of pre-colonial nations, or their disintegration into that 'formless conglomeration of more or less related ethnic groups' described by Samir Amin. On the other hand, colonialism united different African nationalities and peoples under a single territorial and institutional framework, widened their social space as a result of greater inter-ethnic interaction through the institutions and practices of the colonial system and thus created a common historical experience of economic exploitation, political and administrative oppression and cultural oppression. [20]

In spite of their racist and evolutionist perspectives,, the colonialists were perceptive enough to recognize that they were laying the foundations of nationhood in their artificially created territories. In defending the idea of a unitary Congo before the Katanga Provincial Council on 1 September 1958 in Elisabethville, Belgian Colonial Affairs Minister Léon Pétillon had this to say about the Belgian Congo as a nation.

> We have created the Congo and...given it highly centralized institutions...which have inevitably engendered over the long run among the inhabitants, who were at one time ignorant of each other's existence, the concept of a nation and the budding of a kind of nationalism. [21]

Although the people of the Zaire River basin were not 'ignorant of each other's existence', having interacted with one another through trade and war long before the Belgians conquered them, it was their unification by the colonialists which created a sense of common destiny and a commitment to realize that destiny within the territorial boundaries inherited from colonialism.

There are those who argue that despite the unification and centralization achieved under colonialism, Africa does not as yet have nations. For some, the stability that existed during the colonial period is likely to disappear under the weight of centrifugal forces, unless these destabilizing forces are checked by strong arm rule. This, in fact, is the Western prescription for order in Africa today: rule by Machiavellian strongmen who would stop at nothing to attain their objectives and serve Western interests. [22] For others, African countries are not yet nations because of their continued subjection to imperialist domination. According to this school of thought, the nation becomes possible only as a result of a successful national liberation struggle, through the dual transformation of a dependent country by national self-determination and socialism.

A major representative of this orthodox Marxist school in Africa today is Professor D. Wadada Nabudere. [23] Starting from Stalin's formulations on the national question and the contribution to orthodox theory by Lenin and Mao Zedong, [24] Nabudere maintains that in the colonial and neo-colonial countries 'a "national state", although possible at the political level, is historically impossible under capitalism'. [25] For 'national exploitation and oppression' by imperialism continue even under the conditions of political independence. There are no nations in Africa today, only oppressed countries and peoples. At the same time, Nabudere recognizes the fact that capitalism has introduced an 'awakening to nationhood' in these dependent countries and admits that the people do suffer a national oppression.

The question that Nabudere and his friends need to answer is what constitutes the 'national' dimension of oppression and the 'national awakening', in the absence of a nation. Do oppressed people come to their 'awakening to nationhood' on any basis other than that of being economically exploited and politically oppressed as a labour force essential to Western capitalist accumulation? That something else is involved in this awakening can be seen from the following example on the differential positions of black and white workers *vis-à-vis* colonial oppression in Angola.

The poor whites did not share a common experience of oppression with African workers, in spite of the fact that many were in wage employment, including unskilled jobs such as being waiters, taxi-drivers, doormen, lottery-ticket vendors, maids and market women.[26] Even though they experienced the fascist repression unleashed by Antonio Salazar's *Estado Novo* on Portuguese citizens and subjects alike, they escaped the systematic and most vicious manifestations of political and cultural oppression to which Africans were subjected on the basis of their race and to which the poor whites as a group made their own deadly contribution. It was in response to this racially based exploitation and oppression that African nationalism developed among black Angolans, as it did elsewhere in reaction to the violence and Manichean world of colonialism.[27]

That is to say that Africans experienced capitalist exploitation and colonial oppression as blacks or as Arabs and this experience had a lot to do with their response to the colonial situation. Denied their human and democratic rights, they were also victims of discrminatory practices with regard to economic and social justice: lack of equal employment opportunities, investment credit, property rights, access to the better social services and amenities reserved for Europeans. Consequently it was their common identification of the colonial society as the general obstacle to social and economic progress that made it possible for all social classes to unite in a common struggle against colonialism.

In black Africa, this struggle was also inspired by the fight against racism and oppression in the African diaspora of North America and the Caribbean, home of the intellectual pioneers of Pan-Africanism (H. Sylvester Williams, W.E.B. DuBois, Marcus Garvey). As an intellectual movement Pan-Africanism represented the rise to self-assertion of Africans and peoples of African descent outside the continent with the overriding goal of regaining their social dignity as a people and eventually establishing an independent *nation* in the African homeland. This was especially true for Garveyism, the prophetic and mass-based wing of the movement, whose influence was felt all over black Africa.[28]

With Pan-Africanism the national question became more complex as political entrepreneurs or would-be founders of nations had to grapple with the problem of determining the most relevant socio-historical entity to develop as a nation. To which of the following three entities was the new African nation to correspond: 1) the *ethnic nation* of ancient glory whose construction was arrested by colonialism or the one born out of the contradictions of the colonial situation (Luba Kasai, Ibo); 2) the colonially created *territorial nation*, or 3) the *Pan-African nation*, of which diaspora Africans were to be a part?

Each of the three positions had its defenders, including the first which received a passionate though unconvincing defence in Chief Obafemi Awolowo's 1947 book *Path to Nigerian Freedom*, in which he argues for a multinational state based on a federation of ethnic nations.[29] At the other end of the spectrum were people like Kwame Nkrumah, who advocated a Pan-African entity and proposed the creation of a 'United States of Africa'.[30]

Generally, it can be said that the Pan-African ideal, however attractive it might have been to African nationalists between 1945 and 1960, was in flagrant contradiction to both the neo-colonialist strategy of imperialism and the class interests of the African petty bourgeoisie, the class leading the nationalist struggle. The basic thrust of neo-colonialism was for the imperialist powers to grant independence to the colonial territories while retaining control over their economies in order to keep these countries within the world capitalist system as indispensable sources of raw materials and cheap labour for the imperialist countries. Amilcar Cabral has described the imperialist strategy of decolonization as follows:

> The objective of the imperialist countries was to prevent the enlargement of the socialist camp, to liberate the reactionary forces in our countries which were being stifled by colonialism and to enable these forces to ally themselves with the international bourgeoisie. The fundamental objective was to create a bourgeoisie where one did not exist, in order specifically to strengthen the imperialist and the capitalist camp.[31]

The aims and objectives of imperialism were basically compatible with the class interests of the African petty bourgeoisie. Both the imperialists and the African nationalist leaders opted for the dismantling of the colonial empires into their constituent territories, as these would prove easier to manipulate and to control from the standpoint of the imperialists and provide a more fertile terrain for the advancement of the economic and political interests of the petty bourgeoisie. Balkanization gave even mediocre leaders the chance to become heads of state or cabinet ministers at the national level, something that might have escaped them altogether within larger and more complex units.

Consistent with this process of balkanization, administratively centralized units that were under the control of a single governor-general like French West Africa, French Equatorial Africa and the Belgian Congo and Ruanda–Urundi were split up into eight, four and three countries respectively. Efforts to retain French West Africa as a single entity or to salvage the larger portion of it into a federation were sabotaged by the French imperialists, with the help of African politicians like Félix Houphouet-Boigny, a major leader of the region-wide nationalist movement, the *Rassemblement Démocratique Africain* (RDA). Radical parties in Guinea, French Sudan (Mali) and Niger joined progressive elements in Senegal, Upper Volta (Burkina Faso) and Dahomey (Benin) to keep up the fight for unity, but lost. The Pan-African ideal had fallen victim to imperialism and petty bourgeois opportunism. As Walter Rodney writes, the African petty bourgeoisie 'reneged on a cardinal principle of pan-Africanism: namely, the unity and indivisibility of the African continent.' [32]

Thus did the concept of the nation become attached to the territorial entities of the colonial partition, not as a matter of necessity in the organization of the anti-colonial struggle, as Crawford Young maintains, but as the result of the interplay of imperialist and African petty bourgeois interests. [33] The year 1956 can be taken as a benchmark in the annals of African territorial nationalism. It is not only the year of the Suez crisis and the preservation of the independence and national sovereignty of Egypt. It is also the year of the independence of Morocco, Tunisia and Sudan, the *loi-cadre* establishing territorial governments in the French colonies of West Africa, Equatorial Africa and Madagascar, the end of the Mau Mau war, which signalled the beginning of the decolonization process in Kenya and the emergence of modern nationalist politics in Zaire, Angola and Guinea-Bissau. [34]

In 1958, when the All-African Peoples Conference was held in Accra, Ghana, the talk of a Pan-African nation had become a rhetorical exercise. Most of the delegates to this conference were representatives of nationalist movements seeking the independence of their respective colonial territories. Territorial nationalism had established itself so strongly as a norm that one of the delegates was pressured to abandon the tribal anachronism of his movement. The delegate in question was Holden Roberto, then representative of the Union of the People of Northern Angola (UPNA), which he renamed overnight in response to this pressure as the Union of the People of Angola (UPA). The UPNA was the political voice of the separatist movement of the Kongo of Angola, which had sought to restore the old Kongo Kingdom. [35] The pressure exerted on Roberto at Accra was symptomatic of the new African commitment to build new nations out of the arbitrarily created colonial territories.

On the whole, the political map of Africa represents a double failure: the failure of the Pan-African ideal of a single nation under one continental state or under several regional federations and that of reactionary nationalism, which had sought to recreate or revive pre-colonial nations. Neither the Pan-African nation nor the pre-colonial nation had well organized class forces capable of realizing them as political projects. It was shown above how the petty bourgeois intellectuals who once championed Pan-Africanism quickly embraced the European architects of decolonization as fathers of their respective territorial nations. As for the natural rulers of Africa, their alienation from the mass of the people in most colonial territories was irreversible.

The new African nation was born in the struggle against colonialism. It had its class base in the African petty bourgeoisie, the class to whose interests it corresponded within the colonized society. In addition to the petty bourgeoisie, the proletarianized and semi-proletarianized masses had also developed some emotional identification with this new socio-historical entity before independence. [36] This is especially true of those fractions of these classes which had become urbanized and had migrated to urban and industrial centres out of their areas of origin. Their class interests as workers and informal sector entrepreneurs were better served within a territorial entity in which they both felt at home and did not have to compete with too many other people for jobs, resources and means of livelihood. Thus, if the petty bourgeoisie was the standard-bearer of territorial nationalism, these class fractions were among its most active supporters.

National Construction and the Crisis of Instability

Most of the countries of the African continent are arbitrary colonial creations. Of the 53 internationally recognized entities (the 50 OAU members plus Morocco, Namibia and South Africa), only ten correspond to historical states, while four others have a clearly defined cultural identity. The first group, already identified above, includes Ethiopia, but not Zanzibar, which is now part of the United Republic of Tanzania. The second group consists of Algeria, Botswana, Somalia and Western Sahara. [37]

With few exceptions, the remainder 39 states each comprise a mixture of peoples without a core cultural tradition around which all others may coalesce. For these countries, national construction involves the development of a multi-ethnic entity based on a common history of colonial oppression and a common commitment to forging a new cultural identity linked to all the traditions of the past without at the same time being strongly attached to one of them. [38] Most of the historical states are also faced with this challenge, inasmuch as the state itself is linked to a dominant cultural tradition that has been imposed on peripheral groups and minorities.

The process of national construction must therefore reflect the commitment to unity in diversity. This implies not only the need to integrate all the common traits of all cultures in order to forge a new historical identity, but also a scrupulous respect for the language, originality and specificity of each group. Such respect is essential to national unity, particularly in those countries where one or several major groups may assert their cultural and political dominance at the expense of minorities. It is essential also to the task of mobilizing progressive forces to continue the struggle against imperialist domination through neo-colonialism. By destroying this domination, the country resolves the national question by achieving a greater ability to freely determine its own destiny and to transform the economy so that it may serve the interests of workers and peasants.

This aspect of the national question is the one that Nabudere and others evoke to deny the very existence of nations in Africa. However, there must be a nation, or at least its material foundations of territory and a people, before there can be a national liberation struggle. Preoccupied as we ought to be with the anti-imperialist struggle, we should not forget that this struggle takes place within a given territorial entity and that the specific characteristics of, and the contradictions among, the people of that territory will have definite consequences for the struggle.

The remainder of this paper is devoted to an analysis of the national question as it relates to the political map of Africa. It will examine the problem of colonial territories that have been denied their right to self-determination as well as the conditions under which ethnic groups, nationalities and national minorities seek to achieve regional autonomy within existing territorial boundaries or to modify these boundaries in order to establish themselves as sovereign nations. More specifically, an attempt is made to explain how ethnic nationalism, the rise to self-assertion of national minorities and the quest for national self-determination give rise to the crisis of instability and to armed conflict in post-colonial Africa.

Ethnic nationalism refers to the specific relationship of politicized ethnicity—or the mobilization and organization of an ethnic group for collective action—to the national question.[39] According to Crawford Young, ethnicity in general differs from nationalism as an ideological formulation of identity 'in the absence of any serious aspiration to the total autonomy required by nationalism'.[40] For our purposes, ethnic nationalism implies at the very least an aspiration to regional autonomy in a multinational state and as a maximal project a commitment to independent nationhood. In the latter case, the people involved attain this objective either by creating a state of their own or by joining an already existing state to which they are ethnically related. In post-colonial Africa, ethnic nationalism with secessionist tendencies has risen in the form of irredentism, revanchism, or as a result of violent conflicts stemming from inter-ethnic competition for economic resources and political power. A constant factor of regional instability in the Horn of Africa, ethnic nationalism was one of the root causes of major crisis in Uganda and of civil war in Zaire and Nigeria.

Irredentism: The Somalia Question

The main instance of irredentism in Africa has been the determination of ethnic Somalis in the Ogaden and sections of the Haud and Bale in Ethiopia, in Djibouti (formerly French Somaliland or French Territory of the Afar and Issa) and in the North-eastern Frontier District (NFD) of Kenya to seek unification with Somalia. The Somali question was a direct consequence of the arbitrary manner in which Africa was partitioned and the establishment of independent states on the basis of colonial frontiers. A culturally homogeneous and distinct people made up of related clans of nomads, the Somalis were divided between four powers: Britain, Ethiopia, France and Italy.

Somali nationalism, inspired by the heroic resistance to colonial conquest led by Mohamed Abdille Hassan between the early 1900s and 1920, was given a new impetus after the defeat of Italy in 1941. The dream of a Pan-Somali territorial unity was reinforced by the seemingly approving attitude of the major regional power, Britain, which actually promised to create such an entity by incorporating all the Somali-inhabited areas. Despite these promises, Britain recognized Ethiopian sovereignty over the Ogaden in 1942, relinquished control over most of it in 1948 and ceded the Haud to Ethiopia in 1954.[41] Only British Somaliland and Italian Somaliland were united at independence in 1960 to form the Somali Democratic Republic.

As a result, irredentist movements arose in the Ogaden and the Haud and in the NFD. In October 1962 the leaders of the approximately 200,000 ethnic Somalis in Kenya demanded the integration of the NFD into Somalia. This was rejected by both Britain and the transitional government in Kenya. No sooner had Kenya become independent on 12 December 1963 than Somali pressures forced the new state to declare a state of emergency two weeks later. The Council of Ministers of the newly created OAU intervened on 12 February 1964 to mediate what the OAU simply took to be a border dispute between the two countries. Tensions seem to have diminished since then and Kenya appears to be making an effort to integrate the Somalis into the country's multi-ethnic society. There is no doubt, however, that a great deal remains to be done in this regard.

With over one million Somalis the Ogaden had a stronger irredentist movement, the Western Somalia Liberation Front (WSLF), created immediately after Somalia's independence. There has been a close collaboration between the Somali government and the WSLF. However, the double nature of the Ogaden question as both a territorial dispute between two sovereign states and as a question involving the right to self-determination of an oppressed national minority creates tensions and differences between the two. This seems to be the case today, as a more radical WSLF sees itself not as an irredentist movement but as a liberation movement demanding self-determination and having the option of either merging with Somalia or remaining within Ethiopia as an autonomous region.[42]

Ethiopia and Somalia went to war over the Ogaden in 1964 and in 1977. The 1964 war was a simple border war and one for which OAU mediation was sufficient to help bring an end to the hostilities. Mindful of the OAU position favouring Ethiopia's retention of the Ogaden, the Somali government launched the 1977 war in collaboration with the WSLF so as to hide its real expansionist aims. This is the war in which the Soviet Union and Cuba gave military support to Ethiopia, including the deployment of Cuban troops in the Ogaden, resulting in the internationalization of the conflict. With the United States backing Somalia militarily in what has become a theatre of global strategic confrontation, but refusing to endorse Mogadishu's position on the Ogaden, the Somali state is totally isolated on this issue. The international community appears to be unanimous in its support for the OAU principle of the non-inviolability of colonial frontiers.

Revanchism: the Case of Buganda

Revanchism or the attempt to recover lost territory or status is the second form under which ethnic nationalism has manifested itself as a destabilizing force in Africa. Buganda, the traditional homeland of the Baganda of the

Republic of Uganda, is virtually the only case of revanchism with major consequences for peace, development and the social order in post-colonial Africa. This ancient kingdom has enjoyed a special status as an autonomous region of Uganda between 1900 and 1966. Established by a 1900 agreement between Britain and Buganda, this status was preserved at independence in 1962, with the Lukiko or Ganda legislature electing Buganda's representatives to Uganda's Parliament and the Kabaka or Ganda king as Uganda's head of state.

Kabaka Edward (Freddie) Mutesa II succeeded for a while in running his own show in an autonomous region of Uganda. However, the attempt to develop a modern Ganda nation within an independent Uganda fell foul of the centralizing tendencies of territorial nationalism and the new states of Africa. It was at the origin of the crisis of instability in Uganda between 1962 and 1966, which resulted in the *coup d'état* of Prime Minister Milton Obote and the flight of the Kabaka to exile in Britain in May 1966.

The ousting of the Kabaka, the desecration of his kingdom and the abolition of the Ganda monarchy by Obote helped to reinforce Ganda nationalism and to breed revanchist sentiments among the Baganda. Ethnic mobilization was pervasive but lacking in effective leadership. Having lost the battle to head the Ganda masses to the Kabaka and his sectarian political party, the *Kabaka Yekka* (the Kabaka only), and being for the most part committed to the unity of Uganda, the Ganda petty bourgeoisie was prepared to abandon the idea of a special status for Buganda. [43]

In the countryside, on the other hand, the active popular demand was for the restoration of the kabakaship and the reunification of the kingdom; ordinary people felt an intimate bond between the monarchy and their own identity. Their revanchist disposition is aptly summarized in the following description of the political climate in Buganda between 1966 and 1971.

Buganda lay sullen and brooding, a reservoir of discontent awaiting the day of deliverance. There was no organized resistance, but a series of isolated attacks, the most serious of these being an assassination attempt on Obote in 1969 in which he survived miraculously a bullet through the jaw. Obote felt unable to travel publicly through Buganda, the silent hostility of the Ganda countryside hung oppressively over the presidential palace. [44]

The colonial policy of divide and rule had laid the foundations for reactionary politics in Buganda. The conferring of a special status on this territory had not only cultivated chauvinism among the Baganda, but also created tensions between them and other Ugandans. Although the Baganda constituted only 16% of the total population of Uganda, their relatively privileged access to colonial educational institutions and their close collaboration with the British colonialists in the administration of the colony had earned them a position of strength in inter-ethnic competition. This position was eroded by the arithmetic of electoral politics, which gave the rest of Uganda a decisive advantage with regard to the exercise of political power.

The special status of Buganda was an anachronism that needlessly impeded the process of national construction in Uganda. At the same time the repression to which the Ganda masses were subjected because of their misguided revanchism worsened the situation by making them feel excluded from Uganda's national fold. The second Obote administration is now faced with the challenge of healing the wounds that his first administration left unattended.

Inter-ethnic Conflict, Ethnic Nationalism and Secession: Biafra and South Kasai

A third instance of ethnic nationalism as a destabilizing factor is the autonomist or secessionist drive by a major ethnic group resulting from an inter-ethnic conflict situation in which the group perceives its own survival as being threatened. The intensity of that perception is a function of the gravity of the situation and its political repercussions in the ethnic homeland. If violence and the perceived threat to the group's socio-economic status or existence itself are the necessary conditions for the autonomist or secessionist option, the sufficient conditions include the relative weakness of the central state machinery, the political ambitions of the group's petty bourgeois leadership and the latter's ability to organize and sustain the struggle for a separate political entity.

Biafra (Nigeria) and South Kasai (Zaire) are two secessionist attempts that answer perfectly to this description. The parallels between them are so striking that one wonders why students of ethnicity and secessionist movements have not seen fit to compare them. Usually, when mention is made of ethno-regional challenges to central authority, the secessions of Katanga and Biafra are cited as though they were comparable.[45] As I have argued elsewhere, ethnicity and the national question were not central issues in the Katanga secession.[46]

It is true that the Lunda and other ethnic groups of southern Katanga (now Shaba) were resentful of their lower socio-economic status in comparison to the predominantly Luba-Kasai settlers of the urban and mining centres. In defining these settlers as strangers who ought to be sent home, the authentic Katangans were hoping to eliminate them from inter-ethnic competition for jobs, social welfare and political power. However, the secession itself was clearly an instance of internal settlement as the work of European settlers,[47] who had determined since 1958 that the only realistic way to advance their interests was to have Africans assimilate their secessionist views and defend them as their own.[48] The party of secession, Moïse Tshombe's *Confédération des Associations Tribales du Katanga* (CONAKAT), was the auxiliary arm of white settlers' politics and their voice through African intermediaries.[49]

The secessionist attempts in Biafra and South Kasai, on the other hand, were entirely the work of Africans. The external factor did eventually assume importance in Biafra though arms sales, mercenaries and the economic and strategic interests of the major powers that were at stake. This is one aspect in which Biafra and Katanga share a number of common traits as large territories with enormous mineral wealth and belonging to two strategically important countries in West and Central Africa. From the standpoint of external involvement, South Kasai was merely an appendage of Katanga which served it as an indispensable source of light arms, a few mercenaries and other imported commodities.

More important than the external factors, which admittedly prolong and exacerbate the crisis, are the internal factors which give rise to it. And these are primarily related to the differential adaptation of a country's ethnic groups to the political economy of colonialism and the nature of inter-ethnic competition for economic resources and political power.

Like the Baganda, the Ibos of Nigeria and the Luba–Kasai people of Zaire adapted themselves so well to the colonial system that their representation in the African petty bourgeoisie was considerably higher than their respective proportions in the general population. In their relentless pursuit of material and social progress, they became the trusted auxiliaries of the colonialists in the administration of territory outside their areas of origin; they also became channels for the penetration of capitalist commodity relations in the countryside and the proselytization of Africans to the Christian faith.[50] Consequently, they were favourably stereotyped by the colonial establishment as intelligent, aggressive and hard-working people, which tended to facilitate their access to education, wage employment and other economic resources. At the same time, their position of relative strength in inter-ethnic competition earned them unfavourable stereotypes from their fellow citizens who tended to see them as arrogant, chauvinist and bent on dominating the rest of the society.

Unlike most other ethnic groups, whose separate identities as people predates colonialism, the Ibos and the Baluba of Kasai emerged as separate and cohesive ethnic groups within the colonial context. 'Being Ibo,' Crawford Young writes, 'is a modern identity.'[51] It was born through the mobilization of this acephalous society of linguistically and culturally related villages in the fight for economic and social progress. The aim was to accelerate the development of its productive forces within the colonial political economy so as to catch up with those areas of Nigeria with a better economic and social infrastructure like the Lagos–Ibadan region and to attain a higher socio-economic status for Ibos. Active self-awareness was forged in the urban communities of Ibo settlers all over Nigeria, starting with Lagos, where the Ibos began to pose a challenge to the social hegemony of the Yoruba petty bourgeoisie in the mid-1930s.

Luba–Kasai ethnicity had a more solid foundation in the pre-colonial Luba Empire which emerged on a large scale in northern Shaba between the 16th and the 18th Centuries among people possessing a common religious culture based on the veneration of ancestors.[52] Despite this foundation, Luba–Kasai identity developed in a similar context of inter-ethnic competition and involved the progressive division of Luba migrants from the Shaba heartland who had settled in the Kasai region before the 19th Century into two separate ethnic groups: the Lulua and the Baluba of Kasai.

Neither group ever organized a single centralized state. They each form a lineage-based segementary society whose highest form of political centralization is at the level of the maximal lineage or chiefdom. [53] Until 1870 all the separate Lulua chiefdoms designated themselves as Luba migrants from the south. [54] According to Vansina, the name 'Lulua' was given to them as inhabitants of the Lulua River valley by the Cokwe. [55] Sharing a single cultural tradition consisting of a common origin, history, language, religion, family structure and the form of economic and political organization, the Lulua and the Baluba were so clearly differentiated politically that they engaged in a bloody fratricidal war between 1959 and 1961.

The differentiation process was the result of the contradictions of colonialism. Between 1880 and 1890, the Luba populations of South Kasai were being decimated by the slave raids of the Cokwe and the Songye auxiliaries of the Arab-Swahilis under Chief Lumpungu. After 1885 thousands of Luba villagers fled to the Luluabourg (now Kananga) area where they were welcomed and given refuge by their Lulua kin. Later on large numbers of young people seeking to escape the burden of traditional economic and social relations left the Luba homeland in South Kasai to seek education, jobs, and new economic opportunities in the Luluabourg area, on the line of rail between Port Francqui (Ilebo) and Elisabethville (Lubumbashi) and in the urban and mining centres of Katanga. Important communities of Luba settlers thus arose in these areas, where they were readily available for recruitment to wage labour and to the churches and schools of the Christian missions. Meanwhile, their ethnic homeland remained one of the most underdeveloped regions in the Belgian Congo.

Pursuing the goal of uplifting themselves through education, wage employment and commerce, Ibo and Luba-Kasai communities outside their respective ethnic homelands attained a relatively higher socio-economic status than most of the groups among whom they lived. The crystallization of their ethnic identity, together with its mobilization for collective action, clearly demonstrates the urban and therefore petty bourgeois origin of politicized ethnicity as a result of inter-ethnic competition. The medium through which politicization takes place is the ethnic association which was initially an urban-based organization set up to help migrants from the same geographical area, ethnic homeland or lineage resolve some of the problems that they are faced with in the absence of social welfare agencies capable of dealing with them effectively.

Once they are politicized, ethnic associations turn their energies to the task of politically awakening their rural homelands in order to enlist them in their battles against rival groups. Since ethnic antagonisms are less strongly felt in the countryside, the associations must endeavour to mobilize support through a process that some have called 'ethnic evangelization'. [56] This process is described by David Abernethy.

What was the best course of action open to the urban migrant who was acutely concerned lest his ethnic group fall behind others in the struggle for wealth, power and status? Certainly the rural masses had to be informed of the problem. If the masses were not aware of their ethnicity, then they would have to learn who they really were through the efforts of 'ethnic missionaries' returning to the homeland. These 'missionaries' would also have to outline a strategy by which the ethnic group, once fully conscious of its unity and its potential, could compete with its rivals. [57]

The quest for a better life also involved struggling against colonialism. Erstwhile auxiliaries of the colonialists, Ibo and Luba urban settlers were quickly converted to radical nationalism once it became evident that the colonial system was an obstacle to social justice and to their fuller social and economic development. As pointed out above, such groups were strong supporters of national unity, as this would best serve their interests. Led by Dr Nnamdi Azikiwe, Ibo intellectuals, workers and youth joined the NCNC, the foremost nationalist party in Nigeria. [58] A Luba intellectual, Joseph Ngalula, was one of the founders in 1956 of the *Mouvement National Congolais* (MNC), the political party whose banner Patrice Lumumba was to hold high in the fight for Congolese unity. [59]

Consistent with their determination to weaken the national liberation struggle and to transfer power to a more moderate leadership, the colonialists fed the fears of other groups concerning the prospects of being dominated by ambitious groups like the Ibos and the Baluba of Kasai. Thus the very colonial officials who had invented the myth that from the standpoint of agricultural productivity one Luba cultivator was 'worth seven Lulua', were now calling for the Baluba to vacate Lulua lands. [60] The Belgian colonial administration and the Catholic Church were instrumental in the creation in 1952 of an exclusive Lulua ethnic association, the Lulua-Frères, devoted to promoting greater social mobility among the Lulua in order to allow them to catch up with the Baluba.

Perceived as a threat by other groups, who feared losing all the political and economic benefits of independence to them, the Ibos and the Baluba of Kasai became politically isolated on the eve of independence. The marriage of convenience between the NCNC and the Northern People's Congress (NPC) for purposes of putting together a federal government in Lagos helped to diminish Ibo isolation; it did not end it. In the Congo, Lumumba's associates on the MNC executive committee attempted to depose him as president in July 1959 but failed. They then set up their own dissident wing of the MNC under the leadership of Luba leader Albert Kalonji who had a popular following in his capacity as MNC leader for the Kasai province. In the poisoned atmosphere of the Lulua-Baluba war, which erupted after months of heightened tension on 11 October 1959, this popular following was virtually Luba. Thus, in spite of the fact that non-Luba leaders as prominent as Cyrille Adoula and Joseph Ileo continued to be associated with this party, the MNC-K simply became a Luba party. [61]

The events leading to the secession of Biafra are widely known. Suffice it to say that it all began with the *coup d'état* of January 1966 by a group of Ibo majors, whose purpose was to purify Nigeria by ending corruption and mismanagement. The fact that not a single Ibo politician was found among the leaders killed convinced the rest of Nigeria that the coup was but a prelude to the establishment of Ibo domination. As a coincidence, the senior army officer who inherited the reigns of power was himself an Ibo. The politically inept regime of Major General Johnson Aguiyi-Ironsi only helped to worsen matters. His decision to set up a unitary system of government was interpreted as the final move by his entourage of mostly Ibo aides to cement Ibo domination of the country through control of civil service and other public sector jobs and of access to government contracts, services and development projects.

Anti-Ibo pogroms in the north and the assassination of Ibo officers during the counter-coup of July 1966 created a catastrophic situation in which the Ibos were justifiably worried about their survival as a people. The call went forth to Ibo settlers all over Nigeria to return to the homeland. Here the Ibo bourgeoisie and petty bourgeoisie saw their chance of doing whatever was necessary to make up for their political and economic losses elsewhere. In a situation in which the federal government was weak and unsure of its future direction, the one option that appealed to these classes was secession. With the intensification of ethnic nationalism this option was readily embraced by the mass of the Ibo people who endured countless sacrifices in its support between 30 May 1967 and 10 January 1970.

The story of South Kasai is not as well-known and is seldom a subject of serious scholarly inquiry. However, students of the national question will find a wealth of information on this secession in a yet unpublished study by a leading Zairian scholar, Professor Ilunga Kabongo. [62] Ilunga's work is outstanding in its comprehensive analysis of all the complex issues involved, chief among which were the political bankruptcy of the Luba petty bourgeoisie, the arrogance and excessive ambitions of Albert Kalonji, Lumumba's political error in siding with the Lulua at a time when a civil war opposed them to the Baluba, the complicity of the moderate anti-Lumumba leadership in Léopoldville (Kinshasa) in aiding and abetting Kalonji for purposes of fighting Lumumba and his followers and the internal contradictions of the secessionist state that helped to facilitate reunification.

Like Ibo nationalism, Luba ethnic nationalism was 'the result of frustration and political defeat'. [63] Luba political isolation at the national level was exemplified by the failure of Kalonji to win an influential position in the national government. [64] In Katanga, his federalist stand and selfish political calculation in supporting Tshombe militated against the interests of the Luba-Kasai settlers, who subsequently stood alone—rejected by Tshombe's authentic Katangans and accused of betrayal by their Luba-Katanga kin who were staunch unitarists and Tshombe's enemies. In the Kasai province itself, the national and provincial elections of May 1960 'took on the aspect of an anti-Baluba plebiscite'. [65] Although the MNC-K had won 21 seats out of 70 in the provincial assembly it failed to win the control of the government since Lumumba was able to put together a coalition totalling 50 votes and handed the provincial leadership to Barthelemy Mukenge, a Lulua.

As a result, the same Luba leaders who had rejected the idea of repatriation contained in the Lake Munkamba accords of January 1960 were ready by

14 June 1960 to put out an emotional call for all Luba settlers in Lulua inhabited areas to return to their South Kasai homeland. Anti-Luba voilence all over Kasai and in Katanga reinforced this basically opportunistic drive by politicians seeking to make up for their political failures. The original plan was for the creation of an additional province whose legislation and government would consist of the MNC-K provincial representatives elected in May. Kalonji's personal ambition was such that although he was elected to the national parliament he saw in the chaotic environment of the period the opportunity to realize his dream of becoming a supreme leader somewhere. On 8 August 1960 he proclaimed the secession of South Kasai, from Elisabethville, where he received encouragement and support from Tshombe.

Until Kalonji's rebellion was ended in a *coup d'état* by one of his army officers acting on orders from Leopoldville on 29 September 1962, South Kasai enjoyed the ambiguous status of being neither a totally independent and separate entity nor simply a self-governing region within a country. It had some of the trappings of sovereignty such as a flag and an army and directly exported the diamonds mined by a Belgian company without passing through the central government and without paying any taxes to the latter. On the other hand, not a single country accorded it diplomatic recognition—in contrast to Biafra which was recognized by four countries—and the Congolese currency remained in circulation. As for the people, their emotional identification with the Congo was still evident, being daily reinforced by the beautiful sounds of Congolese music and the leadership's involvement in all the discussions concerning the future of the country as a whole.

Ironically, it was the obsessive opposition to Lumumba by the moderate Congolese leadership and the Western powers and their agents at the United Nations which gave South Kasai not only a breathing space but also the *de facto* recognition it needed to survive as a separate entity for two years. Kalonji's independence proclamation had invoked both the right of his people to self-determination and his opposition to Lumumba's supposedly Communist regime. The cold war became part of the crisis when the *Armée Nationale Congolaise* (ANC) troops sent to crush the secession were flown to the Kasai in Soviet-supplied Ilyushins. The ANC met little resistance when it occupied the South Kasai capital of Bakwanga (Mbuji–Mayi), the diamond capital of the country, on 27 August 1960. In retaliation for the sniping death of a comrade two days later, the ANC massacred 270 innocent civilians who had taken refuge in a Catholic church.

The world was rightly shocked upon hearing this news; but UN Secretary General Dag Hammarskjold went too far in calling it an act of genocide. Taking advantage of the anti-Lumumba climate thus created, President Joseph Kasa-Vubu dismissed the prime minister on 5 September 1960, using the Bakwanga episode as a ground for the dismissal. From then on, the Leopoldville authorities treated with Kalonji and his ministers as though they were a legitimate government until Parliament legalized the existence of South Kasai as one of 21 provinces on 14 August 1962. They also used Bakwanga as their 'butcher's' or the place where any undesirable Lumumbist could be sent to be murdered.[66] By 1962, internal contradictions, due in part to Kalonji's self-styled coronation as the first *Mulopwe* or sacral king of the Baluba of Kasai, had favourably disposed most of the people toward reunification. There was no alternative to being Congolese.[67]

The Rise of Oppressed Minorities: Chad, Ethiopia and Sudan

Conflicts involving the rights of national minorities are perhaps the greatest challenge to national construction in contemporary Africa. Unlike the experience of South Kasai and Biafra, where major ethnic groups were attempting to break away from countries in which they felt unwanted, these conflicts have to do with the rise to self-assertion of national minorities seeking to exercise either their full citizenship and democratic rights or their right to self-determination and, if necessary, independence and secession. In asserting their dignity as peoples, the minorities reject what they perceive as the imposition by the majority or dominant group of its language and/or culture on them and their treatment as second-class citizens.

Sociologically, minority status has little to do with numbers. A numerical majority will be reduced to the status of a minority—a sociological minority, to use Balandier's expression—in either a situation of ethnic stratification or in a colonial situation where a numerical minority holds state power.[68] A good example of minority status in a multinational context is the case of Oromo people of Ethiopia, who are the most numerous national group in that country and on whom Ethiopian rule was imposed during the 19th Century. Resulting from the fact of conquest, their minority status was existentially a daily experience under imperial rule through excessive payment of tribute to feudal lords who took up to three-quarters of the tenant's harvest, a 10% land tax and *corvée* labour.[69] For the Oromos, the Ethiopian state has for over a hundred years been closely linked to the Amhara cultural tradition and it is still perceived as being inseparable from it. Hence the struggle for self-determination which has been organized since 1975 by the Oromo Liberation Front (OLF).

The perception of Amhara domination is shared by the Somalis, whose situation is already described above, and by the Tigrayans. Historically, Tigray has been part of the Ethiopian Empire. It is in Tigray that the central Ethiopian state emerged during the fourth century AD with the Christianization of the ancient kingdom of Axum. The imperial state shifted from place to place before it was settled at Shoa, in the Amhara heartland, by the end of the 19th Century.[70] Thus, unlike the Oromos and the Somalis, who were forcibly incorporated into Ethiopia as part of the expansion of the empire and who base their claim to self-determination in part on this history of conquest, Tigrayan resistance to the central state is basically related to contemporary issues, namely, the Tigrayans' perceptions of cultural oppression, economic neglect and discriminatory practices by the state.

The post-war modernization undertaken by Emperor Haile Selassie seems to have favoured the Amhara ruling classes and petty bourgeoisie. Although they formed only one quarter of the Ethiopian population, the Amharas were heavily represented in all state organs, including the armed forces, where in 1970 70% of all officers were Amhara.[71] Given the predominance of the Amharas and their language and culture, members of other nationalities saw themselves as second-class citizens and 'found it much harder to reach middle or high ranks in the public service'.[72] Members of the Tigrayan People's Liberation Front (TPLF) underline the economic neglect of their region by Addis Ababa as one of their major grievances against the state.[73] The neglect of peasant agriculture and social welfare did have devastating consequences for ordinary people in Tigray. The 1972-3 famine in Wollo and Tigre provinces which claimed over 100,000 lives is a clear testimony to that official indifference. This was a salient factor in the overthrow of Emperor Haile Selassie and the destruction of the imperial state.

The fact that all the three minorities (Somali, Oromo, Tigrayan) have not only continued to struggle for self-determination after the 1974 Revolution but also created new organizations (OLF, TPLF) for that purpose is an indication of how deep-seated their autonomist sentiments are. The Revolution itself helped to release their energies and to mobilize support for their struggles. Rightly or wrongly, they feel that the central state must first of all recognize their right to self-determination before any meaningful negotiations can take place. The government, on the other hand, refers to the insurgents as bandits, thus suggesting that they have no legitimate grievances. In this impasse, and given the fact that the rest of Africa is unlikely to address issues that everyone rightly regards as the internal problems of Ethiopia, civil war and the suffering of millions of people now also faced with famine are likely to continue in the foreseeable future.

Chad and Sudan have situations that are not only less complex than Ethiopia's but present a number of parallels in the underlying causes of their unending civil wars.[74] Both countries have a north–south problem that generally revolves around the co-existence of two cultural zones: the zone of Arab culture, exclusively Islamic, and the zone of black African culture, in which African religions, Christianity and Islam are to be found.[75] Co-existence does not necessarily imply confrontation. For if that were the case, all other African countries with similar cleavages should by now have witnessed their share of civil wars. Violent conflict in both countries was part of the minorities' response to powerlessness, economic neglect and cultural oppression.

The north–south cleavage in Chad and Sudan is primarily a function of the legacy of the colonial political economy. For the colonialists, it was only those regions which were economically useful that were to witness the development of the infrastructure and that of supportive social services such as education and health. In the Sudan it was the north, with its historical and economic links with Egypt, that was deemed useful to British imperialism. It was administered by the elite Sudan service while the south was run by military officers until the 1920s and by a special group of administrators thereafter. With the active help of Christian missionaries, who had a vested interest in recounting the tales of the nineteenth-century slave traffic, everything was done to keep out of the south anything Arab or Muslim: Arab language, names, dress, traders and Islam.[76]

With independence, Arabic became the national language and Islam the state religion in a unitary state system. Given the economic backwardness of the south, Arab civil servants were generally the only ones qualified to occupy the higher ranks in the administration of the south. For the south, this meant Arab colonialism, which had to be resisted. Southern demands for federalism were rejected and rebellions in the south led to the imposition of military rule on the region. This is the background to the emergence of the secessionist movement of the *Anya-nya* which fought a bloody civil war with the Sudanese army between 1963 and 1972. The Addis Ababa Agreement of 1972 officially ended the civil war and gave regional autonomy to the south, while several top *Anya-nya* leaders became members of the national leadership in Khartoum.

However, the agreement did not contribute to improving the material conditions of the broad mass of the people who remained receptive to the idea of continuing the struggle. By 1983, a new and more radical political organization, the Sudanese People's Liberation Movement (SPLM), had assumed the leadership of the popular struggle, not for another secessionist drive, but for the liberation of the Sudan as a whole. The SPLM benefited greatly from President Jaafar el Numeiry's amazing decisions to split the south into smaller administrative units and to impose the *Sharia* or Islamic Code, on all Sudanese, including non-Muslims. By the end of 1984, these decisions had been reportedly rescinded; but the struggle for genuine regional autonomy in the south continues.

Like the British in the Sudan, the French imposed two separate administrations in the two cultural zones of Chad. For them the *Chad utile* (or 'useful Chad') was the southern region, where the cultivation of cotton, the major export crop, was made compulsory in 1926. Before World War II the major portion of the south was incorporated in the French territory of Oubangui-Chari (now the Central African Republic), whose people have close cultural ties with the people of southern Chad.[77] The Sara people constitute the major ethnic group in this region and their language dominates the African culture zone. The Saras were to the French in Chad what the Baluba were to the Belgians in Kasai and Katanga and the Baganda to the British in Uganda. After independence, southern and for the most part Sara administrators took over from the French all over Chad, including the north, where the transition took several years to be completed.

Greatly underpopulated, especially in the vast desert region of Borkou-Ennedi-Tibesti (BET), the north was for a long time subject to French military administrators. In spite of the importance of its cattle, which provided beef to all of French Equatorial Africa and for export, it was completely neglected in the provision of economic and social services. There were few or no schools, health centres and government-provided wells in most parts of the region. This tradition of neglect continued after independence, with President Ngarta Tombalbaye even deciding to ignore the Libyan occupation of the Aozou Strip in exchange for Libya dropping its support for Chadian insurgents in 1972. Chadian administrators in the north were more preoccupied with the collection of revenue than with serving the people. Corrupt bureaucrats extorted as much money as they could by overtaxing the pastoralists, sometimes collecting the cattle tax two or three times from the same individual. The fact that the collector was a southern Christian and his victim a northern Muslim did help enhance the feeling of belonging to an oppressed minority among the nomads.

The major difference between Chad and Sudan, at least before the 1980s, was that the leadership which attempted to organize and guide the popular resistance to the post-colonial state was secessionist in orientation in southern Sudan while it was committed to national unity in Chad.[78] From its creation by Ibrahima Abatcha and others in 1966, the *Front de Libération Nationale du Tchad* (FROLINAT) has seen its task as that of overthrowing a neo-colonial state and replacing it with a people's state committed to resolving the national question—in part by giving equal status to French and Arabic as official languages—and to building socialism. Since 1978, however, the Chadian situation has changed dramatically. There has been a shift of power from the south to the north, and we are now seeing the south acquiring minority status and autonomist sentiments emerging among the Sara. According to Gérard Galtier, southerners 'are particularly hostile to Mr Hissein Habre, who had a very unfavourable attitude toward Christians in 1979 (which resulted in intercommunal massacres) and whose troops are now lording it over everyone in the South.'[79]

As a recent editorial in *Le Monde diplomatique* suggests, it is an error to think that once Libyan troops are withdrawn, Hissein Habre's Chad will miraculously find peace and stability.[80] National reconciliation will require greater respect for all the different regions and peoples of Chad.[81] A necessary condition for that will be the espousal by all concerned of the nationalist ideals for which Ibrahima Abatcha and thousands of FROLINAT militants laid down their lives in the struggle against French imperialism and its neo-colonial allies in N'Djamena.

The Struggle for Liberation in Colonial and Former Colonial Territories: South Africa, Namibia, Eritrea and Western Sahara

The greatest threat to regional stability in Africa today arises from armed conflicts involving the struggle for liberation in colonial and former colonial territories which have been denied their right to self-determination and independence in accordance with universally accepted principles. With the possible exception of Eritrea, whose history is little known to Africans outside of the Horn, the cases which fall into this last category of crises related to the national question in Africa are so well-known that they do not require elaborate discussion.

South Africa and Namibia are the last two major territories of the African continent to remain under European colonial rule. Sociologically, they are both colonial–settler states, even though they each have a different status in international law: South Africa as a sovereign state and Namibia as a UN trust territory illegally occupied by South Africa. It is their colonial form of state which reduces the African majority, with all the violence and viciousness of the apartheid system, to the status of a sociological minority and unites all the different ethnic groups into a single oppressed nation. In order to defeat the struggle that this nation has been waging for its liberation for decades in both countries, the white ruling classes are attempting all kinds of political schemes to keep themselves in power in South Africa and to impose an international settlement in Namibia likely to appease their Western allies. More importantly, they have greatly expanded their defence establishment and are now engaged in destabilizing their African neighbours. South Africa has occupied portions of southern Angola, is actively supporting dissident right-wing movements in Angola and Mozambique and is giving aid and comfort to a number of opposition forces in Zimbabwe and Lesotho. By weakening socialist-oriented regimes in Angola and Mozambique and by making the economic survival of these war-torn countries contingent on Western economic involvement, the destabilizing effort of Pretoria is serving the economic and strategic interests of imperialism in Southern Africa. This is why it goes hand in hand with the constructive engagement policy of the United States.

Whereas the liberation of South Africa and Namibia evokes unanimous support among Africans, the questions of Eritrea and Western Sahara are more controversial since they involve the interests of two major African states and their strategic alliances in the world. Here again, as in the case of South Kasai and Biafra, we have striking parallels that are seldom underlined in the debate on the national question in Eritrea and Western Sahara. Both were colonial territories that were claimed by a neighbouring state which based its claims on historical grounds. For Morocco, these claims included Mauritania and parts of Algeria, notably the iron ore areas of Tindouf and Gara-Djebilet and involved a border war with Algeria in 1963. In the case of Ethiopia, few people seem to notice the paradox that a state that seems comfortable with the OAU principle of maintaining colonial frontiers with respect to the Somali claim on the Ogaden is content to invoke similar reasons for its claim on Eritrea. The majority of African states have rejected all of Morocco's claims but remain conspicuously silent on the question of Eritrea.

An Italian colony whose borders were set in an 1889 treaty with Emperor Menelik II of Ethiopia, Eritrea became a British protectorate in 1941, after the defeat of Italy. For Eritreans, the periods of Italian and British rule did forge a common and separate identity which was manifest in their demand for self-determination and independence after World War II. For evident strategic considerations, which included the desire to gain a foothold in north-east Africa and the Red Sea region,[82] the United States manoeuvred at the United Nations to satisfy the wishes of Emperor Haile Selassie. Thus, when the vote was taken on the UN resolution concerning the future of Eritrea in 1950, the United States voted for federation with Ethiopia while the Soviet Union passionately defended the right of the people of Eritrea to self-determination. Later on, the rationale for the US position was stated by US Secretary of State, John Foster Dulles.

From the point of view of justice, the opinions of the Eritrean people must receive consideration. Nevertheless, the strategic interests of the United States in the Red Sea basin and considerations of security and world peace makes it necessary that the country has to be linked with our ally Ethiopia. [83]

In 1962, one year after the Eritrean liberation struggle began, Emperor Haile Selassie annexed Eritrea. Born a year later, in 1963, the OAU accepted the Emperor's *fait accompli*, in contrast to its later position *vis-à-vis* King Hassan II with respect to Western Sahara. Eritreans dispute the view that this annexation was achieved democratically with a majority vote of the Eritrean Parliament, pointing out that the vote was literally obtained at gunpoint by hand-picked legislators who were very conscious of the fact that an armed police was surrounding the parliament building in Asmara at the time of the vote. [84] Whatever the truth might be, the fact remains that the Eritrean people are committed to the struggle for self-determination, as shown by their massive support for the Eritrean People's Liberation Front (EPLF), the movement that has been leading this struggle since 1970.

This paper has attempted to show that not all the movements seeking self-determination in Africa should be automatically dismissed as separatist or secessionist movements which are detrimental to Africa, or the lawless activities of bandits. Each movement ought to be examined on its own merits through careful scholarly analysis, with a view to distinguishing petty bourgeois opportunism and externally-sponsored destabilization from the expression of legitimate grievances involving the rights of minorities and the rightful quest for nationhood by the inhabitants of colonial or former colonial territories who have been denied their right to self-determination. The dogma of the preservation of colonially-inherited boundaries should not become a licence that governments can use to oppress minorities or the screen behind which to hide their incompetence and indifference to the suffering of their peoples.

Unless they are based on clear cut evidence of oppression, irredentist movements have no justifiable claim in contemporary Africa. To claim, as some Somali nationalists do, that Somali-inhabited territories outside Somalia are colonies whose struggles against African colonizing powers 'are no different from the struggles that brought about the end of the British, French and Portuguese empires', is to exaggerate. [85] There are many other peoples in Africa whose unity has been lost as a result of the European partition. The Bakongo, for example, are found in three different countries today: Angola, Congo and Zaire. If we were to redraw the map to accommodate those among them who want to recreate a Kongo nation as well as similarly placed peoples elsewhere, Africa would become a madhouse. Since the national question cannot be fully resolved without national liberation, the priority item on the agenda for Somali progressives today is to liberate Somalia from neo-colonial exploitation and oppression. For if Somalis are being oppressed in Kenya and Ethiopia, they are equally repressed in Somalia itself. Over 200,000 Somalis have fled repression in Somalia to seek refuge in Ethiopia. [86]

What is true for irredentism is equally so for revanchism and for secessionist movements resulting from inter-ethnic conflict. Fortunately, the experiences of Biafra and South Kasai do suggest that the ethnic antagonisms which gave rise to the secessionist option are not irreconcilable. Much of the conflict arose from petty bourgeois opportunism and the youth of the states involved, which had not learned how to institutionalize inter-ethnic competition in ways that would lessen violent conflict. Nigeria and Zaire, like multi-ethnic societies all over the world, are condemned to inter-ethnic competition in social, economic and political arenas as long as they remain class societies marked by inequality and scarcity.

As for those conflicts involving the rights of minorities and the quest for self-determination in Africa today, the only principled position is that of genuine respect for the democratic rights of peoples in accordance with UN and OAU principles. In the interest of peace, development and regional stability, prominent African leaders and concerned organizations should offer their good offices to help resolve these conflicts in a manner that will be satisfactory to all parties. A first step in that direction is the recognition by all sides to a conflict of the legitimate grievances and concerns of their adversaries. Satisfying those concerns will certainly be different but not impossible; it is a matter that can better be resolved through diplomacy than through the barrel of a gun.

A major factor in the revolt of oppressed minorities in Chad, Ethiopia and Sudan is the uneven development of capitalism within African countries. Such a pattern was the inevitable result of the colonial policy of divide and rule in Chad and the Sudan. In imperial Ethiopia, it was the effect of the indifference, neglect and incompetence of a decadent political order. In all three cases, as in all similar contexts, successor states have both the opportunity and the obligation to transform the situation by correcting the pattern of regional inequality inherited from the past.

Another greatly needed alteration today is in Africa's position on the Eritrean question. The case for Eritrean independence is virtually identical to that of Western Sahara. The OAU should therefore apply the same standard to both of them. And the United Nations has its share of responsibility in the matter, given its 1950 resolution on federation with Ethiopia.

Once the people of Eritrea have exercised their right to self-determination, progressive forces in both Eritrea and Ethiopia should be able to work together to establish some type of association between them. Such an association will be useful not only for the purposes of developing the economic complementarities between the two states but also for the sake of promoting a larger union of states in the Horn of Africa. For it is only by the creation of viable sub-regional federations that both the Pan-African ideal of unity in a continent free of all foreign domination and the economic development goals of the Lagos Plan of Action can be realized. The only positive way to resolve the national question in post-colonial Africa is to realize the socialist and anti-imperialist goals of the national liberation struggle by defeating imperialism through greater economic and political integration at the regional and sub-regional levels.[87]

Notes

1. See, for example, Zdenek Cervenka, *The Organization of African Unity and Its Charter*, Praeger, New York 1969 on the OAU commitment to maintenance of the inherited state system of colonial partition as a charter principle.

2. I am referring to the nationalist movement of French Canadians led by the *Parti Québecois* and to the radical autonomist movement of Native Americans under the leadership of the American Indian Movement (AIM).

3. Clifford Geertz, 'The Integrative Revolution: Primordial Sentiments and Civil Politics in the New States', in Clifford Gerrtz (ed.), *Old Societies and New States*, Free Press, New York, 1963.

4. The major statement on the subject is in Aristide R. Zolberg, 'The Structure of Political Conflict in the New States of Tropical Africa', *American Political Science Review*, vol.62, no.1, 1968, pp. 70—87, especially pp. 73—4. Zolberg was also influenced by the theories of modernization of his comparative politics teacher at the University of Chicago, David E. Apter, who saw the tribal system as being in conflict with modern (i.e. Western) patterns of social and political organization. See D.E. Apter, *Ghana in Transition*, Atheneum, New York, 1963, pp. 80—81 and *The Political Kingdom in Uganda*, Princeton University Press, Princeton, 1961, pp. 18—20. On the political significance of primordial lines of cleavage, see his *The Politics of Modernization*, Univeristy of Chicago Press, Chicago, 1965, p. 197.

5. See Goran Hyden, *Beyond Ujamaa in Tanzania: Underdevelopment and an Uncaptured Peasantry*, University of California Press, Berkeley, 1980, *No Shortcuts to Progress: African Development Management in Perspective*, University of California Press, Berkeley and Los Angeles, 1983 and his 'Fostering Progress in Africa: The Need to Think about the Present Crisis Historically', Background Paper for the Committee on African Development Strategies (A Joint Project of the Council on Foreign Relations and the Overseas Development Council), presented at the 2nd session of the Committee in Washington DC, 23 October 1984.

6. This critique of Hyden's positions is part of my 'Governance and Economic Management: Historical, Social and Institutional Issues', paper presented at the 2nd session of the Committee on African Development Strategies, Washington, DC, 23 October 1984.

7. J.V. Stalin, 'Marxism and the National Question' in J.V. Stalin, *Works*, vol.2, Foreign Languages Publishing House, Moscow, 1913(?), p. 307, emphasis in original.

8. Linda Burnham and Bob Wing, 'Toward a Communist Analysis of Black Oppression and Black Liberation', Part I: 'Critique of Black Nation Thesis', *Line of March 7*, vol.2, no.1, 1981, p. 40.

9. Ibid., p. 41.

10. Nicos Poulantzas, *L'Etat, le pouvoir, le socialisme*, Presses Universitaires de France, Paris, 1978, pp. 102—33; Samir Amin, *The Arab Nation*, Zed Press, London, 1978. Contrary to his earlier formulations on the concept of the nation in this book as well as in his *Unequal Development*, Monthly Review Press, New York, 1976, where he allows for 'at least an embryonic stage of national development' (p. 29) for the tributary and trading formations of black Africa, Samir Amin seems to have moved closer to the orthodox Marxist theory in his *Class and Nation*, Monthly Review Press, New York, 1980, where he limits the appearance of nations to two types of society: 'complete tributary' and capitalist societies (p. 20). Most of the tributary formations of black Africa are thereby

excluded, as they were 'incomplete' and lacking in irreversible state formation', which seems to be tied to the use of animal energy in agriculture and of writing (p. 42). Needless to say, it is his earlier formulations which retain our attention.

11. Poulantzas, 1978, pp. 105—6, emphasis in original.

12. Amin, 1978, p. 10.

13. Ibid., p. 11.

14. Poulantzas, 1978, p. 124.

15. Ibid., pp. 110—127.

16. Amin, 1978, p. 81.

17. The Kuba people of Zaire are a particularly good example of a pre-colonial nation. In his authoritative history of the Kuba peoples, *The Children of Woot*, University of Wisconsin Press, Madison, 1978, Jan Vansina presents them as a multi-ethnic society consisting of five ethnic groups. From his analysis, it can be shown that the Kuba Kingdom consisted of one nation—a Kuba nation—relying heavily for its identity on the central Kuba chiefdoms led by the Bushoong as its core group and supported at different levels of attachment by the peripheral Kuba chiefdoms, which shared a common culture with the core group, and by four ethnic minorities (Kete, Coofa, Cwa, Mbeengi), which were for the most part oppressed minorities (see p. 166).

18. For a brief history of these states, see David Birmingham, 'Central Africa to 1870: Zambezi, Zaire and the South Atlantic', chapters from the *Cambridge History of Africa*, Cambridge University Press, Cambridge, 1981.

19. Nzongola-Ntalaja, 'Les chefs traditionnels dans l'administration locale coloniale au Dahomey et en sierra Leone', *Cahiers Zaïrois d'Etudes Politiques et Sociales*, no.1, 1973, pp. 95—116.

20. Jean Suret-Canale, *Afrique noire occidentale et centrale*, vol.2: *L'ère coloniale (1900-1945)*, Editions Sociales, Paris, 1964, defines colonialism as a system of economic exploitation, political and administrative oppression and cultural oppression.

21. Léon Pétillon, cited in Jules Gérard-Libois, *Katanga Secession*, University of Wisconsin Press, Madison, 1966, p. 24.

22. Eric Rouleau, 'Guerre et intoxication au Tchad', *Le Monde diplomatique*, September 1983.

23. D. Wadada Nabudere, *Imperialism, the Social Sciences and the National Question*, Tanzania Publishing House for the African Association of Political Science, Dar es Salaam, 1977.

24. See V.I. Lenin, *Critical Remarks on the National Question and The Right of Nations to Self-Determination*, Progress Publishers, Moscow, 1974 and Mao Tse-tung 'On New Democracy', in the *Selected Works of Mao Tse-tung*, vol.11, People's Publishing House, Peking, 1952.

25. Nabudere, 1977, p. 57.

26. Gerald J. Bender, *Angola Under the Portuguese: The Myth and the Reality*, University of California Press, Berkeley, 1978, pp. 222—3.

27. On racism and violence as defining characteristics of European colonialism in Africa, see Frantz Fanon, *The Wretched of the Earth*, Grove Press, New York, 1963, pp. 35—106.

28. A good example of how the influence of Garveyism went beyond English-speaking Africa is its penetration of the Belgian Congo, where the colonialists had tried their best to shield the country from the winds of change. See Muzong Kodi, 'Garveyism and Kimbanguism: Belgian Reactions to a Messianic Movement

in the Congo', *The Panafricanist*, 3, 1971, pp. 1—8 and Wyatt MacGaffey, *Modern Kongo Prophets: Religion in a Plural Society*, Indiana University Press, Bloomington, 1983, p. 7.

29. Obafemi Awolowo, *Path to Nigerian Freedom*, Faber, London, 1947. This thesis was further developed in most of Chief Awolowo's later publications.

30. Kwame Nkrumah, *Africa Must Unite*, Heinemann, London, 1963.

31. Amilcar Cabral, *Revolution in Guinea: Selected Texts*, Monthly Review Press, New York, 1972, p. 71.

32. Walter Rodney, 'Toward the Sixth Pan-African Congress: Aspects of the International Class Struggle in Africa, the Caribbean and America', in Horace Campbell (ed.), *Pan-Africanism: The Struggle Against Imperialism and Neo-Colonialism*, Afro-Carib Publications, Toronto, 1975, p. 21.

33. Crawford Young, 'Patterns of Social Conflict: State, Class, and Ethnicity', *Daedalus*, vol.111, no.2, 1982, pp. 80—81.

34. On the year 1956 as a crucial date for the liberation and international working class movements, see Yves Benot, 'Amilcar Cabral and the International Working Class Movement', *Latin American Perspectives*, Issue 41, vol.11, no.2, 1984, p. 82.

35. See John Marcum, *The Angolan Revolution*, vol.1, MIT Press, Cambridge, 1969, pp. 49—100, for a history of Kongo nationalism in Angola.

36. Like the petty bourgeoisie, they were subject to the integrative mechanisms of an inter-ethnic urban or semi-urban milieu: living and working together, speaking the same lingua franca of the territory or the region and developing a common culture in lifestyle, popular music and entertainment.

37. According to Tony Hodges, *Western Sahara: The Roots of a Desert War*, Lawrence Hill, Westport, CT, 1983, pp. 149—50, the Sahrawi people of Western Sahara never formed a nation in pre-colonial times and were more conscious of their tribal or clan identity than of any notion of supra-tribal or national identity. 'Nevertheless', Hodges writes, 'as men of the desert, great camel-herding nomads and speakers of the Hassaniya dialect of Arabic, the Sahrawi did, in a broad cultural sense, regard themselves as a very different people from the predominantly Tashelhit-speaking sedentary or seminomadic Berbers to their immediate north.'

38. Crawford Young, *The Politics of Cultural Pluralism*, University of Wisconsin Press, Madison, 1976, p. 93.

39. Ethnicity *per se* is understood here as simply denoting ethnic identity. By and in itself, it does not imply political mobilization with a view to advancing or defending the interests of a given ethnic group. C.K. Lumuna-Sando, *La Question tribale au Congo (Zaïre)*, AFRICA, Brussels, 1978, makes an interesting distinction between ethnic nationalism (or what he calls 'tribal nationalism') and tribalism, the first being a necessary condition of revolutionary nationalism, and mass political participation, and the second, the ideology of the comprador bourgeoisie.

40. Young, 1976, p. 72.

41. Bereket Habte Selassie, *Conflict and Intervention in the Horn of Africa*, Monthly Review Press, New York, 1980, pp. 102—5.

Bereket Habte Selassie, 'The American Dilemma on the Horn', *Journal of Modern African Studies*, vol.11, no.2, 1984, p. 266; Osman Mohamoud, 'Somalia: From Irredentism to Insurgency', *Horn of Africa*, vol.5, no.4, 1982/3, pp. 26—31.

43. Young, 1976, p. 264. For more information on this status and on Buganda's history, see D.E. Apter, 1961, and Crawford Young, 'Buganda', in René

Lemarchand, (ed.), *African Kingships in Perspective*, Frank Cass, London, 1977, pp. 193—235.

44. Young, 1976, p. 265.

45. See, for example Robert H. Jackson and Carl G. Rosberg, 'Popular Legitimacy in African Mulit-Ethnic States', *Journal of Modern African Studies*, vol.22, no.2, 1984, pp. 196—7, Crawford Young, 'Comparative Claims to Political Sovereignty: Biafra, Katanga, Eritrea', in Donald Rothchild and Victor A. Olorunsola, (eds), *State Versus Ethnic Claims: African Policy Dilemmas*, Westview Press, Boulder, Colorado, 1983, pp. 199—232.

46. Nzongola-Ntalaja, 'Imperialism and the Political Economy of Southern Africa', in David Wiley and Allen R. Isaacman, (eds), *Southern Africa: Society, Economy, and Liberation*, Michigan State University, East Lansing, 1981, pp. 302—3.

47. On the notion of internal settlement as the desperate strategy of a dying colonialism, see Nzongola-Ntalaja *Class Struggles and National Liberation in Africa*, Omenana, Roxbury, MA, 1982, pp. 79—90.

48. Gérard-Libois, 1966, p. 24.

49. See ibid., pp. 24—7, on the links between CONAKAT and the *Union Katangaise*, the political party of the white settlers, which was officially admitted as an affiliate of the CONAKAT in June 1959. In addition to the settlers, imperialist forces in Western Europe and their allies in Southern Africa were actively promoting the Katanga secession between 1960 and the end of 1962.

50. Ilunga Mbiya Kobongo, 'Ethnicity, Social Classes, and the State in the Congo, 1960-1965: The Case of Baluba', unpublished PhD dissertation, University of California, Berkeley, 1973, writes that the Baluba of Kasai were 'co-colonizers with the Belgians' (p. 268): 'As Belgian colonization expanded in Kasai and Katanga, the Baluba became the best agents of the colonizer, who used them as catechists, teachers, clerks and manual workers. Their language, *Tshiluba*, was even imposed upon the entire Kasai Province, becoming one of the four "national" languages of the Congo' (p. 220).

51. Young, 1976, p. 461.

52. Thomas Q. Reefe, *The Rainbow and the Kings: A History of the Luba Empire to 1891*, University of California Press, Berkeley, 1981, p. 5.

53. On Luba social and political organization, see Ilunga, 1973, pp. 228—50; Théodore Kanyinda-Lusanga, 'Institutions traditionnelles et forces politiques au Congo: le cas de la société luba du Kasai', *Etudes Africaines du CRISP*, Travaux Africains nos. 104—105, 1970, Léonard Mukenge, 'Croyances religieuses et structures socio-familiales en société luba: "Bena Muntu", "Bakishi", "Milambu",' *Cahiers Economiques et Sociaux*, vol.5, no.2, 1967 and Mabika Kalanda, *Baluba et Lulua, une Ethnie à la recherche d'un nouvel équilibre*, Editions Remarques Congolaises, Brussels, 1959.

54. A Van Zandijcke, *Pages de l'histoire du Kasayi*, Collection Lavigerie, Namur, 1953, p. 7.

55. Jan Vansina, *Kingdoms of the Savanna*, Univeristy of Wisconsin Press, Madison, 1966, p. 221.

56. Young, 1976, p. 463.

57. David Abernethy, *The Political Dilemma of Popular Education*, cited in ibid., p. 464.

58. National Convention of Nigerian Citizens, formerly National Council of Nigeria and the Cameroons.

59. Most writers, including the author, have erroneously dated the creation of the MNC from 1958, the year Lumumba became its president and revived the party by giving a popular following to what had hitherto been a political club of nationalist intellectuals.

60. Henri Nicolaï and Jules Jacques, *La transformation des paysages congolais par le chemin de fer: L'exemple du B.C.K*, ARSC, Brussels, 1954, p. 103.

61. The two wings of the party became known by the names of their respective leaders as MNC-Lumumba (MNC-L) and MNC-Kalonji (MNC-K).

62. Ilunga, 1973.

63. Ibid., p. 301.

64. Kalonji reportedly refused the offer of the agriculture portfolio in Lumumba's cabinet, despite the fact that he was an agronomist. Four years later, and after his secessionist adventure and nearly twenty months of exile in Spain, he became Minister of Agriculture in the Tshombe government. This is at the time when the former secessionists had become the leaders of the unified country.

65. Crawford Young, *Politics in the Congo: Decolonization and Independence*, Princeton University Press, Princeton, 1965, p. 537.

66. According to some accounts of his death, Lumumba himself was en route to Bakwanga on 17 January 1961 when the two Luba-Kasai officials escorting him aboard the plane decided instead to take him to Elisabethville, in Tshombe's Katanga, where he was murdered upon his arrival.

67. This is a paraphrase of Young's conclusion on Biafra, which is even more applicable to the case of South Kasai. See Young, 1976, p. 474.

68. See Georges Balandier, *Sociologie actuelle de l'Afrique noire*, 2nd edition, revised and enlarged, Presses Universitaires de France, Paris, 1963, pp. 3—38.

69. See René Lefort, *Ethiopia: An Heretical Revolution?*, Zed Press, London, 1983, for details on this aspect of Ethiopian history.

70. Robert Cornevin, 'La longue et difficile histoire de l'Erythrée', *Le Monde*, 26 December 1974.

71. Lefort, 1983, p. 18.

72. Ibid., p. 36.

73. Personal notes from the Howard University Conference on the Horn of Africa, Washington, DC, 25 August 1984.

74. See Robert Buijtenhuijs, *Le Frolinat et les révoltes populaires du Tchad, 1965-1976*, Mouton, The Hague, 1978, pp. 439—41.

75. Gérard Galtier, 'Culture arabe at culture africaine: comment reconstruire l'Etat tchadien', *Le Monde diplomatique*, November 1984, pp. 18—19.

76. Young, 1976, pp. 489—501.

77. Galtier, 1984, p. 19.

78. Buijtenhuijs, 1978, p. 440.

79. Galtier, 1984, p. 19.

80. Claude Julien, 'Erreurs', *Le Monde diplomatique*, December 1984.

81. Galtier proposes to rebuild Chad as a multinational state with two dominant cultural zones, a Sara language zone and Arab language zone.

82. See Richard Pankhurst, 'Decolonization of Ethiopia, 1940-55', in UNESCO, *The Decolonization of Africa: Southern Africa and the Horn of Africa*, UNESCO, Paris, 1981, pp. 129—130.

83. John Foster Dulles, cited in Linda Heiden, 'The Eritrean Struggle for Independence', *Monthly Review*, vol.30, no.2, June 1978, p. 15.

84. Herrick and Anita Warren, 'The US Role in the Eritrean Conflict',

Africa Today, vol.23, no.2, 1976, p. 46.

85. Said Yusuf Abdi, 'Decolonization in the Horn and the Outcome of Somali Aspirations for Self-Determination', in UNESCO, 1981, p. 103.

86. Personal communication from Osman Mohamoud.

87. Some of the ideas expressed in this conclusion became clearer to me as a result of the discussion on this paper at the Addis Ababa Seminar on 3 January 1985. I am very grateful to all the participants who commented on the paper, particularly Peter Anyang' Nyong'o, Michael Chege and Emmanuel Hansen.

5. Conflict in the Horn of Africa

Michael Chege

After Southern Africa, the Horn of Africa is potentially the most explosive sub-region in the continent. By the sheer size of recent armaments build-up, troop mobilization and superpower involvement, the Horn of Africa overshadows other African flashpoints such as Chad and Western Sahara. More than anywhere else in Africa, war in the Horn of Africa has brought unprecedented social dislocation and human suffering in its train. Of the estimated five million refugees in Africa, about one half are to be found in the Horn of Africa; and nearly all have been rendered refugees by reasons directly or indirectly associated with war. The conditions they are living in— difficult at the best of times—have been exacerbated by drought and continued warfare.[1] Even more worrying, while in crisis areas outside South Africa some formulae for peaceful settlement have been adumbrated, the genesis for a negotiated solution to the problems in the Horn is not even on the horizon. On the contrary, the maelstrom threatens to encompass an even greater number of contiguous states in Africa, the Middle East and the Gulf which, for one reason or another, have taken sides in the conflict. The bellicose sabre rattling of the superpowers has been reinforced by their growing military involvement in the area. Superpower involvement is in itself a prime explanation for the intractability of the problem and the lining up of states in the Horn and its environs on one side or the other.

This paper is an outline of the origins and progression of political conflict in the Horn of Africa, whose core area is defined as Somalia, Djibouti and Ethiopia. But the geographical limits of the conflict, which must also be addressed, extend to other African states, notably Sudan and Kenya, while diplomatic and military involvement brings in states yet further afield. After discussing the character and development of the conflict, the paper attempts to assess the social, economic and geostrategic permutations of warfare in the Horn of Africa. The final part is devoted to an analysis of attempts at negotiated solutions to the problem and to some thoughts on the lessons gained by the major participants from the largely indecisive and exhausting military engagements in the recent past.

Origins and Outbreak of War in the Horn of Africa

In highly abridged form, the origins of contemporary conflict in the Horn of Africa are to be traced to the problem confronting ruling classes in the region: the creating of national states within the international boundaries established in the interests of European colonialism at a time when the post-colonial states have little economic surplus and a weak economic base. Nationalism and the preservation of territorial integrity of the state have become dominant regime objectives. Conflicts arise because nowhere are territorial boundaries co-extensive with the natural boundaries of the nationalities which inhabit the area.

In the circumstances the regimes in the area are compelled to whip up nationalistic ideologies and to crush resistance to nationalist policy (whether internal or external) by force of arms. But being in no position to procure the necessary arms with their own resources, the states are forced into military dependence on either one of the two major superpowers, the USA and the USSR. In their own competition for the world's natural resources and strategic advantage, the superpowers are not only willing to oblige, they are ready to provoke and fan the flames of political conflict in the Horn and thus render themselves indispensable. In this fashion the stage is set for a murderous see-saw of military escalation: local conflict invokes external intervention which in turn expands the scope of local confrontation making it necessary to import more sophisticated armaments for the next round of military engagements, and so on.

Although some specialists on the Horn of Africa like to harp on the long tradition of external involvement in the region, it is important to remark that foreign military involvement was in the past quantitatively and qualitatively different from that of the present. In the third and fourth decades of the 16th Century, for instance, the Christian Ethiopian highlanders resisted imposition of Islam by the invading forces of Imam Ahmed Ibn Ibrahim Al-Ghazi or Gran, the Left-Handed. The invaders were Somalis, Arabs and Turks, their assault was so fierce that the Ethiopians had to call in 400 fellow Christian Purtuguese musketeers to repulse them. But the affair and others which followed it were probably less devastating than the bloody European wars of religion which characterized European history for a good deal of the latter half of the 16th Century and the early part of the 17th. Thus Tom J. Farer invokes the imagery of religious rivalry in the Horn to explain the historical sources of the current conflict.[2] Just as it would be considered far-fetched to draw on the imagery of the Thirty Years War (1618–48) to explain the outbreak of the Second World War in Europe, so it is fanciful to see recent military conflict in the Horn of Africa as a continuation, however modified, of rivalries existing in pre-modern times.

The seeds of the current crisis are to be found in the competing ambitions of European imperialists in the Horn in the closing years of the 19th Century. British interests in the area were restricted to securing the Suez route, important for the lucrative trade with their dominions in Asia. In practice, Aden as a port of call and a supplies base had to be maintained and for this to happen the British needed the yield of beef produced by the Somali hinterland opposite Aden. Thus British Somaliland came into being. The French, for similar reasons, kept Djibouti, then referred to as French Somaliland, but only after some challenge from the British. The Italians, minor players in the imperialist league, had annexed a 50,000 square mile triangle along the Red Sea coast with its apex in the Tigrayan highlands in the mid-1880s. In their quest for imperial grandeur, the Italians received ambiguous support from Emperor Menelik II in return for giving him access to European arms. The British also gave succour to Italian ambitions in the area to provide a counter-weight to French interests.

But, as was very soon clear, the Italians sought more than Eritrea and their Somaliland—Italian Somaliland—along the East African Coast. In 1889 they negotiated the Treaty of Uccialli with Emperor Menelik. Each party interpreted the treaty differently. The Italians claimed that the treaty gave their country protectorate status over Ethiopia. Menelik thought otherwise and was in any case too busy with imperial conquests in the Horn far beyond the traditional highland Amhara-Tigre areas. He made military forays deep into Somaliland and the South-west to establish, as he put it, 'the ancient frontiers of the Ethiopian empire'. He was anything but modest. These old frontiers, extended 'up to Khartoum, and as far as Lake Nyanza', he claimed in an unabashed, bellicose declaration. [3] Menelik more than anybody else is associated with the delimitation of modern Ethiopian boundaries. yet he also fought back against the European imperialist conquest of Ethiopia, casting himself in the role of a flawed hero. To this day the struggling nationalities in Ethiopia take sides for or against the state Menelik created.

At the Battle of Adowa in 1896 the Ethiopians defeated the Italians and shattered their dream of an Italian dependency extending from the Red Sea through the Ethiopian Highlands to the Indian Ocean. Adowa also marked the beginning of successive territorial concessions to the Ethiopian emperor; after the Italian defeat neither Britain nor France was interested in a military confrontation with Menelik. A Franco-Ethiopian convention specifying the French Somaliland border was quickly reached in 1897. The British ceded considerable territory from their Somaliland to Ethiopia in the same year. The Italians, for their part, agreed to limit the boundaries of Italian Somaliland to a line 180 miles parallel to the Indian Ocean.

With these agreements the major international boundaries in the Horn were set. Not only was the Somali population scattered into French, British and Italian Somaliland, the Ethiopian Empire now included many nationalities besides the Amharic-Tigre core. There were also the Somali—Abo, Oromo, Afars—in outlying areas. With today's boundaries basically in place only two later adjustments were made. In 1925 the British handed over Jubaland in Kenya to Italy in recognition of its support in opposition to Germany during the First World War. Secondly, Ethiopia formally incorporated Eritrea into its empire in 1962 after ten years of relative Eritrean autonomy. Ethiopian rule had been established there by the UN following the defeat of Italy in the Second World War.

The establishment of political boundaries served to demarcate future battle lines. A resurgent Somali nationalism after 1960 would be founded on the reunification of the Somali people left resident in five territories: British Somaliland, Italian Somaliland, French Somaliland, Ethiopia and Kenya. This task was to fall to the independent Somalia Republic born out of the union of British and Italian Somaliland in 1960. Ethiopia, racked in pre-colonial times by the jockeying for power among Amharic and Tigrayan nobility, rebellion in distant fiefdoms and external invasions, had now to contend with governing a disparate and vast empire. For, in the last decade of the 19th Century, Menelik had doubled the geographical size of the state. At independence in 1963 Kenya inherited a restive Somali population in its North-eastern quadrant, previously known as the Northern Frontier District. Politics in Djibouti under the French seethed with rivalry between the Afars extending out to Ethiopia and the Issas (Somalis). Both Ethiopia and Somalia kept threatening pre-emptive intervention and occupation of this mini-state right down to the time when it became independent in 1977. To this complicated equation was added, as we have already seen, the factors of superpower involvement and the interests of other states in the greater Horn region. The latter generally followed the contours set by the superpower state which they happened to be supporting in the region.

War Comes to the Horn of Africa

The Ogaden refers to that mass of land lying to the east of the Ethiopian Highlands and deep into Somalia. It is mostly poor land, part desert and part scrub. Yet with its vegetation alternating with the seasons, and its network of wells, the Ogaden forms an ecological zone which has been the habitat of Somali nomads over the centuries. Between late 1977 and mid-1978, the Ogaden witnessed some of the most extensive conventional warfare seen on the African continent since the Second World War.

Skirmishes between Ethiopia and Somali forces had repeatedly occurred along the common border, particularly in 1961 and 1964. The Imperial Government in Ethiopia had, since the early 1950s, entered into a military assistance agreement with the United States granting the latter facilities at the Kagnew Base outside Asmara.[4] 'Between 1953 and 1977, Ethiopia received some US$279 million in American military aid, while 3,552 members of the armed forces were trained in the United States.'[5] The Somalis, in contrast, had to make do with dilapidated weaponry donated by Egypt or Italy. This guaranteed Ethiopia military superiority and victory in the military clashes of the 1960s.

Between the early 1960s and 1974, however two important developments took place throwing this uneasy equilibrium out of balance. In October 1969 the military in Somalia took over from the corrupt and ineffective civilian regime of Prime Minister Ebrahim Egal. The first order of business for the new regime was to refurbish the administration and expand the size and capability of the armed forces. From the modest Soviet arms and training and the antiquated Egyptian armaments which had characterized the pre-1969 period, the military government, with increased Soviet aid, created a 25,000 strong army and provided it with modern weaponry including the most potent air-strike capability in sub-Saharan Africa. The Soviet Union signed a Treaty of The Friendship and Cooperation with Somalia in 1974. High level diplomatic and state visits took place. The Soviets constructed extensive facilities at Berbera on the Red Sea Coast. All this alarmed the West and the conservative Arab regimes across the Red Sea. Kenya too felt menaced by this armoury. Senator Patrick D. Moynihan, then ambassador to the UN, said the Soviets had 'colonized' Somalia. 'Globalist' analysts in the USA said the Gulf to Cape route was under Soviet threat.

The second important development was the outbreak of the Ethiopian Revolution in February 1974 bringing in its wake the demise of the imperial and feudal order, and more. By October 1974 the Ethiopian military was firmly in control of the state machinery and soon at virtual war with the Marxist intelligentsia, especially the EPRP. Specifically, the fratricidal struggles between the *Dergue* and the Ethiopian Left between 1975 and 1978, which reached their peak in the Red Terror of 1977-78, provided too great a temptation for the new Somali military regime to attack Ethiopia with the intention of recovering the Ogaden. Though direct evidence is hard to come by, it seems that the Somali regime underestimated the internal factionalism in Ethiopia.

Between June and July 1977, and facing virtually no resistance, the Western Somali Liberation Front, with the support of Somali regulars, occupied most of the Ogaden and besieged Harrar, Jigjiga and Dire Dawa on the eastern foothills of the Ethiopian Highlands. The gains Menelik had made in the 19th Century had been reversed by a Somali population which had always resented them. The Ethiopian military regime's initial reaction was to seek additional armaments from the Unites States; but in vain. Relations between them and US had soured over American protestations at the sweeping nationalizations in Ethiopia in 1975, and the *Dergue's* human rights record. This period coincided with President Carter's crusade in favour of human rights promotion worldwide. So the Somalis dug in their heels in the Ogaden, little aware of what was to come.

It was the Soviet Union, as is by now well-known, which came to Ethiopia's rescue with one of the largest and most efficient armaments airlift in modern history. Over one billion US dollars worth of arms were flown into Ethiopia from USSR over the twelve-month period beginning September 1977.[6] With the armaments came some 3,000 Soviet military advisers and an estimated 20,000 Cuban regulars who could handle Soviet weaponry. The Ethiopian army, better armed, even better clothed, gained fresh confidence. With Soviet logistic aid the Ethiopian army and the Cubans launched a blitzkrieg in the Ogaden in February 1978. A few thousand South Yemenis joined them within six weeks. At the cost of 25,000 lives, the Somalis were summarily routed from the area. The Somali regime watched with bitterness as its former allies now turned the guns against them. In the past, the Soviets and more openly the Cubans, had supported Somalia and Eritrea against Ethiopia.

With the Ogaden now disposed of, Eritrea was the main theatre of war in the Horn of Africa. A war of national liberation against the imperial regime had simmered in the region since its forced incorporation into Ethiopia in 1962. Under the aegis of the Eritrea Liberation Front (ELF), and with support from some Arab states, notably Syria, Iraq and Libya, guerrilla war increased after 1969 breaking out into more or less open warfare after 1974. In the meantime the ELF had acquired a rival in the EPLF (Eritrean Peoples Liberation Front) and later in another splinter group, ELF–PLF (Eritrean Liberation Front— Popular Liberation Forces).[7] Despite over six major military offensives against the Eritreans, and in spite of sporadic and other intense intra-Eritrean warfare, the Ethiopian military had failed to break the back of the Eritrean resistance by 1984. In the first half of 1985, the situation appeared at best stalemated: the Ethiopian government had control of the major towns while the guerrillas controlled the countryside.[8] Indeed, a rising complaint from food aid agencies involved in Ethiopia in 1985 was that the Ethiopian government allowed food distribution only within the geographical limits of their control. Eritrean resistance movements in the Sudan were used to distribute food in areas they controlled.

The 1974 revolution also unleashed pent-up nationalist opposition among long oppressed nationalities elsewhere in Ethiopia. These included the Tigrayans and the Oromo. The latter constituting 40% of Ethiopia's population, is the largest ethnic group in the country. Other peoples were the Somalis and Afars. At that time the *Dergue* saw fierce internal struggles for power and had to face the militant Ethiopian Peoples Revolutionary Party. By 1977 it faced localized rebellions among the Oromo in the South, the Afars in the East and the Tigrayans in the north-west, quite apart from the larger struggles in Eritrea and Ogaden. This gave an added twist to the geopolitics of the Horn of Africa. In the absence of a politically acceptable nationalities policy from the Addis Ababa government, imposition of a military solution called for a strong army and forced increased dependence on external—in this case, Soviet— arms. Each of the local resistance movements in turn acquired sanctuaries (for guerrillas and refugees) in the neighbouring states. The Eritreans and Tigrayans took sanctuary in the Sudan, as did the EPRP. Both Eritrean movements had considerable support from the Arab states. Publicity and propaganda was put out in Europe. Thus, military and diplomatic support could be obtained from regimes, both local and external, which were hostile to the Ethiopia government for one reason or another. Sudan, besides receiving close to half a million refugees, also provided the rearguard bases if not arms for all the Eritrean movements. Also based in Sudan were the Tigrayan Peoples Liberation Front (TPLF), the Oromo Liberation Front (OLF) and the reactionary Ethiopian Democratic Union (EDU) which comprised the old feudal nobility. Somalia was the nominal home for the Western Somali Liberation Front and the Somali-Abo Liberation Movement. Only the Afars, it appears were content to operate from within, owing to lack of resources and personnel.

Apart from the main theatres of war in the Ogaden and Eritrea and the theatre-at-large within Ethiopia, conflict simmered on and off in Kenya's North-eastern Province, which is predominantly Somali in ethnic composition. From 1963, when the Somalia government contested the British government's decision to incorporate the old Northern Frontier District into independent Kenya, local guerrillas, with Somalia's backing, fought the Kenya Army for four years. As in most guerrilla wars, civilian casualties were inflicted on both sides. In October 1967 an armistice was negotiated between Kenya and Somalia through the good offices of President Kenneth Kaunda of Zambia. The then civilian regime in Mogadishu pursued a peaceful and pragmatic policy of unifying the Somali nation. Somalia's claims to the area were never renounced however, for no regime could survive in Somalia if it gave up the struggle for Somali unification. Although the Barre government has continually claimed that the Kenya Somali problem is of a different order from that of the Ogaden, this conflict was scaled down considerably after 1967 at which point Somali denied arms and facilities to guerrillas operating in Kenya's North-eastern Province.

Sporadic Somali incursions actually continued in the North-eastern Province, often followed by severe Kenyan retribution. A significant episode in June 1981 received considerable international coverage. In this case Somali civilians received the full wrath of the Kenya Army after Somali bandits had ambushed and killed Kenya government personnel. In yet another incident some 400 civilians died in early 1984.

Yet one sequel to the Ogaden war was a growing rappprochment between Kenya and Somalia, even as Kenya was strengthening its traditional Ethiopian links. In July 1979 President Moi of Kenya visited Ethiopia. He received a red carpet welcome from a regime foaming with anti-capitalist rhetoric. Chairman Mengistu in turn visited Kenya, a country then in grip of anti-Marxist rhetoric, in December 1980. Yet this did not prevent a Kenyan-Somali rapprochment. After all, Kenya and Somalia had a common arms supplier in the USA. In December 1984 the two countries signed an extensive cooperation agreement greatly relaxing tensions along their common border. The role of the superpowers in the Horn of Africa, once again, had much to do with this and other major political developments in the region.

Superpower Involvement and Local Alignments

After the Ogaden war and the sudden rupture of the Somali–Soviet accord, the United States moved swiftly to secure a foothold in Somalia with a view to strengthening its strategic advantage in the Horn of Africa, the Persian Gulf and the Indian Ocean. Part of this policy consisted of direct US intervention; the other part required client states in the region to fall into place and act as surrogates.

With the radicalization of the Ethiopian Revolution and its increasingly anti-American tone, the Jimmy Carter government instructed the US Secretary of State Zbigniew Brzezinski in April 1977, 'to get Somalia to be our friend'.[9] This came hot on the heels of Fidel Castro's tour of the region and his suggestion for a socialist federation combining Somalia, Ethiopia and South Yemen. Dr Kevin Cahill, an American who happens to be the personal physician and friend of President Siad Barre, was dispatched to Mogadishu with conciliatory messages from Washington. Barre believed, or was made to believe, that the United States would condone a Somali takeover of the Ogaden.[10] But in rapid succession the United States made a diplomatic turnabout, leaving Somalia to face single-handedly its erstwhile allies, Cuba and the Soviet Union, on Ethiopia's side. Evidence suggests that the Carter administration became increasingly impressed by the weight of African opinion regarding the inviolability of colonial boundaries. Not a single African state was prepared to support Somalia's forced occupation of the Ogaden.

After the defeat it suffered in 1978 Somalia woke up to an offer of American defensive arms and economic aid. In return, the United States acquired former Soviet military facilities at Berbera and Kismayu. The facilities were part of a network intended for the American Rapid Deployment Force. The other facilities in the region were at Mombasa (Kenya) and Muscat in Oman. In addition, the United States began planning for a fifth fleet based in the Indian Ocean and for increased military aid to Sudan and Egypt. With the United States now firmly in the position of the major arms supplier to Kenya and Somalia and enjoying military facilities in both countries, it was only a matter of time before a rapprochement between Kenya and Somalia was arrived at, as indicated above. The United States government assured the Kenyan government that provision of armaments to Mogadishu were conditional upon a non-aggressive posture towards Kenya by Somalia.

The United States also urged third parties to meddle in the Horn as surrogates of US interests. Saudi Arabia encouraged Somali belligerence in the last quarter of 1977 and supplied Somalia with $200 million worth of arms. Dr Henry Kissinger admitted that the Saudis were 'partly' pushed by the United States into the decision.[11] Iran under the Shah supplied Somalia with second-hand military equipment. Egypt, waxing anti-communist, also ferried arms to Somalia and threatened to invade Ethiopia should she consider tampering with sources of water in the Nile.

For its part, the Soviet Union as already noted, gradually moved towards Ethiopia from early 1977, finally denouncing the Ogaden invasion in August.[12] With the die cast, Somalia abrogated its 1974 friendship treaty with the Soviet Union, and in November 1977 expelled all Soviet experts and denied them access to all military installations in the country. Soviet reaction was as swift as it was brutal. They pulled out to punish, in some cases heading directly for Ethiopia. With them the Soviets took plans and components for development aid programmes, in much the same way as the French had done in Guinea in 1958.[13]

The Soviet exit from Somalia preceded a *demarche* by Warsaw Pact experts who also left promptly. It also had considerable repercussions in the geopolitics of the region. Socialist South Yemen threw its support behind Ethiopia, sending a detachment of several thousand to join the Cubans and Ethiopians in the Ogaden. With Egypt and Sudan firmly lined up against Ethiopia, Libya cast its lot in with Ethiopia, as incidentally did Israel which operated more or less openly, down to February 1978.

With this swift change in inter-state loyalties, the Eritreans found new adversaries in the South Yemenis and Cubans who had previously supported them. The pro-Western and anti-socialist regime in Kenya found itself supporting the self-declared Marxist-Leninist regime in Ethiopia alongside the Soviet Union and other socialist states. For once, Libya and Israel found common cause in supporting the Ethiopian regime.

Among specialists in the Horn there is as yet no consensus on the rationale behind the superpower switch in clients and the new regional line-up which it triggered. Attempts to explain the events in terms of conflicting economic systems—socialist advance versus monopoly capitalism—founder on the problems encountered in rationalizing the Soviet decision to abandon nominally Marxist-Leninist Somalia for the nominally Marxist-Leninist *Dergue* which was then engaged in an all-out war of elimination against Marxist-Leninist militants and intellectuals in Addis Ababa. For, while it must be readily admitted that a social revolution has indeed occurred in Ethiopia, it is debatable whether the sequel has been a socialist society, let alone a Marxist-Leninist one.[14] Indeed a notable recent development in Ethiopia is a number of programmes by the World Bank in favour of private foreign investment and the use of market incentives in agriculture.

American interests in the region are often explained in terms of securing access to oil in the Arabia peninsula and the Persion Gulf for the capitalist West. In practice this calls for American military presence on Africa's eastern seaboard and the Gulf, and more importantly, for planting pro-American regimes in the region. Hence, it is argued, American policy is predicated on pre-empting progressive political regimes and undercutting revolution.

This is a more plausible explanation than theories which presume that American presence is necessitated by a need to counter increasing Soviet presence in the Horn and the Indian Ocean which could supposedly imperil oil tankers bound to the West via the Cape of Good Hope or the Suez Canal. As Tom Farer notes, the Soviet Union must be credited with enough intelligence to realize that a blockade of sea routes leading to the Gulf would almost certainly lead to war with the West, which could not be confined to the Gulf and the Horn.[15]

In summary then, conflict in the Horn of Africa must be seen as a confluence of two forces: local and international. The local input is the violence arising from attempts by states in the region to forge nations within boundaries which are incompatible with the existing mosaic of nationalities in the region. The international input is superpower rivalry, essentially in the quest of national self-interest. The Soviet Union promotes its credibility as a superpower by arming clients while paying little more than rhetorical attention to their socialist content.[16] The United States camouflages its control of energy sources in the greater region in terms of promoting regional stability (i.e. opposing revolutionary changes) and counteracting Soviet military threats in the Gulf, Horn of Africa and the Indian Ocean. The dialectic of internal causes and international intervention is one in which alterations in one induce changes in the other. The social and economic costs to the people of Horn of Africa have been tremendous.

Socio-economic Consequences of War in the Horn of Africa

The effects of warfare and external involvement have been felt directly and indirectly by the inhabitants of the Horn of Africa and its surroundings. There has been an exodus of refugees from the main areas of conflict to neighbouring states. It is not easy to get reliable statistics as the picture is complicated by displaced persons (in UN parlance) who have relocated on account of such natural catastrophes as drought and the inaccessibility of many localities by modern or even ancient means of transport. Nevertheless, the Horn of Africa has seen some of the gravest human suffering in memory; there are approximately two million refugees in Somalia and half a million who have fled Eritrea for the Sudan.

The already impoverished economies in the region have had to bear the increased defence expenditure necessitated by additional military mobilization and importing of arms. Table 5.1 illustrates the increase in armed forces in the Horn between 1976 and 1982. It is clear from the statistics that the Ethiopian armed forces increased nearly fivefold between 1976 and 1982, creating the largest army in sub-Saharan Africa. Kenya and Somalia doubled their armies while there was a marginal increase in the Sudanese army. To the armed forces in official uniform we must add an estimated 40,000–120,000 irregular forces (i.e. guerrillas) said in 1984 to have been operating in the Horn. Of these half were in Eritrea.

Table 5.1
Military Mobilization in the Horn of Africa

Country	Total Number of Armed Forces 1976-7	1982	Growth
Ethiopia	50,800	250,000[a]	492%
Kenya	7,600	16,650	219%
Somalia	25,000	60,000	240%
Sudan	52,600	58,000	110%

[a] Includes the 150,000-strong people's militia.

Source: *Military Balance*, International Institute of Strategic Studies, London, 1976/77 and 1982.

The scale of mobilization is reflected in the increased proportion of national resource devoted to defence. Table 5.2 demonstrates the changes between 1976 and 1982. The percentage of GNP allocated to military expenditure in the four states was generally modest (1.3% for Kenya and 5% for Somalia) before 1976, even for Somalia which undertook a substantial military build-up between 1970 and 1976. The national resources going into defence grew at phenomenal rates thereafter. Kenya quadrupled its defence expenditure in money terms between 1976 and 1979, principally in response to Somalia's defence policy and consequent US defence support. Even more spectacular was Somalia's sixfold, money-terms rise in military spending to the point where defence consumed over a fifth of GNP. Ethiopia experienced a fourfold increase in the military budget which in 1982 took 9% of GNP.

Table 5.2
Trends in Defence Expenditure

Country	1976/77 Defence Expenditure (US $)	As % of GNP	1982 Defence Expenditure (US $)	As % of GNP
Ethiopia	84m	2.9	362.8m	8.87
Kenya	35m	1.3	160m[b]	2.5[b]
Somalia	15m	5.0	95m[c]	22.1
Sudan	120m[a]	4.3	333m	3.6

[a] Refers to 1975/76
[b] Refers to 1980
[c] Refers to 1979.

Source: *Military Balance*, International Institute of Strategic Studies, London 1976/77 and 1982.

Robin Luckham and Dawit Bekele have dwelt at length on the impact of arms imports on the balance of payments of the states in the Horn of Africa.[17] The index they use is the ratio of imported arms to export earnings. A better measure would be the percentage of external debt service accounted for by repayment for imported arms. This however, is not easy to obtain. But it would appear, so far, not very substantial for countries like Ethiopia which have been importing arms from the Soviet Union on fairly easy credit terms and whose overall debt burden is comparatively slight.[18] It is probable that the harder military credit terms offered by the United States have had the effect of raising the external debt burden being borne by Kenya and Sudan.

The overall picture of economic change in the area has been one of declining or sluggish growth. Between 1960 and 1982, GNP per capita in Somali declined at 0.1% per year on average, while that of the Sudan declined at the rate of 0.4% per year. Ethiopia's per capita income growth rate was 1.4% over the same period, while Kenya's was 2.8%.[19] Per capita food production has declined in all of them, in some cases disastrously. Industrial growth has been either marginal or declining, with the possible exception of Kenya. Laitin and

Samatar provide a distressing picture of the Somali economy after the Ogaden war. [20] Somalia in 1984 was marked by a collapsed economy in the agricultural and industrial sectors.

The blame for this cannot be placed entirely on the states of the region. Destabilizing factors arising from the structure of the world capitalist system— the oil crisis, inflation, recession—are certainly part of the explanation. So is drought. But so too are the disastrous economic policies which governments in the region have pursued over the years and the political instability and domestic chaos which we have already discussed. The peoples of the Horn have been visited not just by the calamities of war, but also by a continuous deterioration in their standards of living because of a conflation of natural disasters, their own rulers and strongly vested international interests. And in the process of it all nobody has cared much for their opinions as a possible beginning to the solution to the central problem.

Conclusion: Prospects for Political Settlement

If, as we have seen, conflict in the Horn of Africa can be explained by a dialectic of local causes aggravated by superpower involvement which further escalates local conflict, political settlement must be sought essentially from initiatives by states of the Horn. A settlement to the problem must also preclude intervention by the superpowers.

The most proximate point of departure must be the resolution to the national question *within* and *between* the states of the Horn. As long as some communities within the states are economically and politically oppressed, chances of revolt will remain high and with them prospects of regional and extra-regional intervention. It is therefore incumbent upon the governments in the Horn area to develop policies towards dissident nationalities based on democratic practice and a large degree of political and economic autonomy, This suggests some form of federal or confederate political system.

The basic problem is the extent to which political autonomy should be sacrificed. Somalia's support for irredentist movements in Ethiopia and Kenya testify to her quest for the integration of all Somali-speaking peoples in the region under one flag. As evident from diplomatic reaction to Somalia's invasion of the Ogaden, most African states are likely to oppose forced alteration of colonial boundaries precisely because they are all vulnerable to irredentist and secessionist claims. A compromise needs to be found between the extreme policies of boundary change demanded by Somalia and the miitary occupation of dissident territories now being pursued by Ethiopia. And when the principles of full autonomy and political rights are conceded to the Ethiopian nationalities they cannot be denied to the Somali population in Kenya and Ethiopia or Africans in Southern Sudan. The only possible exception to this rule would appear to be Eritrea whose colonial boundaries were erased in the era of African decolonization by the Ethiopian *ancien regime*. Eritrean nationalists have therefore argued that their secession should not be construed in the same light as that of Katanga or Biafra.

To introduce the necessary flexibility in inter-state discourse it is imperative that the profile of involvement by USA and USSR in the region be scaled down considerably, and with it that of their allies and local proxies. External powers lie behind the hardening of attitudes among the major contestants in the Horn and reduction of external influence would be conducive to a political settlement and lowering of tensions.

But this is easier said than done. We have attempted to explain that none of the leading powers in the world has intervened in the Horn of Africa in the interests of the African people resident there. It would be futile to plead with them for a reduced role in the interests of welfare of the peoples of the Horn. Initiative, therefore, must come from the governments in the region. The problem here, unfortunately, is how few if any of them have a genuine commitment to the improvement of material conditions and social welfare of their citizens. The governments in the Horn are part of the problem rather than part of the solution.

Notes

1. See Roland Stanbridge, '1980—Africa Refugee Year', in *Africa Contemporary Record 1980-81*, Africana Publishing, New York, 1982, pp. 94—103.
2. Tom J. Farer, *War Clouds in the Horn of Africa*, Carnegie Endowment for International Peace, Washington, DC, 1976, pp. 8—11.
3. Ibid. p. 56.
4. The Kagnew Base was vital to American geostrategic concerns in the Middle East and for monitoring communications further afield, especially in the Middle East including southern parts of the USSR.
5. Bereket H. Selassie, 'The American Dilemma on the Horn', *Journal of Modern African Studies*, vol.22, no.2, 1984, p. 260.
6. Colin Legum and Bill Lee, *Crisis in the Horn of Africa*, Africana Publishing, New York, 1979.
7. The standard reference work on Eritrean history is G.K.N. Trevaskis, *Eritrea: A Colony in Transition: 1941-1952*. Royal Institute of International Affairs Series, London, 1980. Some interpretations impute a class conflict between the Muslim and traditionalist ELF and the Christian and progressive EPLF. Others emphasize ethnic cleavages between lowland peoples and the highlander Tigrayans.
8. See, for instance, Lionel Cliffe, 'Dramatic Shifts in the Military Balance in the Horn: The 1984 Eritrean Offensive', *Review of African Political Economy*, vol.30, 1984, pp. 93—7.
9. Robert F. Gorman, *Political Conflict in the Horn of Africa*, Praeger, New York, 1981, p. 70.
10. On 17 October 1977, the United States called for a UN-supervised referendum in the Ogaden, a move which was roundly condemned by African diplomats at the UN.
11. Bruce Oudes, 'The United States Year in Africa: Reinventing the Wheel'

in *Africa Contemporary Record, 1977/78*, Africana Publishing, New York, 1979, p. A73.

12. Gorman, 1981, p. 117.

13. Legum and Lee, 1979.

14. James F. Petras and Morris H. Morley, 'The Ethiopian Military State and Soviet-US Involvement in the Horn of Africa', *Review of African Political Economy*, no.30, 1984, minimizes internal structural reforms and predicates Ethiopia socialism on state to state relations with the Soviet Union. In stressing the thoroughness of domestic social transformation and the limits imposed on genuine Marxist thought and democracy by the military, Addis Hiwet (in the same issue of *Review of African Political Economy*) probably comes much closer to reality than most people who have written on this issue.

15. Farer, 1976, pp. 114—16.

16. Petras and Morley, 1984, insist that relations between USSR and Ethiopia are opportunistic on both sides.

17. Robin Luckham and Dawit Bekele, 'Foreign Powers and Militarism in the Horn of Africa', *Review of African Political Economy*, no.30, September 1984, pp. 16—18.

18. Luckham and Bekele, ibid., p. 16, put the Ethiopian military debt to the USSR at US$ two billion by 1982, payable over 10 years beginning 1983/84 at 2% interest. World Bank statistics put Ethiopia's debt service (as a percentage of exports) at 9.5% in 1982 and that of Somalia at 7.2%. Sub-Saharan Africa's average is 12.6%.

19. All the statistics have been obtained from the World Bank, *Towards Sustained Development in Sub-Saharan Africa*, Washington, DC, 1984, p. 57.

20. David Laitin and Said Samatar, 'Somalia and the World Economy', *Review of African Political Economy*, no.30, September 1984, pp. 58—72.

6. Conflict in Southern Africa

Ibbo Mandaza

The basis and nature of the current conflict in Southern Africa have to be understood in the context of the global struggle between imperialism as represented by the United States and its NATO allies, and the Socialist bloc as represented by the Soviet Union and its allies. This conflict expresses itself in the case of South Africa specifically in the contradiction between an imperialist policy which, in pursuit of its regional economic and strategic interests, is invariably supportive of the South African apartheid state and the struggle by the black people of Namibia and South Africa for national independence and economic self-reliance. It is a struggle supported by the Organization of African Unity through its Liberation Committee, for the complete liberation of Africa from colonialism and racial domination.

It is a struggle that has also prompted the formation of the so-called frontline group of states bringing together Angola, Botswana, Mozambique, Tanzania, Zambia and Zimbabwe. It functions as both a sub-committee of the Organization of African Unity, as well as the main political, diplomatic and (in some cases) military rear bases of the South African and Namibian liberation movements.[1] The frontline group also forms part of a broader network of African states known as the South African Development Co-ordination Conference (SADCC) and which includes Malawi, Lesotho and Swaziland. SADCC's main objective is the quest for economic disengagement from South Africa[2] but it has acted more as a forum within which to mobilize a common outlook on the problem of Southern Africa and against which the South African state has increasingly appeared politically and diplomatically isolated in Africa.[3]

The conflict in Southern Africa is complicated by the race factor which acts as the most important political and popular basis for mobilizing internal and external forces against the South African regime. Against this background imperialism finds itself unable to reconcile its economic and strategic interests in Namibia and South Africa with the need to condemn apartheid which, although morally indefensible, is nevertheless inextricably bound up with imperialist interests and the need for a strong South African state to support its global struggle against the Soviet Union and its socialist allies.

Imperialism's fear is that the destruction of the apartheid state might constitute a major threat to international capital and imperialist strategy in

Southern Africa since the fundamental changes that will bring about democracy and majority rule are more likely to be the outcome of a violent struggle in which it fears that the Soviet Union and its allies might become involved, than by a peaceful transition. Consistent with their declared anti-imperialist stance and commitment to decolonization and liberation the world over, the Soviet Union and socialist bloc is naturally concerned with the struggle in Southern Africa and provides material, political and diplomatic support to both the liberation movement and the frontline states. However, there is as yet no indication that the Soviet Union is prepared to be directly involved in the Southern African conflict.[4] Both Soviet and Chinese foreign policy on Southern Africa—and on Africa in general—has tended to be confined to the kind of limited involvement referred to above. They have always acted at the request of the movements or countries concerned and with the specific objective of ensuring both that the Africans themselves maintain the initiative and to avoid providing the US and its NATO allies with a justification for a major showdown in an area which it regards as part of its own sphere of influence.

The main thrust of the US foreign policy in Southern Africa is largely preemptive, propagandist and jingoist, designed to prevent its global enemies from establishing a foothold in the region. Consequently, any state associated with any member of the socialist block is quickly branded as communist and subjected to a combination of economic boycott and military destabilization by its regional 'policeman'—South Africa. This perhaps explains why countries like Mozambique have not readily sought the direct involvement in their affairs of the Soviet Union, China or other socialist countries, even when subject to direct military aggression. It also explains the current insistence by the USA that the withdrawal of the Cubans is a pre-condition for both the withdrawal of South African troops from Angola and the resolution of the Namibian question.

These and other developments in Southern Africa highlight the relative dominance of imperialist policies in the region. They indicate that the west will stop at little to ensure the maintenance of its economic and strategic interests. It does not mean actual opposition to the attainment of national independence in Namibia and South Africa but an anxiety that it should happen without undue threat to its economic and strategic interests. Needless to add, this policy has been the cause of much conflict and bloodshed in the region and the indications for the immediate future are that this will continue.

The Main Focus of Analysis

The purpose of this paper is to outline briefly the historical basis of imperialism in Southern Africa. A central feature will be an analysis of the main elements of United States policy in Southern Africa in the last two decades, highlighting the modifications that have been necessitated by the intensification of armed conflict which brought national independence to Angola, Mozambique and Zimbabwe, and will inevitably do so in Namibia and South Africa.

The analysis of the South African state itself will be confined mainly to a consideration of whether or not it can be described as a sub-imperial power, [5] taking into account the configuration of US–South African relations and the role of the South African state in the destabilization of the frontline states. It will throw into sharp focus the aggressive and dominant role of this policy in influencing not only the Frontline and SADCC states but also the Southern African liberation movements. Accordingly, the Lancaster House Agreement on Zimbabwe, the Lusaka Accords on Namibia and Angola, the Nkomati Accord between South Africa and Mozambique and the recent talks about talks between South Africa and the ANC will all be described below in the context of a framework of overall US policy on Southern Africa.

This analysis will challenge the view prevalent in some radical analyses of the Southern African situation that its liberation will be synonomous with socialist construction under the leadership of a vanguard party of the revolutionary working class. [6] This argument is based partly on the conventional conception of white settler societies as ones which, because of a large presence of whites and a strong state and military machinery, are incapable of accepting the deal of decolonization, as there is little or nothing to gain from it. The high level of development of productive forces, the industrial base and the large wage-earning class are also cited as factors that preclude a neo-colonial solution, particularly in South Africa. Furthermore it is argued, this settler intransigence, concretized in the apartheid state (with its linkages to imperialism) necessitates the inevitable development of a formidable and ideologically revolutionary machinery of resistance in the form of national liberation movements which aim to establish socialism under a revolutionary democratic alliance dominated by the proletariat and the peasantry.

This argument is not challenged in an attempt to disparage the revolutionary philosophy that inspires our radical tradition in Africa. Nor should the critique be misconstrued as giving credence to those outdated analyses that talk of prospects of peaceful change in South Africa. The purpose is to put the historical and material conditions of South Africa in a correct analytical framework. [7] The history of Southern Africa itself negates the peaceful change scenario. The sub-region has been a battle-ground ever since the arrival of the Dutch at the Cape in 1652. Indeed, it has been through violent struggle that Southern Africa finds itself at this juncture and it will be through continued armed struggle and intense class struggle that national independence will be attained in Namibia and South Africa. But violence in itself is neither synonomous with nor the midwife of genuine liberation and socialism.

It is ideologically proper that comrades in South Africa should hope that there will emerge out of the liberation struggle 'a revolutionary democratic alliance dominated by the proletariat and peasantry' as 'a first stage in a continuous process along the road to socialism'. [8] However, we must base our analysis on what is, rather than on what ought to be, and recognize that events will fall short of these expectations. The new states that will emerge in Namibia and South Africa out of the liberation struggles will be dominated by the black petty bourgeoisie—a class which will more likely be the tool of neo-colonialism rather than the agent of revolutionary change. It is for this reason that the focus of our analysis is US foreign policy in the region, its interaction with and influence upon both the South African state and the frontline and SADCC states and upon how all this relates to, and impinges upon, the strategy and tactics of the Southern African liberation movements. These latter are not analysed in great detail except to assert the need to understand these movements as consisting of a variety of classes and ideological outlooks bound together in a common desire for national independence and democracy in the form of majority rule.

An issue that will receive only brief mention is the growing strength of the anti-apartheid lobby in North America and Western Europe.[9] Active for many years, the lobby has recently developed apace mainly on a popular conception of the South African problem as a 'human rights' issue rather than one with its origins in the contradiction between imperialism and the aspirations of the black majority in Namibia and South Africa. Nonetheless the growth in the power of the lobby has some important implications in the current phase of the conflict in Southern Africa.

First, it has become an important weapon which both the national liberation movements and the frontline states can use, at least on the political and diplomatic front, to extend and intensify the isolation of South Africa throughout the world. Secondly, the recent anti-apartheid demonstrations by groups of American Jews are an indication that South Africa cannot indefinitely rely on its alliance with Israel.[10] More importantly, it may yet influence the USA into a significant discrmination between the respective situations of two vital outposts of the imperialist global network and establish in Western minds the notion that the South African apartheid state is even less legitimate than its Zionist counterpart.

There is also evidence that this lobby is causing some embarrassment to the US government and its NATO allies, particularly over the question of human rights and racism.[11] This is the situation that the South African human rights leader, Archbishop Desmond Tutu, has effectively exploited, not only in the human rights movement tradition but also in the form of subtle support for the national liberation movement.[12] His Nobel Peace prize added impetus to the lobby throughout the world but it will cause only a modification rather than fundamental change in the conventional imperialist policy on Southern Africa. Another consequence will be a close association of the anti-South Africa lobby in the West and the national liberation struggle in Southern Africa which will increase pressure for a negotiated settlement along the Zimbabwean model.

Imperialism in Southern Africa

In an earlier work I outlined the main features of imperialism, based on a Marxist-Leninist characterization;[13] here, the essence of modern imperialism is summarized. It is characterized by: 1) the gap in economic development between the industrialized Western (and European-settled) countries and those restricted to primary production. The gap is widening under continued imperialist domination; 2) the export of capital from the more developed countries to the less; 3) the division, especially in the late 19th Century, of territories throughout the world by the more developed nations as part of the rivalry and competition for strategic and economic advantages. This competition for colonies led to two world wars; 4) the further concentration and centralization of capital and the integration of the world capital economy into the structures of the giant US-based multinational corporations or integrated monopolistic enterprises. These multinational corporations not only accelerate technological change but also control trade, prices and profits; 5) the decline in the period since the Russian Revolution of national rivalries among the leading capitalist countries as an international ruling class has been consolidated on the basis of ownership and control of multinational corporations; the world capital market has been internationalized by the World Bank and other agencies of the international ruling class. This has led to, 6) the evolution of global imperialist foreign policy which corresponds to the global interests and perspectives of the multinational corporations and, 7) the intensification of these tendencies under the threat from world socialism to the world capitalist system.

Emphasis should, however, be placed on the foreign policy of imperialism, with particular reference to the means whereby the more economically developed nations seek to maintain and extend their political, military and economic hegemony over the less. Ever since the Russian Revolution of 1917, the major objective of the USA and its allies has been to prevent the contraction of the world capitalist system. To this end, imperialism—and particularly its US manifestation—has developed a complex strategy that includes, *inter alia*, 'regional and defence arrangements which provide and take advantage of shared responsibilities' among the capitalist countries and their outposts. [14]

In examining the specific nature of imperialist domination in Southern Africa it is important to understand its relationship to the emergence in particularly Namibia, South Africa and Zimbabwe of white settler colonialism, what could be described as a particular expression of imperialist domination or as colonialism *par excellence*. Historically, South Africa has been at the centre of imperialist operations in the region from as long ago as the 15th Century when the Cape was recognized as a vital strategic centre on the route to India and the Far East. This continued to be the case through three successive stages of capitalist imperialism—mercantile, free trade and modern monopoly imperialism. These stages cover the modern history of Southern Africa, from 1652 when the first Europeans settled at the Cape, to the present.

Significantly the era of modern monopoly imperialism coincided with the discovery in the late 19th Century of gold and diamonds which so influenced the pace of developments in both South Africa and most countries of the sub-region. The era also produced the partitioning of Africa, and prompted Cecil John Rhodes and his fellow imperialists to begin to plot the Cape to Cairo road as part of the British colonial strategy in Southern Africa and beyond.

In our analysis, the domination of South Africa of the sub-region resulted from the strategic importance of the South African land mass; its attractive natural resources; its immense mineral deposits that in time became central to the economies of the Western countries; its abundant and cheap human resources constituting a source of accumulation (and appropriation) of surplus and its geographical position in the path of imperialist expansion from the Cape northwards. These same factors—especially the quest for minerals, land and labour—determined the colonial histories of Zimbabwe, Namibia, Angola and, to a lesser extent, other Southern African countries. [15]

Consequent to the establishment of imperialist domination in Southern Africa a significant white settler population developed, which in turn became imbued with a virulent ideology of white racial domination. This ideology has been used to mobilize all white classes behind the apartheid state, even including the white working class despite their exploitation by imperial capital and the white bourgeoisie. This racial polarization of the working class has been a complicating factor for the national liberation struggle. [16] Further to its role as a mobilizer of the white working and other classes, the ideology of racism has also been an effective instrument in the exploitative process as evidenced by the high rate of accumulation (and appropriation) of surplus by the imperialist system. South Africa provides very favourable conditions for the capitalist super-exploitation of labour in particular and material resources in general. Thus, contrary to the imperialist (and liberal) myth which views the phenomenon of racism in Southern Africa as extraneous to the economy, we see it as central. Imperialism profits directly from apartheid and at a higher rate than elsewhere in Africa and, most other areas of the world.

A recent work has shown the following as the average yield on direct investment in South Africa as compared with other countries between 1972 and 1981. [17]

Table 6.1
Investment yields

Country	Yield %
Australia	14.5
Canada	10.9
New Zealand	10.0
Norway	16.5
Spain	9.9
South Africa	15.8

The study goes on to explain why South Africa has become so attractive to US and Western European investment. [18]

The Republic of South Africa has always been regarded by foreign investors as a gold mine, one of those rare and refreshing places where profits are great and problems small. Capital is not threatened by political instability or nationali-zation. Labour is cheap, the market booming, the currency hard and convertible, such are the market's attractions that 292 American Corporations have established subsidiaries or affiliates there. Their combined direct investment is close to $900 million, and their returns on that investment have been romping home at something like 19 per cent a year, after taxes. [19]

The quotation describes the situation in the early 1970s; but other analysts have shown that between 1943 and 1978, 'US direct investment in South Africa grew from $50 million to $2 billion—an increase of 4,000 per cent;' [20] had reached US$7,200 million by 1980; [21] that '15% of foreign investment to South Africa from the dollar area comes from the US Corporations, and that most of that investment is in heavy industry;' [22] that US$3,000 million are sent out of South Africa every year as profits and dividends for overseas international monopolies; [23] that Britain and American 'account for 70% of the total foreign investment' [24] in South Africa and that there are now 350 US companies involved in South Africa. [25]

Ample documentation also exists on the pattern and rate of investment in South Africa on the part of Britain, West Germany, France and other Western and NATO countries. Always, however, there is a need to relate such invest-ment to the industrial and military build-up in South Africa and, in turn, to US policy on South Africa and the latter's role in the sub-region. This military factor is a further implication to be drawn from the relationship between imperialism and the apartheid state.

> International credit, provided the margin of funds needed by South Africa in the 1974-76 period to finance its military build-up, its stockpiling of oil, and its major infrastructure projects in strategic economic sectors such as transport-ation, communications, energy, and steel production, all of which are related to security needs... [26]

More recently emphasis has been placed upon the relationship between US and Western investment and South Africa's growing military technology and nuclear capability as well as its policy of 'total strategy'. This involves, *inter alia*,

> a militarized national security system, integrating all branches and levels of the state machinery, industry, business, the educational system and all other institutions to ensure that political control remain in white hands, more specifically those of the Afrikaner group of the ruling class. [27]

This 'total strategy' has equipped South Africa to play a role as a sub-imperial centre preserving regional political and economic 'stability' [28] as a junior partner in a general imperialist strategy against the Soviet Union.

US Policy in Southern Africa and South Africa's Role in the Sub-region

There are numerous studies of US policy in Southern Africa; but the best rely heavily on an analysis of National Security Study Memorandum 39 (or NSSM 39) of 1969, a US policy document that outlined the Nixon-Kissinger strategy on Southern Africa. The editors of a popular version of it have dubbed it *The Kissinger Study of Southern Africa*,[29] emphasizing that the policy is based on a careful consideration, by the USA of its strategic and economic interests in the sub-region. But these are, in turn, related to US global interests as a whole.

The editors have summarized the 'real-world considerations' affecting US policy towards Southern Africa:[30]

● the strategic importance of Southern Africa, particularly with the closing of the Suez Canal following the 1967 Middle East War and the increased Soviet naval activities in the Indian Ocean;
● the US need to use overflight and landing facilities for military aircraft heading to and from Indo-China;
● significant investment and balance of trade advantages to both Britain and the US in South Africa;
● South Africa's status as the major gold supplier in the capitalist world and its importance of guaranteeing the useful operation of the two-tier gold price system.

On the basis of the above, the objectives of US policy in Southern Africa were stated to be:[31]

● to improve US standing in black Africa and internationally on the racial issue;
● to minimize the likelihood of an escalation of violence in the area and the risk of US involvement;
● to minimize the opportunities for the USSR and Communist China to exploit the racial issue in the region for propaganda advantage and to gain political influence with black governments and liberation movements;
● to encourage the moderation of the current rigid racial and colonial policies of the white regimes and
● to protect economic, scientific and strategic interests and opportunities in the region, including the orderly marketing of South Africa's gold production.

The development of this policy initiated a directly interventionist role by the USA in Southern African affairs in a role surpassing even that of the former colonial master of the sub-region, Britain. Thus the 1970s witnessed the heavy hand of the USA in the detente exercise, particularly after the Portuguese coup of 1974 which brought a successful conclusion to the liberation struggles in Angola, Mozambique and Guinea-Bissau. Perhaps more than Britain itself, the USA was instrumental in the Lancaster House Agreement on Zimbabwe of 1978-80, on the basis, it has been argued, of option two (out of the five options which constituted the policy alternatives for the USA in Southern Africa).

Broader association with both black and white states in an effort to encourage moderation in the white states, to enlist cooperation of the black states in reducing tensions and the likelihood of increasing cross-border violence and to encourage improved relations among states in the area. [32]

It has also been argued by those who designed the policy that this option two was based on the belief that 'blacks cannot gain political rights through violence' and that therefore only a combination of persuading whites into 'acquiescence' and 'increased economic assistance' could bring about constructive change. [33] It also revealed a 'complete lack of concern over the aspirations and fate of the African people', and that the USA 'had no genuine interest in solving racial and colonial conflicts in Southern Africa'. It became involved, 'not out of commitment to fundamental human rights and basic democratic principles', but 'because other countries have made it so'. [34]

Other analyses have pointed to the coincidence of US and South African interests. M.M. Ncube has noted that:

The interests of the two now coincide. They must protect apartheid together, which means they must from now plan together and fight together! Defence of apartheid has become an objective though the US ruling class may, for tactical reasons, express its interests in language which camouflages that truth. Consequently, the US involvement in destabilization in Southern Africa is an open secret. It is carried out both in support of the apartheid regime as well as a generalized strategy against the national liberation movement, socialism and communism. [35]

Accordingly, Ncube sees the USA and South Africa as almost synonomous in acts of destabilization [36] as Operation Savannah, which in October 1975 was designed to overthrow the MPLA government in Angola; Operation Cobra (of September 1977) against Angola's oil-fields in Cabinda and the related abortive attempt to set up an independent state in Cabinda; another invasion of Angola in 1978 by a joint force of the South African army, foreign mercenaries and UNITA; Operation Protea (of 1981) which led to the invasion and occupation by South African troops of the southern part of Angola; the building up and support for the Mozambique Resistance Movement (MNR) in Mozambique; military attacks on Zimbabwe, including the sabotage of Air Force planes, the threat of the 'estimated 500 former Rhodesian Soldiers in camps in northern Transvaal', and the arming of bands of dissidents [37]; the numerous acts of aggression against Lesotho; the occasional threats against Botswana and the training of the Mushala gang to destabilize Zambia. [38]

Also seen as evidence of US involvement in these acts of destabilization are the accounts of CIA operations in Africa in the Congo crisis and the assassination of Patrice Lumumba as well as close links and exchanges of information between the CIA and Pretoria's State Security Council. [39] Likewise, Ncube sees the recent US policy of 'constructive engagement' as synonomous with option one of NSSM 39, [40] namely, 'closer association with the white regimes to protect and enhance our economic, strategic and scientific interests'. [41]

It is on the basis of this that he concludes that because the USA is anxious to prevent Namibia, South Africa and Southern Africa in general from falling into the Soviet sphere of influence, it is therefore at one with South Africa in denying to 'the people of the region self-determination'.[42] He concludes,

> In short, 'constructive engagement' is the modern version of the Monroe Doctrine in which the US is blatantly telling those who are not yet free that they dare not choose self-determination lest they be labelled communists and therefore be candidates for massacring... Meanwhile South Africa, the local policeman for US interests, will see to it that Washington's edicts are carried out![43]

All this constitutes a gross misunderstanding of US imperialist policy in Southern Africa and arises out of a confusion of the means and goals of such a policy. More than that, it is the kind of analysis which suggests that liberation is an unattainable goal—not only in Southern Africa but perhaps even the world over. It is in opposition to this view that we now outline some of the pertinent elements of US policy in Southern Africa in relation to both South Africa, the frontline states and the national liberation movements of Namibia and South Africa.

The major objective of US policy is the pursuit of stability so that its economic and strategic interests will, as far as possible, be maintained intact. In pursuit of these it will use military means but it prefers a political solution. It is in this respect that NSSM 39 is most instructive, particularly in the choice of option two as the major guiding line of US policy in Southern Africa, an option which, however, should be seen only as a broad outline of policy. Modifications have had to be made in the light of changing regional circumstances since 1969. One rationale for option two was that 'blacks cannot gain political rights through violence'.[44] However, since NSSM 39 was formulated in 1969, armed struggle has led to independence for Angola, Mozambique and Zimbabwe.

Contrary to Ncube's analysis, therefore, constructive engagement should be viewed as a modification of option two, as required by the changing circumstances of the Southern African situation. Accordingly, Rod Bush's interpretation[45] of constructive engagement is, on one level closer to our understanding of US policy than Ncube's, though, on another level, he reveals a misunderstanding of certain aspects of that policy by concluding that because of the presence of the white settler government in South Africa, 'a neo-colonial solution or the deal of decolonization is extremely unlikely'.[46] In fact the major objectives of option two and constructive engagement are decolonization and neo-colonialism. What are the *goals* of constructive engagement? To quote Bush,

> 1) an internationally acceptable settlement in Namibia, preferably excluding SWAPO or severely limiting its options; 2) foreclosure of opportunities for the growth of Soviet influence; and 3) greater acceptance of South Africa within the global framework of Western Security.[47]

Accordingly, the *policy* of constructive engagement consists of a 'skilful combination of bullying and intimidation with negotiation'.[48] It is in this context that the USA supports South African raids into neighbouring territories to soften up the national liberation movements before negotiating for a political settlement or to counter Soviet influence in a particular country, especially if its government has left-wing leanings. This explains recent events in Angola and Mozambique, in particular the fact that the Lusaka and Nkomati Accords[49] are both designed to soften up the ANC and SWAPO as well as to counter Soviet influence in Angola and Mozambique. This is all with a view to bringing about neo-colonialism in Namibia and South Africa within the context of imperialist stability. It should be recalled that there was a similar pattern of events in the period immediately before independence in Zimbabwe.

Another feature of US policy in Southern Africa concerns what has been described by some as a fundamental contradiction in its policy 'since it has apparently tried to strike a balance between conflicting and irreconcilable objectives of African and white-minority ruled states'.[50] But given the African reality referred to above, and the diminishing area of white rule in the period since the formulation of NSSM 39, this dilemma has become less glaring. There now appears to be a general acceptance on the part of the current architects of US foreign policy that black majority rule in Namibia and South Africa is now only a matter of time. It is now a question of how best to prepare the white minority for it, what safeguards—as happened in Zimbabwe—can be formulated for it and how to ensure that there will be an orderly and non-communist transition. Furthermore, there are even suggestions among senior US officials themselves that the US has been over-anxious and pre-emptive about the Soviet and communist threat in Africa. At the time of the Lancaster House talks on Zimbabwe one US official was heard to comment that all that Africans wanted was black majority rule and the sooner they were allowed to get it, the better for Southern Africa and the USA itself.[51]

But another important consideration is the position of both the frontline states and the national liberation movements in response to US policy in Southern Africa. Like option two which, in its original formulation, assumed that the white minority states were unassailable, so too, in 1969 at least, were African states in general more conciliatory towards white settler colonialism. In this respect, the Lusaka Manifesto has been described as reflecting not only the ideological deficiency of neo-colonial Africa but also its abject weakness in the face of imperialism and an aggressive South Africa. The most abject of the states even entered into the open cooperation—the dialogue and detente of the 1960s and 1970s—with the South African government under the pretence that this would bring about a change of heart in white settler colonialism.[52]

But since then it has been the intensification of the national liberation struggle in Southern Africa which has bolstered the diplomatic leverage of the African states in their opposition to the white south. Certainly these liberation struggles gave rise to the frontline state lobby that is today the guiding force of African diplomacy in Southern Africa. Yet the basic economic, political and military vulnerability of most SADCC states has generally meant that, individually or jointly, they have had to operate within the ambit of the imperialist strategy in Southern Africa. The major objective of the frontline states is now the decolonization of Namibia and South Africa, and they have therefore acted as a kind of bridge between the national liberation movements and the USA and its NATO allies, sometimes breathing fire but, like the USA itself, ultimately supporting negotiation. The extent to which the violence and upheavals that accompany the liberation struggle have had an adverse economic and military effect on them is also the extent to which they have increasingly been able to negotiate for, and on behalf of, the national liberation movements. Sometimes this has even meant arm-twisting the latter into compliance with whatever formula might be seen as producing a solution. This is in fact what happened over the Zimbabwe issue in 1979-80 and what is currently happening with regard to Namibia, and will certainly happen with regard to South Africa if and when the circumstances appear ripe enough for fully-fledged negotiations.

A major concern of the frontline states has been the need to maintain a united front in their dealings with South Africa, the national liberation movements and US imperialism and its NATO allies. It is a measure of their strength and influence with regard to these imperialist forces and in defining the African reality. It also coincides with the tendency of the USA and its allies to always solicit the views and support of the frontline states on matters affecting the sub-region. But the unity of purpose of these frontline states relates mainly to the basic objective of black majority rule. This commitment to basic and minimum conditions has meant that they have been able to project themselves as a freedom—and peace-loving group of states, especially when either a national liberation movement, South Africa, the USA or one of their number has been intransigent on particular issues.

In this way the frontline states have contributed significantly to the isolation of South Africa in many parts of the world and caused a measure of embarrassment to those, like the USA and some of its allies, who openly deal with South Africa. It is in this respect, perhaps, that SADCC has become, for North American and Western countries who trade with South Africa, 'a soft option, a face-saving commitment, a dubious counter balance to their involvement in South Africa'. [53] Yet it is also an indication that Africa—and in particular the frontline states—has progressed significantly from the political condition it found itself in in 1969.

It is, of course, common to regard such recent events as the Lusaka and Nkomati Accords as a reflection of the current unassailable position of South Africa. But the point, surely, is that South Africa is besieged enough by the unfolding reality around it, enough, at least, to realize that black Africans—at home and abroad—are a force to reckon with.

The Accords might be a vain attempt at warding off the inevitable through some kind of revival of the constellation of states. But there can be no doubt now that the South African state is a declining factor in the overall consideration of the relation of forces in the Southern African sub-region.

For as long as the apartheid state is a reality, neither the Lusaka Accords, Nkomati Accords, nor any arrangement that is designed to bolster the South

African state at the expense of the basic political demands of black Africans in South Africa and beyond its borders, can be sustained. It will be recalled that the dialogue and detente of the 1970s failed dismally for the South African state and that we saw the emergence then of the new states of Angola, Mozambique and Zimbabwe.

The Current Crisis

This brings us to a brief consideration of whether or not South Africa is indeed a sub-imperial power and the implications for the future of the sub-region. Ruy Mauro Marini was, perhaps, the first writer to use the concept of sub-imperialism in his account of Brazilian sub-imperialism. [54] He defined sub imperialism as essentially 'the form which dependent capitalism assumes upon reaching the stage of monopolies and finance capital'. [55] But within the context of the overall imperialist strategy of trying to contain revolution and so keep the capitalist system intact, Brazilian sub-imperialism represents the counter-revolutionary role that Brazil plays in Latin America on behalf of the USA. Viewed in the latter context, it is not surprising that the concept of sub-imperialism came to be applied to South Africa. [56] There are other factors that support such a characterization. The first is South Africa's economic strength in the sub-region and the fact that most of the frontline and SADCC states are dependent upon it for trade, transport and even employment. The second is its military strength and the ease with which it can invade and occupy any state in the sub-region. Its aggression is sometimes part and parcel of the US policy in the region and would tend to justify Dan Nabudere's view that 'it is the US imperialist running all over, telling Vorster and Smith what to do'. [57] Yet there are also occasions when South Africa's actions have caused, especially in this current stage, even Reagan to feel 'a moral responsibility to speak out...to emphasize our concern and grief over the human and spiritual costs of apartheid.' [58]

This is precisely the point at which there appears to be a distinction between South Africa and other so-called sub-imperial countries like Brazil and Israel. A comparison was made earlier between South Africa and Israel on the human rights question and the fact that the world in general regards South Africa as having less validity than the Zionist state. The South African regime lacks legitimacy in the eyes of not only the majority of its inhabitants but also of Africa and the world in general. This does suggest that even if there are economic and strategic reasons why South Africa should be described as sub-imperial, political circumstances have now changed and are likely to lead to a new political equation in the sub-region. As we have seen, its leverage at the sub-regional level has consequently become more limited; and where it has had to assert itself, this has been done so aggressively as to make such gains as might be attained rather limited. Thus, while the concept of sub-imperialism does help us to understand the South African state's role within the imperialist network, it is less precise and valid in the South African situation than in the Brazilian one.

The main question, however, is whether or not the USA and its NATO allies are prepared to sustain and support an apartheid state in its present form or whether they will increasingly pressurize South Africa into some kind of settlement that takes into account African reality. A point has already been made about the growing pressure on the USA and its allies from the human rights movement both within South Africa itself as led by Archbishop Desmond Tutu and other liberal organizations (for example, the UDF), and in North American and Western European countries. An additional pressure for the USA in particular is the fact that it now has to relate the human rights issue in South Africa to its self-appointed role of the policeman of human rights throughout the world, including in the Soviet Union. It cannot therefore be seen to be openly decrying human rights abuses in other parts of the world while keeping silent on the question of South Africa's denial of political rights to the great majority of its inhabitants.

With the increasing unrest and violence in South Africa and the pressure of the national liberation movement and the frontline states, the issue of human rights cannot be ignored by the USA and its allies. Whether or not this will provide a sufficient basis for intervention is not clear. But there can be no doubt now that South Africa is beginning to feel the pressure of isolation and criticism in a world that has become conscious of the South African reality and the need for national democracy in that country.

The South African state was forced to adopt a total strategy as the basis of state policy after 1978 'as a response by a new alignment of forces within the ruling class to the gathering crisis during the 1970s'. [59] According to Davies and O'Meara,

> This crisis can be broadly characterized as the product of the collapse of the economic, political and ideological conditions which had hitherto sustained a form of capital accumulation based predominantly on forms of cheap, unskilled black labour. [60]

It was a crisis that led to an attempt at modifications at the internal and regional level. But as we have seen, the total strategy has not only failed but has helped to mobilize blacks within South Africa and in the frontline states against the apartheid state. The Nkomati Accord was undoubtedly a blow to the ANC[61] but it will prompt the latter into a more careful consideration of the home situation and the extent to which new strategies and tactics have to be adopted in a world that has generally become conscious of the evils of the apartheid system. The ANC leadership has the knowledge and experience derived from the Southern African terrain of political struggles to be able to recoup and advance further. More than that, much will depend on their ability to link the favourable home situation, the human rights movement at home and abroad and the armed struggle within a broad strategy for national liberation in South Africa. There is evidence that the Nkomati Accords have helped fuel the anger of the black masses of South Africa. The anger appears to be 'confined and directed to black sell-outs in the black townships'. But the South African authorities are evidently worried about it; and it is a matter of time, as happened in Zimbabwe, before the tremors begin to affect the white population. We are already beginning to see signs of this.

In general, therefore, the total strategy has failed on the internal level. The new constitutional provisions failed in their attempt to co-opt so-called 'Coloureds' and Asians into the South African governmental system. And history—particularly Zimbabwean—has shown that the attempt to incorporate selective elements among the oppressed classes is always bound to be limited in political impact and certainly doomed to failure.

> The acceptance of incorporation on the terms of the 'Total Strategy' would require the black petty bourgeoisie to abandon its political trump card—its real and potential leadership role with respect to the masses and its ability to use mass struggles to advance its own position. Moreover, it would require this to be done in a phase of heightened mass struggle when the present ruling class can be seen to be vulnerable. [62]

But history has also shown that attempts by a ruling class to adjust in the face of growing opposition is, more than anything else, a sign of weakening and a beginning of the end.

Finally, if the Zimbabwe model is anything to learn from, the indications are that imperialism will settle with the African nationalists in Namibia and South Africa, seek safeguards for the white settlers and impose direct and indirect constraints on the new states so as to ensure stability and the maintenance of their well-known economic and strategic interests in Southern Africa. Certainly the frontline states would want to pressurize the USA and its allies towards such an outcome and a large section of the ANC, PAC and SWAPO leadership would favour a negotiated settlement if and when the conditions appear appropriate. A negotiated settlement is certainly on the cards for Namibia and everything now depends on what guarantees the USA and its allies can extract to ensure that Soviet influence will not become a force in both Angola and the future Namibia. Any guarantee to the USA and its allies will, of course, be acceptable to South Africa, especially if the latter is able thereafter to view itself as part of the world anti-communist crusade. But Namibian independence will bring closer that of South Africa itself and the momentum is certainly growing.

There is as yet much to happen in South Africa itself. There will be more violence and unrest and international and sub-regional pressure will mount. It is too early to speculate about the talks about talks between representatives of the South African state and those of the ANC in Lusaka. But what has been so far reported in the South African press may be only the tip of the iceberg, suggesting that there may already be serious exploratory talks— involving even such persons as Archbishop Tutu and some members of the frontline states—taking place in secret. [63] Both the South African state and the ANC might well wish to talk with different aims in mind. The ANC might want to use talks as a public relations exercise in a situation where it is quite inconceivable that they will agree to anything less than that which will lead to national independence. The South African state might view talks as another ploy to divide African nationalist ranks. But the pressure is now more on the South African state to concede than on the ANC, though it would be naive to expect results in a process that is only just beginning.

The South African government has denied its direct involvement in the talks, but those who did go to Lusaka to speak with the ANC are not only members of the South African Nationalist Party but are regarded as representing opinion within a broad section of the South African ruling class. A national survey conducted in September 1984 revealed, among other things, that 43% of the South African whites were in favour of the government negotiating with the ANC and 44% against the idea.[64] In an editorial entitled 'Talk it Out', a pro-government South African paper, *Die Beeld*, urged the government to talk 'while there is time' and drew comparisons with the Zimbabwean situation.

There are, of course, numerous differences between the Zimbabwean and South African situations, both in terms of the imperialist and colonial experiences as well as in the impact of capitalism and the resultant class structures. But these are differences of degree rather than of kind and are in any case relative. The point which is often made about the larger white population that has its roots in South Africa can often be exaggerated and might even be suggestive of a racist (or inverted racist) posture that sees history from the point of view of the whites alone. At any rate, population sizes and ratios are quite relative; and we must recall that hardly ten years ago there was a commonly held belief, in colonial Zimbabwe and beyond, that Zimbabwe would not be independent for many years. Ian Smith himself said then that it would not come in a thousand years and, at least, not in his lifetime. But the Zimbabwean example also illustrates how even the most rabid racists can learn to live under black rule. Those not willing to do so, have other options, they can simply leave and make homes elsewhere in the world. Yet, in comparison to Zimbabwe, South Africa has always had a stronger and larger group of individual whites who have shown a total commitment to the liberation of their country.

There can be no doubt as to the relative dominance of imperialist strategy in a Southern African sub-region whose economic, political and ideological terrain is currently indicative of the inevitability of a neo-colonial settlement in both Namibia and South Africa. But this should not be regarded as a hopeless situation for the forces of freedom and national liberation. It is but a stage in a process that will see not only the new South African state but Southern Africa as a whole in a better position for the greater struggle for peace and development.

Notes

1. For a brief analysis of the origins and politics of the frontline states, see Ibbo Mandaza, 'Imperialism, the "Frontline" States and the Zimbabwe "Problem",', *UTAFITI* (*Journal of the Faculty of Arts and Social Sciences*, University of Dar es Salaam), vol.5, no.1, 1980, pp. 129—163.

2. 'Southern Africa: Toward Economic Liberation: A Declaration by the Governments of Independent Africa Made at Lusaka on the 1st April, 1980', *Record of the Southern African Development Coordination Summit Conference*, Lusaka, 1980 (mimeo).

3. For an account of the origins and perspectives of the SADCC see Thandika Mkandawire, 'Dependence and Economic Cooperation: The Case of SADCC', Yash Tandon, 'SADCC and the Preferential Trade Area (PTA): Points of Convergence and Divergence' and Ibbo Mandaza, 'Some Notes and Reflections on SADCC', in Tim Shaw and Yash Tandon (eds) *Regional Development at the International Level: African and Canadian Perspectives*, vol.II, University Press of America, New York and London, 1985.

4. These are conclusions drawn more from general observations than from a careful study—which is rather overdue—of the socialist bloc with particular regard to Southern Africa.

5. For a review of the literature on this concept see Mandaza, 'Imperialism', *op cit.*, 1980, pp. 135—42.

6. My own analysis in the article cited above was tainted with this view until the Lancaster House Agreement on Zimbabwe shattered it. But it is a view which is discernible in what is otherwise one of the best analyses of the South African situation, Joe Slovo, 'South Africa—No Middle Road', in Davidson, Slovo and Wilkinson, *Southern Africa: The New Politics of Revolution*, Penguin, Harmondsworth, Middlesex, 1976, pp. 106—210. But see also the collection of articles on South Africa in *Contemporary Marxism*, no.6, 1983; particularly Rod Bush, 'Editor's Introduction: The United States and South Africa in a Period of World Crisis', pp. 1—13.

7. See, for example, the more recent work by Theodor Hanf, Herbert Weiland and Gerda Vierdag, *South Africa: The Prospects of Peaceful Change: An Empirical Enquiry into the Possibility of Democratic Conflict Regulation*, Rex Collings, London, 1981.

8. Slovo, *op cit.* 1976, p. 148.

9. An example is the daily protests outside the South African embassy in Washington DC, a campaign which began in November 1984.

10. *The Herald*, Harare, 22 December 1984.

11. For example, President Reagan found himself in the embarrassing situation of having to modify within a period of less than a week his earlier stand on quiet diplomacy in South Africa, conceding that such a policy was not the most effective way to persuade Pretoria to 'abandon the contemptible system of apartheid,' *The New York Times*, New York, 12 December 1984. See also *The Sunday Mail*, Harare, 12 December 1984.

12. *The Sunday Mail*, Harare, 9 December 1984.

13. Mandaza, 'Imperialism'.... *op cit.*, p. 131—2; and V.I. Lenin, *Imperialism, The Highest Stage of Capitalism*, Progress Publishers, Moscow, 1978.

14. Cited in the Introduction, by Barry Cohen and Mohamed A. El-Khawas, to

The Kissinger Study of South African Africa, Spokesman Books, Nottingham, 1975, p. 16.

15. For a concise account of these developments, see Giovanni Arrighi, 'The Political Economy of Rhodesia', in G. Arrighi and J.S. Saul, *Essays on the Political Economy of Africa*, Monthly Review Press, London, 1973. Also, Ibbo Mandaza, 'Capital, Labour and Skills in the Context of the Political Economy of Zimbabwe', *Contemporary Marxism*, no.7, 1983, pp. 116—139; and by the same author, *The History of Zimbabwe: From Colonial Domination to National Independence*, Longmans, London, 1985.

16. For some analysis of this historical problematic, see, Bernard Magubane, 'Imperialism and the Making of the South African Working Class', *Contemporary Marxism*, no.6, 1983, pp. 19—56; also his book, *The Political Economy of Race and Class in South Africa*, Monthly Review Press, New York, 1979; and Slovo, *op cit.*, 1976.

17. Karim Essack, *The Road to Revolution in South Africa*, Continental Publishers, Dar es Salaam, 1984, p. 21.

18. Ibid.

19. *Fortune*, July 1972, p. 49. Cited in M.M. Ncube, 'The US, South Africa and Destabilisation in Southern Africa', *Journal of African Marxists*, no.6, 1984, p. 31.

20. Elizabeth Schmidt, 'Decoding Corporate Camouflage: US Business Support for Apartheid', Washington DC Institute for Policy Studies, 1980, p. 4. Cited in Ncube, *op cit.*, 1984, p. 31.

21. Ncube, *op cit.*, 1984, note 43, p. 45.

22. Ibid., p. 30.

23. Essack, *op cit.*, 1984, p. 21.

24. Ibid.

25. Ibid.

26. Quoted from Schmidt, *op cit.*, 1980, p. 60 in Ncube, 1984, *op cit.*, p. 31.

27. Ncube, 1984, p. 32. For an analysis of the total strategy policy and its implications, see also Robert H. Davies and Dan O'Meara, 'The State of Analysis of the Southern African Region: Issues Raised by South African Strategy', *Review of African Political Economy*, 29, 1984, pp. 64—76.

28. El-Khawas and Cohen, *op cit.*, 1975, p. 8.

29. Ibid.

30. Ibid., p. 24.

31. Ibid., p. 24—5.

32. Ibid., p. 84.

33. Ibid., p. 84.

34. Ibid., p. 26.

35. Ncube, *op cit.*, 1984.

36. Ibid., pp. 33—8. Unless otherwise stated, the following references are taken from these pages under the title 'US and South African Destabilization Actions, p. 33.

37. This is my own addition and is not mentioned in Ncube's account.

38. Ncube, *op cit.*, 1984, p. 36.

39. Ibid., pp. 34—7.

40. Ibid., p. 37.

41. El-Khawas and Cohen, *op cit.*, 1975, p. 84.

42. Ncube, *op cit.*, 1984, p. 38.

43. Ibid., p. 38.
44. El-Khawas and Cohen, *op cit.*, 1975, p. 84.
45. Bush in Magubane, *op cit.*, 1983, p. 7.
46. Ibid., p. 10.
47. Ibid., p. 7.
48. Ibid.
49. This was the agreement (of 16 February 1984) between South Africa and Angola on troop withdrawals. It was attended and therefore underwritten by the USA and had the direct support of President Kaunda and the frontline states. It established a Joint Monitoring Commission (JMC) to observe the orderly withdrawal of South African troops from Angola. Nkomati is the agreement (of 16 March 1984) between South Africa and Mozambique. Although not present, the USA is known to have either influenced or at any rate to be in support of an agreement which clearly falls within the broad parameters of constructive engagement.
50. Cited in Mandaza, 'Imperialism...', *op cit.*, 1980, p. 138.
51. These are some of the remarks I had occasion to hear from high placed US officials during a visit to the USA in November 1979 as part of a ZANU (PF) delegation that was sent to the UN to lobby for support during the Lancaster House talks on Zimbabwe.
52. See Mandaza, 'Imperialism..., *op cit.*, 1980, p. 136.
53. Mandaza, 'Some Notes' in Shaw and Tandon, *op cit.*, p. 6.
54. *Monthly Review*, 23, 9., 1972.
55. Ibid., p. 15.
56. See, for example, El-Khawas and Cohen, *op cit.*, 1975; Mandaza, 'Imperialism...' *op cit.*, 1980; Bush, *op cit.*, 1983.
57. Dan Nabudere in *Imperialism, the Social Sciences and the National Question*, Tanzania Publishing House, on behalf of the African Association of Political Science (AAPS), Dar es Salaam, 1977, p. 60.
58. *The Herald*, Harare, 12 December 1984.
59. Davies and O'Meara, *op cit.*, 1984, p. 67.
60. Ibid.
61. Thabo Mbeki, Member, National Executive, ANC, in a televised discussion of the *Monthly Forum*, of the Zimbabwe Chapter of the *African Association of Political Science (AAPS)*, entitled 'Which Way Southern Africa?', Harare, 7 November 1984.
62. Davies and O'Meara, *op cit.*, 1984, p. 74.
63. Archbishop Tutu has been through some capitals of the frontline states and on 30 December 1984 flew to Kasaba on the shores of Lake Tanganyika for talks with Zambian President Kenneth Kaunda before returning to South Africa on 31 December 1984 (*The Herald*, Harare, 31 December 1984).
64. *The Sunday Mail*, Harare, 23 December 1984.

Part 3: Peace and Development: National and Regional Strategies

7. The Role of the Organization of African Unity in Promoting Peace, Development and Regional Security in Africa

S.K.B. Asante

> With the state there comes security
> *Harold J. Laski*[1]

> Economic issues have risen in importance on the agendas of world politics. In such a world, the composition of threats to states has become more subtle and more complex. 'Security' is more than a military matter.
> *J.S. Nye*[2]

> We view, with disquiet, the overdependence of the economy of our continent... This phenomenon had made African economies highly susceptible to external developments and with detrimental effects on the interests of the continent
> OAU, *Lagos Plan of Action*[3]

Although much has been said and written in recent years about the Organization of African Unity (OAU)—the world's largest continental organization—no comprehensive study has yet focused on the Organization's overall objective of promoting peace and regional security in Africa.[4] What has been written so far has focused on the restricted and narrow view of the concepts of 'peace' and 'security', drawing attention mainly to such issues as inter-state and intra-state conflicts and border disputes.[5] Yet these are not the only concerns of the OAU in the important field of peace and regional security in Africa. For while the Organization's jurisdiction is geographically confined to the continent of Africa, the peace and security problems of Africa in a broader sense are not limited to the geographic confines of the continent. As Yashpol Tandon rightly noted a few years ago, some of the major problems of Africa, which threaten peace and regional security, 'have their genesis in its relations with the outside world'.[6] Unity, security and peace among the OAU members are threatened no less by externally generated problems (such as neo-colonialism and under-development as a consequence of Africa's inheritance of unequal exchange and incorporation into the international economic system) than they are by internally generated ones (such as border conflicts). Specifically, although issues of peace and security are domestically rooted, the domestic scene cannot be seen in isolation from regional and international dynamics.

What needs stressing here is that in recent years the concept of security has come to mean something broader and less specific than the original doctrine. There has been a change in the nature of inter-state relations over the past two decades. As indicated in the second opening quotation, the concept of security is now applicable to economic as well as military relations between states. Economic issues and development issues have risen in importance on the agendas of African and world politics. In such a world, the composition of threats to peace and security of African states 'has become more subtle and more complex'. If collective cognizance of the security dilemmas that confront the OAU member states is to be effective, it must take into account the broader aspects of security and the economic dimensions of African politics.

It is against this background that this essay attempts a brief review of OAU's role in promoting peace, development and regional security in Africa. The first part examines the OAU's promotion of peace and regional security in the restricted sense, that is the extent to which the organization has been effective in providing political security in Africa. The second part will, on the other hand, concentrate not only on the broader aspects of the concepts of peace and security, focusing on the organization's confrontation with the issues of development but also the functional inter-relation between security, peace and development. But before considering some of these issues, it would seem appropriate to set the stage with a brief review of the three key concepts—'peace', 'development' and 'security'—of this chapter.

The Key Concepts

The concepts of 'peace,' 'security' and 'development' are closely related. However, while the terms 'security' and 'development' are both rather imprecise and contentious, the concept of 'peace' is less so. According to the *Dictionary of the Social Sciences*, 'peace' in its restricted sense means 'the ending of hostilities as the Peace of Versailles' which brought the First World War to an end. In its more general usage, however, peace refers to the activities of 'certain institutions which have successfully maintained order in the relations of two or more states in general'.[7] Peace in this general sense, then, refers mainly to the operations of international and regional organizations whose major concerns have been the prevention of war and the promotion of the welfare of their members' citizenry. In this study, therefore, the OAU's promotion of welfare as provided in Article II of the Charter can be viewed as a path to peace. Indeed, promotion of welfare or economic development ensures the more basic conditions for peace. This function is mainly based on the idea that war results from distress and that the best way of safeguarding the peace, therefore, is cooperation among the African states for the promotion of the common interest and the solution of common problems in the economic, social and cultural fields. The more an individual nation prospers, the higher its standard of living and the better its social conditions, the smaller the chance that it will resort to war in order to procure advantages at the expense of others.

Generally, therefore, peace is linked to the concept of development, which has attracted much attention and been given increasing prominence and coverage in social science journals and academic discussions in recent years. To Paul Streeten, for example, 'development means modernization, and modernization means transformation of human beings.'[8] The idea of modernization, however, should not be equated with Westernization. In Africa development must be seen as being first of all based on the assertion of cultural identity. Development as an objective and development as a process both embrace a change in fundamental attitudes to life and work and in social, cultural and political institutions. More specifically, development should mean a sustainable process geared to the satisfaction of the needs of the majority of peoples and not merely to the growth of things or the benefit of a minority. Hence development is conceptualized in Mytelka's recent study as a process of 'structural change and capital accumulation that moves a society closer to conditions in which the basic needs of people [for shelter, food and clothing] are met, full employment prevails and socioeconomic equality increases'.[9] This type of development can hardly be achieved in the absence of a viable security framework. Hence, as stated already, development and security are inseparable. The two processes should be parallel and mutually supporting. But what does security mean in the context of African politics?

'Security' is a word we use every day, although it is somewhat more ambiguous than we at first realize.[10] In the literature of international relations, the term 'security' has traditionally been defined to mean the immunity (to varying degrees) of a state or nation to threats emanating from outside its boundaries. In recent years, however, this definition has been extended to cover a wide range of issues. Those who use the terms regional security or national security tend to employ them in such a way as 'to further their own interest and policy preferences'.[11] When European and American policy-makers and writers in the Western strategic literature talk of African security, we suspect that what they have in mind is the security of Western interests in Africa or the importance of Africa to Western security.[12] Likewise, when Soviet writers use the term 'African security', it is likely that they have at the back of their minds the elimination of Western interests and the maintenance and expansion of positions of Soviet influence and countries of 'socialist orientation'.[13] There does exist, however, among OAU member states, implicitly if not explicitly, an African conception of African security. This perspective is the subject of this essay.

Generally, national security can be used to cover a wide range of goals and divergent, even contradictory, policies. In a sense, security is a negative goal—the absence of a sense of danger or threat. Narrowly defined, security means the absence of a threat to survival; but survival is only rarely at stake. Most people want to feel secure in more than just their survival. They wish to feel secure in their continued or future enjoyment of a number of other basic values. Hence Walter Lippman held that a state is 'secure to the extent to which it is not in danger of having to sacrifice core values if it wishes to avoid war and is able, if challenged, to maintain them by victory in such a war'.[14]

Following this line of reasoning we can identify at least three basic clusters of values which Africans and, indeed, nearly all peoples of today's world rank close to physical survival and which national security policies are designed to protect. These basic clusters of values are 1) some minimal expected level of economic welfare; 2) a certain political and social autonomy as a group and 3) a degree of political status as group.[15] Most national security policies in today's world are designed not merely to ensure the physical survival of the individuals within national boundaries but to ensure a certain minimal expected enjoyment of these other basic values as well.[16] If this is what African peoples are demanding from their political leaders through their membership of the OAU, then it is clear that the problem of security in Africa today includes an immediate military component—the defence of national boundaries and interests—and an economic component. For failure to achieve economic growth will threaten both the overall vitality of the state and its internal stability[17].

Briefly stated, therefore, the OAU was not set up with any narrow end in view but rather for the purpose of promoting the common interests of members in peace, security and general well-being. The Organization, like the United Nations, recognizes that it is not enough to deal with inter-state disputes in Africa and threatening political situations as they arise; it is also necessary to create a continent-wide economic, social and political environment which will be favourable to peace and which will make it undesirable and unnecessary for governments to embark on policies and courses of action which will create the danger of violent conflict. It was for this purpose that the Specialized Commissions were set up under Article XX of the Charter. To what extent, then, has the OAU been able to provide political security in Africa during the twenty years of its existence?

The OAU and Political Security in Africa

At the OAU's founding conference in May 1963, the participating heads of state showed considerable awareness of the various security concerns with which an inclusive African regional organization would have to concern itself. Consideration was given to such potential problems as internal disruptions, border disputes, allegations of subversion by neighbouring states, threats of extra-regional aggression and the need for collective action against the remnants of colonialism. Articles II and III of the OAU charter—which define the goals of the organization and the principles that its members agree to adhere to—make clear that the organization was intended to assist members in the peaceful settlement of intra-regional conflict and in defence against extra-regional aggressors. On the whole, there seems to be no doubt that the OAU is, potentially, the most important advance that has yet been made first, in the domain of inter-African cooperation and second, in the provision of security of the newly independent African states. But the question that remains to be answered is whether this potential has so far been realized in these two fields of major concern of the organization.

Three main security concerns of the OAU may be distinguished in the area of crisis management. The first is the intra-state conflict. Committed to the preservation of the status quo and the principle of the territorial integrity of member states (guaranteed under Article III of the charter), the OAU has not generally been effective either in regulating or bringing to a peaceful solution conflicts within member states, particularly those concerning secessionist claims. In the Nigerian civil war, for example, the OAU was extremely cautious in its involvement and was not able to assist in bringing about a peaceful settlement. The organization has had no involvement in the long, highly intense Sudanese civil war or in the continued problem in Burundi. It had very little to do with the civil war in Angola which was terminated not by negotiation but by the forces of external intervention. The current vexed issues of Chad[18] and Western Sahara[19] have effectively exposed the virtual impotence of the OAU. The organization has proved useful in only one situation: assisting President Nyerere to replace British troops with Africans in the aftermath of the Tanganyika army mutiny in 1964.

The second security concern of the OAU is in the area of inter-state conflicts. Although to a large extent the OAU has been effective in dealing with inter-state disputes, particularly during its first decade, its role has been somewhat peripheral. Most of these conflicts were settled through the mediation of heads of state, who acted as 'agents of dissuasion, inhibition, or pacification'. As long as the Arbitration, Mediation and Conciliation Commission instituted under Article XIX of the OAU Charter has not fully materialized ad hoc commissions are the organs used for conflict resolution, 'prudently and methodically utilizing classical procedures for the peaceful settlement of international disputes appropriate to the particular case'.[20] Hence, for example, the Moroccan–Algerian border conflict was settled through mediatory efforts by Emperor Haile Selassie of Ethiopia and President Modibo Keita of Mali in October 1963; Ethiopia and Somalia were offered the good offices of President Ibrahim Abboud of Sudan in February 1964 and Kenya and Somalia received those of President Julius Nyerere of Tanzania in 1965 in their frontier conflict. As David Meyers has rightly observed, this pattern of conflict management can best be characterized as that of 'settlement *within* the organization rather than *by* the organization'.[21] It should be noted, however, that this pattern of handling crisis situations has been less effective during the second decade of the OAU. Since 1973 onwards the organization has not been in a position to prevent inter-state disputes breaking out into war, as evidenced in the 1977 Ethiopia-Sudan crisis, the protracted Ethiopia-Somalia conflict or the Uganda-Tanzania war of 1978-9, or the Malian-Burkina Faso border conflict of 1985.[22]

But much more disturbing is the OAU's show of impotence in its third main security concern: prevention of foreign intervention in African disputes. Despite the organization's commitment under the Charter to opposition to external interference in the continent's internal conflicts, all the major powers, as well as some of the smaller ones, have been, since the Angolan civil war, drawn more deeply into the affairs of the continent. Indeed, in recent years, the 1884 Berlin Conference has been re-enacted in a twentieth-century setting, in Zaire, Chad, Western Sahara, the Ogaden and Eritrea. More worrying, the OAU has been meeting this challenge of foreign intervention with a divided mind, and with no apparent results, as evidenced at the OAU summit meetings at Libreville in July 1977 and Khartoum in July 1978.[23] The best the OAU could offer at Khartoum was to reach a disturbing compromise on this crucial issue of foreign military intervention: the right of African states to appeal for help to countries of their choice. This in effect was an unofficial OAU invitation to foreign powers to intervene in the affairs of the continent. Thus, those that the founding fathers of the OAU in 1963 sought to exclude from shaping Africa's destiny are now being invited to come back to Africa to exploit Africa's political divisions and economic weakness to their own advantage.

Thus, on the whole, except in a few cases, the OAU has not been effective in its three main security concerns in creating what Amadu Sesay has recently termed 'political order' in Africa.[24] What has gone wrong? Is it the fault of the charter? Have African states really exhausted the untried resources and potentialities of the charter? Does the charter obstruct the way to peace and security? To what extent do the principles and objectives enshrined in the charter still hold good? Or can the impotence of the OAU in promoting peace and security be justifiably attributed to the political leadership in Africa?

The charter of the OAU may not be perfect. But much also depends upon the attitudes of the member states towards the organization. Essentially, the OAU depends upon the willing cooperation of its member states. There are no sanctions to threaten them if they do not give this. There is no organ with disciplinary powers. Nowhere in the charter is there a grant of authority to enforce decisions or to expel members for non-compliance with OAU decisions. These decisions are only recommendationsn to the completely sovereign member states. No international force is provided for to intervene in the territories of member states if they do not fulfil the purposes of the charter or comply with the resolutions of the Assembly or the Council of Ministers.[25] The institutions are designed to promote cooperation, not to exact it; to urge collaboration, not to punish for its refusal. The basic fact about the OAU charter, therefore, is that it does not provide for any supra-national institution like the United Nations Security Council but reflects in every respect the principle of sovereign equality of member states. In such a situation, the OAU can hardly be effective in promoting the objectives of peace and security in Africa.

As well as the limitations of the Assembly, the supreme organ of the organization, there are the limitations of the authority granted to the Commission of Mediation, Conciliation and Arbitration under Article XIX of the charter. Like the International Court of Justice, the Commission lacks the authority to require that conflicting states appear before it. It is even weaker than the World Court in that it lacks authority to interpret the OAU charter (whereas the World Court interprets the United Nations') and in that there is no provision for the enforcement of its decisions (whereas under Article 94 World Court decisions may be enforced by the Security Council). It is not surprising, then, that this Commission—which is the OAU mechanism for handling problems—has been inoperative.

Closely related to the limitations of the OAU institutions is the low level of resources available to the organization, which has also limited its ability to become independent of the national leaders. In general, as Meyers has emphasized, 'the OAU was and has remained weak in terms of material resources'. [26] The organization controls few material resources and unlike such regional security organizations as the Organization of American States (OAS), North Atlantic Treaty Organization (NATO) and the Warsaw Pact, it does not include any of the major powers among its members on which it can depend to supply such items when necessary. Important material resources for an international organization include personnel with expert knowledge of political and/or military affairs and with skills in bargaining and diplomacy and control of financial resources. This lack of the necessary resources has not infrequently frustrated many as OAU activity. A clear case in point was the frustration and embarrassment which attended the OAU joint peace-keeping effort in Chad. The organization not only seriously compromised its autonomy during its operations in Chad it also tainted its image by appearing to be a tool of Western imperialist states, as the peace-keeping force relied on the US and the UK for the logistical as well as financial support. [27]

Given the basic charter limitations of the OAU, perhaps the time has come to give the OAU teeth and make it a positive instrument that can shape the destinies of the African peoples. Indeed, there is no reason why many of the present constitutional weaknesses in promoting peace and security cannot be removed if African states so wish. Such reforms are necessary not only for maintaining political order in Africa but also, and perhaps more importantly today, a 'continental economic order', since nearly all the fifty odd African states are experiencing economic insecurity of unprecedented proportions. This is threatening the political stability of these countries for many of which the issue is that of sheer survival. [28] The second part of this study is, therefore, devoted to OAU's role in promoting regional economic development and security in Africa.

OAU, Development and Continental Security

It has been stated earlier in this study that the OAU's promotion of peace and security is functionally inter-related with the issue of African development. This is to be pursued through concerted action and the pooling of economic strategies and resources. And it is for this purpose that the Economic and Social Commission of the OAU was set up. The overall objective was to accelerate the economic development and industrialization of the continent so as to narrow the economic gap between Africa and the industrialized world

129

and eliminate the dependence and exploitation which have been responsible for the distortion of the development process throughout the continent. A high level of dependence on the former colonial powers and attendant underdevelopment would lead to political chaos and instability which would in turn threaten the peace and stability of the continent as a whole.

However, despite the general economic insecurity of many African states at independence, the OAU's activities in this field during the first decade of its existence were minimal. Economic questions, as John Ravenhill has recently noted, merely served at times 'as diversions and as a source whereby the fragile unity of the organization can be maintained'.[29] Consequently, the achievements of the OAU in the promotion of economic security were 'largely of the symbolic variety'. Although resolutions and declarations on economic issues were adopted, these rarely went beyond the stage of theoretical discussion. A clear case in point was the all important 'Declaration on Cooperation, Development and Economic Independence' approved by the OAU Ministerial Council conference in Abidjan in 1973. Such declarations did not commit the OAU members to specific activities nor constrain them from pursuing others.

More significantly, although one of the main objectives of the OAU Economic and Social Commission was to create a free trade area among African countries, the organization's role in promoting regional economic grouping and in assisting in problem resolution was slight. Such regional cooperation schemes as the six nation francophone Economic Community of West Africa (CEAO) set up in June 1973, the Customs and Economic Union of Central Africa (UDEAC) created in January 1966 and the cooperation agreements of the nine member Maghreb Permanent Consultative Committee (November 1965) were established without OAU involvement. Perhaps the only area where the organization was successful as an instrument for promoting collective economic security in Africa was in fostering economic cooperation among its members in their policies *vis-à-vis* external actors. This was evidenced in the OAU's series of talks which led to the unity of Africa and enabled the continent to negotiate with Europe as a group for the Lomé Convention of February 1975. In this respect, the OAU helped to bridge the anglophone-francophone divide that had long bedevilled intra-African cooperation.

On the whole, however, given the importance of the need for economic security in Africa, it is difficult to understand why the OAU's attention to economic matters has been spasmodic. Is it because the member states of the organization have no faith in the efficacy of inter-African cooperation in the economic realm? There appear to be several reasons for this situation. The over-riding aim of almost all the OAU conferences in its first decade was to intensify the political struggle for independence for those countries still under colonial rule. Consequently, economic development, although of vital importance, did not constitute the principal policy objective. President Kwame Nkrumah of Ghana, the spokesperson of the radical school of Pan-Africanism, strongly believed in the supreme efficacy of politics, and therefore constantly called upon other African leaders to 'seek first the political kingdom'. Second, anxious to encourage national integration, the new African leaders were compelled to look inward and to rank as their first priority the political, economic and social developments of their own countries. The immediate concern, then, was to build viable nation states based on their own traditions and customs and on the promises which had been held out to the masses. To the extent that national consolidation was a high priority, OAU resolutions on economic cooperation were given less than serious attention. Third, from a political economy perspective, a variety of factors can also be said to have complicated the functioning of schemes for economic cooperation under the auspices of the OAU. [30] One such factor was the economic and political heterogeneity of the continent. Countries that followed vastly different development paths could not make good partners in economic cooperation schemes. And fourth, there was the complication to the OAU's activities in the sphere of economic cooperation created by the existence of a second all-Africa organization—the Economic Commission for Africa—whose stated goals and organizational mandate are almost identical to those that the OAU set for its own specialized body in this field, the Economic and Social Commission. Not surprisingly, many OAU economic activities during the period under review were devoted to boundary activities.

Given these factors and coupled with the fact that African development constraints had not reached a crisis stage during much of the 1960s, the OAU could afford to be perfunctory in its promotion of collective economic security in Africa. By the mid-1970s, however, deteriorating economic conditions at home, coupled with growing disillusionment with the continent's external economic relations and dependency, had begun to threaten the economic security of many African states whose governments looked to the OAU for leadership in the economic field. And what was the OAU's response to this continental development crisis? A brief review of this crisis would be in order.

Dependent Development and Economic Insecurity

One of the more significant issues which have occupied the attention of many OAU member states is the disappointing African economic performance of the last 25 years. Despite efforts to stimulate growth, supported by massive aid and technical assistance by both bilateral and multilateral agencies, to foster agricultural production and to initiate other development programmes to bring about more fundamental changes in the economic structure inherited at independence, the continent remains the most economically, socially and culturally deprived of all the regions of the world. [31] The transformation of the continent which was expected to follow closely on the heels of political independence still remains a hope. And this is despite the fact that the continent is well known for the abundance of its forestry, mineral and other resources.

In spite of exports, many African countries showed throughout the 1970s a pattern of sluggish economic growth, low levels of productivity, a circumscribed and fractured industrial base, high dependence on a vulnerably narrow spectrum of primary export commodities, low levels of life expectancy and widening deficits on the aggregate current accounts of the balance of payments.[32] Real per capita income declined while the rate of inflation approximately doubled, reaching an average annual rate of over 20% during 1977-9. The combined current account deficit of the balance of payments rose from about $4 billion in 1974 to close to $10 billion annually in 1978-9.[33] Above all, between 1970 and 1979 the external indebtedness of sub-Saharan Africa rose from $6 billion to $32 billion and debt service (for the oil-importing countries) increased from 6 to 12% of export earnings in the same period.[34] If Africa's inheritance from colonialism in 1960 was—to borrow Timothy Shaw's description—inauspicious, the unfavourable auspices had been amply fulfilled by 1980.

More worrying, Africa provides a fertile ground for what has come to be known as neo-colonialism; this has greatly contributed to the continent's problems. By the end of the 1970s Africa's dependency on the economies of the industrialized Western countries had become greater than ever before. Most African countries had become even more heavily dependent on foreign interersts, foreign investments, foreign technology, foreign expertise, foreign theories of development and economic growth, and above all, on exports of raw materials and agricultural primary commodities to the rich industrialized West.

Externally, too, African governments were not faring any better. Although Africa, led by Algeria in 1973 and 1974, had been in the forefront of the demand for a New International Economic Order (NIEO), it had become obvious by the late 1970s that the high expectations held in some quarters for progress towards a new order were being frustrated. The breakdown of the Paris Conference on International Economic Cooperation in June 1977 and the failure of the series of UNCTAD meetings—from Nairobi UNCTAD IV (May 1976) through Manila UNCTAD V (June 1979) and Belgrade UNCTAD VI (June 1983) to the setback of the UNIDO III in New Delhi in January-February 1980—all suggest that the advanced industrialized countries are not prepared to make the sacrifices necessary to achieve a new order. But even if a new order were to be established, Africa was unprepared 'to derive optimal benefit' from it, in view of the continent's high degree of external dependence. As the energetic executive secretary of the ECA, Adebayo Adedeji, recently emphasized,

> what was clear was that unless the continent successfully puts its own house in order by restructuring its economy at the national, subregional and regional levels, it will remain the periphery of the periphery in the international economy even if a NIEO were to come into existence.[35]

Africa's special relationship with Europe through the Lomé system since 1975 was yielding few tangible results and proving to be disappointing, as forcefully expressed by President Kaunda in December 1977 when he claimed that the African states, under the auspices of the OAU,

> negotiated the Lomé Convention in the belief that it would confer on [their] exports terms and conditions more favourable than those granted to the products

of other countries. After some two years of implementation of the Convention, [they] now have many reasons to doubt that this is the understanding and policy of the Community. [36]

Indeed, on the whole, to pin much hope on the Lomé 'regime' is to follow a recipe for perpetual underdevelopment.

Confronted with this implacable reality, African leaders, the OAU and the ECA have been forced into a sobering reassessment of their options, what is the correct path towards economic development? What kind of economic security should OAU initiate and promote in Africa? In any case, how relevant is the inherited colonial and neo-colonial economic policy to African development? Or simply put, how beneficial to Africa are foreign theories of development and economic growth? Is the trickle down approach to development and economic growth relevant to Africa? Closely related to these is the question about the forcible integration of the countries of the continent into the mainstream of world trade and investment and the consequent external orientation of development and economic growth efforts. By the late 1970s, therefore, the OAU was faced with a choice between continuing to support an inherited structure of dependence and therefore subordination of Africa's own development to special interests in the Western international economic system or beginning to break away from this structure and instal in its place, at the national, sub-regional and regional levels, a new economic order based on the principles of self-reliance and self-sustainment.

Under the leadership of the ECA and its dogged determination to change African governments' perception and understanding of policies, strategies and goals, the OAU at its 16th session held in Monrovia in July 1979 opted for the latter choice. Consequently, the organization adopted the Monrovia Strategy for the Economic Development of Africa and the Monrovia Declaration of Commitment on Guidelines and Measures for National and Collective Self-Reliance in Social and Economic Development for the establishment of a New International Economic Order. [37] In April 1980, the OAU at its special economic summit held in Lagos adopted the historic Lagos Plan of Action (LPA) for the economic development of Africa, based on the Monrovia Strategy.

OAU's LPA: Objectives, Goals and Strategies

The LPA constitutes the first comprehensive continent-wide formulation and articulation of the preferred long-term economic and development objectives of African countries that the OAU has produced. Its main theme is Africa's reduction of dependence on external strategy. Hence the Plan identifies as its basic objectives 'self-reliance', both national and regional and 'self-sustained development'. This, in effect, means first, a substantial shift from external to internal demand stimuli i.e. policies, plans, targets reflecting internal demand rather than demand expressed in developed economies; second, a shift from reliance primarily on imported, to reliance primarily on domestically-produced factor inputs.

Described as Africa's 'economic Magna Carta, the LPA is a complete departure from past, inherited externally-oriented development strategy. [38] It puts a substantial question mark against the relevance of 'imitative life styles' and 'borrowed foreign concepts and ideologies to Africa's social and economic transformation'. [39] By adopting the Plan and the Final Act of Lagos (FAL), the OAU has demonstrated, *inter alia*, its desire for a far-reaching, indigeneously determined strategy for promoting Africa's economic security. As an objective of greater economic security, the Plan seeks to reduce the exposure or vulnerability of a national or regional economy to outside forces such as demand conditions in external markets and world commodity prices. Greater economic security could be sought through increased self-reliance. To a large extent, therefore, the LPA is a significant step on the part of the OAU to provide the much needed economic security of Africa.

However, while the Lagos document has been hailed by some observers such as Robert Browne and Robert Cummings, [40] and its authors like Adebayo Adedeji, [41] as constituting the first 'undiluted efforts' of African governments themselves to 'delineate at the continental level', how their economic destinies should be ordered, scholars like Ravenhill simply dismiss the Plan as 'an exercise in cynicism', in view of the absence of specific commitments on the part of the African leaders. [42] But could the OAU have been expected to do more?

It is perhaps easier to be derogatory about the OAU's adoption of the Plan than to measure the complex problems confronting the organization: its assumption of the role of a monitor of sovereign governments supervising the exercise of their own authority in certain aspects and the African and the general international environment under which it is actually operating. We would, perhaps, do well to remember that as far as the organization's adoption of the Plan is concerned, the OAU, like all political innovations, must be judged not only in terms of what is *ideally* desirable but also, and more importantly, in terms of what—in a given setting of African situations, forces and dispositions—is possible. In other words, we should try to make clear what, in the present condition of the international world, as well as the continuing political and economic dependence of many African states on Europe and the industrialized world in general, we can legitimately expect the OAU to be able to do. Perhaps what is important is the political will to implement the Plan. Is the Plan being implemented? What impact, if any, has it had? Or has it suffered the fate of earlier OAU declarations and programmes of action?

Implementation of LPA: Obstacles and Constraints

Although self-reliance and self-sustaining development as a strategy of the LPA and the FAL were adopted in 1980 to provide economic security in Africa its implementation has not yet advanced beyond ratification. Specifically, those concepts are not yet reflected in country as well as regional development plans, as it made evident in a recent ECA report. [43] Particulalry disturbing is the lack of progress in the promotion of regional cooperation and integration, which constitutes an integral condition for the implementation of both the LPA and FAL.

In the number one LPA priority of self-sufficiency in food production and supply, for example, no action 'has so far been initiated in setting up sub-regional food security arrangements and undertaking the feasibility of establishing an African Food Relief Support Scheme'. [44] Neither the Economic Community of West African States (ECOWAS) nor UDEAC has an explicit regional food policy. [45] Similarly, in the industrial sector, in the field of natural resources, promotion of intra-regional trade and in the establishment of multinational regional and subregional institutions, no implementation action would seem to have been made. The most outstanding progress so far made is the establishment of the Preferential Trade Area for Eastern and Southern African States (PTA) in December 1981, the Economic Community of the Central African States (ECCAS) in October 1983 and the founding of the African Federation of Chambers of Commerce (AFCC).

This slow progress in the implementation of the Lagos document does not *per se* suggest any lack of interest on the part of the OAU members in the LPA as an instrument of economic security. Indeed the November 1984 OAU summit at Addis Ababa solemnly proclaimed the firm determination of the African leaders to 'achieve accelerated economic development and independence of Africa', in accordance with the objectives and principles of the OAU Charter and the LPA and the FAL 'through the effective mobilisation of our countries' immense human and material resources'. [46] What is impeding the implementation of the Plan are the current deteriorating socio-economic conditions. [47] As a recent World Bank publication has rightly noted, 'the crisis management of recent years has resulted in widespread neglect of programmes dealing with the long-term constraints on development'. [48] The limited resources available for the implementation of aspects of the Plan and the FAL are now directed to meet emergency crisis situations. This has been exacerbated by the ever-increasing debts of many African countries and the attendant servicing of these debts and the stagnation in official development assistance (ODA) and a 'significant decrease in net capital flows since 1980'. Besides, politico–economic commercial arrangements such as the Lomé agreements have effectively reinforced the North-bound vertical orientation of the African economy and impeded intra-African economic cooperation. For Euro-Africanism exemplified by Lomé not only symbolizes the 'continuity of an unequal division of labor between the two sets of parties', as Timothy Shaw has shown; [49] it is also essentially incompatible with the self-reliance and self-sustainment objectives of the Lagos Plan. [50] It is against this background that the OAU at its 20th ordinary session held in November 1984 directed its ministerial council to review and appraise the implementation of the LPA and the FAL. [51]

Towards Regional Security: Policy Options

It has been stated that one of the major causes of Africa's continued underdevelopment and therefore its economic insecurity, is the external orientation of its economy and its virtually total external dependence. Such excessive external dependence and incorporation into the world system is an obstacle to a self-reliant and self-sustaining strategy of development. Therefore, as the current economic and social crisis that has gripped the continent since 1980 has slowed down economic and social development, the implementation of the LPA and FAL as instruments of Africa's economic security, including some other options, in particular, regional integration schemes, should be adopted in order to reduce the continent's continued vulnerability to outside forces. [52]

As one possible option, the existing regional schemes should diversify their external economic relations—trading partners and sources of technology and capital—to include not only Western Europe, the United States, Canada, Australia or Japan, but also the industrialized countries of the socialist community such as members of the Council of Mutual Economic Assistance (CMEA) or (COMECON). And to achieve rapid industrialization each regional grouping should seek to establish on the strength of its regional policies collaboration with separate developed countries to achieve specific objectives. For example, through CARICOM and the Caribbean Common Market, the countries of the Caribbean have negotiated long-term industrialization arrangements with Canada, the United States and other industrialized countries. A case in point is the Trade and Economic Cooperation Agreement between Canada and the CARICOM members signed in 1979. [53] This kind of arrangement makes it possible for the industrialized country or countries to lend their support through special financing, incentives to private investment, transfer of technology and the protection of the markets of both sides.

Diversification, not elimination, of dependencies in the initial stages of regional adventure would seem to be almost a *sine qua non* for regionalism in Africa today. A more diversified structure of dependencies will, nevertheless, improve the manoeuvrability of SADCC, ECOWAS and PTA which, in a longer-term perspective, bodes well for a collective self-reliance and genuine reduction of dependence. Diversification also has the potential for strengthening the bargaining position of the regional governments by enabling them to play off one developed economy against another. As Ali Mazrui stressed in his recent Reith Lectures,

> there are occasions when freedom begins with the multiplication of one's masters. If one is owned and controlled by only one power, freedom is often particularly restrictive. But if an African society cultivates the skills to have more than one hegemonic power competing for it, this has possibilities for liberation. To be dependent on two giants, especially when the giants have rivalries between them, is sometimes an opportunity to play one against the other—and maximize one's own options. [54]

Another option still available for African regional groupings for transcending dependency is to develop preferential economic links first, among themselves, and second, with integration schemes in the developing countries in Asia (e.g. ASEAN) and Latin America (e.g. the Andean pact). In more concrete terms, this type of horizontal integration implies the promotion of economic cooperation among developing countries, 'the new imperative of the 1980s', to quote Elvin Laszlo. A vast realm is open for joint action in the fields of economic and technical cooperation. Such joint action could be crucial in enabling African countries to defend the prices of their exports of raw materials and to enhance their sovereignty over their natural resources. It could also encourage the growth of indigenous capacities in science and technology, facilitate the marketing of their products, help to increase their industrial capacity and, above all, strengthen their decision-making power in multilateral institutions. [55] By taking full advantage of opportunities of mutual interdependence and complementarity of their economies, the countries of the South, concludes Adedeji in an important address, 'will sooner or later put themselves in a position to seize the initiative and assume the leadership for bringing about the establishment of the new international economic order'. [56]

Then, too, African countries and leaders should be willing to introduce fundamental policy and institutional changes. These should include a redefinition of the development objectives at national and regional levels to recognize fully regional integration as an effective approach to the issue of dependency and underdevelopment. But a regional development strategy cannot be fully realized unless countries develop a common policy toward the problem of foreign investment and technology dependence through regional regulation and planning. This should be backed by a serious policy directive designed to build a joint industrial research and development institute which would also look into the appropriateness of foreign technology, its purchase, acquisition or adaptation for use in joint development projects. [57]

To this may be added the need for the mobilization of public support. Like the OAU itself, the present regional schemes were and are very much an act of will on the part of their political leadership. Yet in order for them to achieve their most fundamental aims they will have to enlist the active support and cooperation of the masses. Specifically, the success of any regional strategy for collective self-reliance hinges on a common political will of national governments, which in turn requires backing from societal leaders and citizens generally. What appears to be lacking in African integration movements is a group or popular dynamic supporting integration: private sectors, interest groups or pressure groups for the mobilization of public opinion in the direction of integration. The group or popular dynamic gives a momentum propelling integration forward. It means, as well, an attachment or commitment to integration and action to give effect to the attachment or commitment. Indeed, it is the dynamic which would provide the motivation for actions to promote integration and support for actions taken. And as long as groups in West, Central, Eastern and Southern Africa remain more or less on the sidelines or as limited participants, there will be little or no dynamic supporting integration. For though economic integration may be a powerful means for the acceleration of development, in the final analysis 'man is both the means and the end. The best study of the strategy of economic integration is man'. [58]

Furthermore, whatever strategy is adopted for transcending dependency, priority should be given to internal policy reforms or a 'new domestic order', to which the ECA has already drawn attention in recent years. [59] For to think that the way for a spontaneous development of the economy is free when external difficulties are overcome is a dangerous self-deception. Far-reaching internal changes are necessary, particularly in the area of military establishment. African states spend several billion dollars a year to purchase military hardware. Africa's imports of foreign arms between 1976-80, for example, amounted to $55.5 bilion while the rest of the Third World imported arms to the value of $26.5 billion during the same period. And while public expenditures in Africa in 1980 were estimated at $26 per capita, expenditure per soldier averages $9.449. [60] These arms imports serve only the interests of the manufacturers of arms and not those of the African masses. Hence internal policy reforms are required for establishing a new domestic order if Africa ever hopes to transform its relationship with the industrialized nations from one of permanent dependence to one of beneficial interdependence which can generate within the African society itself the engine necessary for sustained economic growth.

However, the implementation of internal policy reforms as well as the various strategies espoused in the LPA—be they 'indigenisation or domestication, diversification or horizontal interpenetration, autarkic self-reliance or vertical counterpenetration'—in the quest for economic sovereignty should not be seen in isolation from the prevailing political environment in Africa. For intra-state or inter-state or regional conflicts prevalent in contemporary Africa are 'quintessentially baneful' to economic stabilization or progress in Africa; they ensure the persistence of neo-colonial forces which seek to influence the economic policies and directions of African states and thereby conspire to perpetrate the economic subjugation of the continent. Hence, as Celestine Bassey has persuasively argued, the collective self-reliance strategy of the LPA has to be 'developed as an integral aspect of a political and military-strategic program (regional security system) for continental collaboration'. [61] In other words, to ensure the success of the goals and objectives of the LPA or any other internal policy reforms, the process of regional military security and collective economic self-reliance should be parallel and mutually supporting.

One useful function that the OAU can perform is to develop a mechanism to resolve disputes among the member states. Indeed, for the organization to be more of a directing force in African affairs—filling the vacuum that presently invites foreign interference—may require, as John Ostheimer has recently put it, 'major surgery and resuscitative measures'. [62] Charter revision may be necessary in some important areas. For example, there appears to be a contradiction between the charter and the principles governing the organization, offering all parties some ground for justifying their conduct. The principle of self-determination is not in conformity with the principle of maintaining inherited colonial boundaries. Consequently, any attempt on the part of an OAU member to support the right of self-determination for a subject people would imply interference in the affairs of other member states. And moreover, the charter's prohibition of interference fails to make a clear distinction between legitimate concern for problems within states that must be countered in the 'interests of humanitarianism and development', and the disruptive (often ethnically-based) disputes that exist in most African countries. [63] There is therefore a need for African countries to evolve a more sophisticated policy towards each other's internal problems so as to prevent the intrusion of East–West or neo-colonialist ambitions into the African vacuum.

The need to strengthen the powers of the OAU secretary-general can hardly be overemphasized. With an office constitutionally similar to that of the secretary-general of the Arab League, but weaker than that found in the OAS and the United Nations, the OAU's officer was clearly not intended to play a major role in conflict management activities. Such activity was to be left to the Assembly or the Council of Ministers. Indeed, with a small budget and a small staff, including senior officials who still maintain special links with their own governments, the OAU secretary-general is greatly handicapped in his efforts to build an effective secretariat.

Significantly, therefore, the OAU lacks executive machinery for handling problems of peace and security. There is thus the need to equip the organization in terms of mechanisms and organs to have a body which would have the power to react to conflict situations before they get out of hand. The present ad hoc approach towards conflict resolution efforts would seem to have outlived its usefulness. Some form of institutionalization is now necessary to conform with the provisions of the OAU charter. The experience of recent years in handling African conflicts would seem to have convinced many African leaders themselves that the organization needs a machinery that can act with effectiveness, mobility and promptness to maintain peace and security and prevent the escalation of conflicts in Africa. In this regard, the creation of an OAU Political and Security Council or, preferably, a Peace Council to replace the defunct OAU Commission on Mediation, Conciliation, and Arbitration, as Berhanykun Andemicael and Davidson Nicol have suggested in their recent study, is now essential. [64]

Conclusion

This study has attempted to review the security problem in Africa, which is a manifestation of yet another critical phase in the political evolution of the continent reflecting the process of nation-building. It has been shown that the security concerns of Africa are crucially linked with the issues of peace and development. While these problems are domestically rooted, the domestic scene is related to externals—dependency, neo-colonialism and East–West intrusion into African affairs. The OAU, which is the collective African machinery for meeting the challenges and threats to African sovereignty, African stability and African solidarity, has over the years proved to be generally ineffective. This has created a security dilemma for Africa, as the strategy of collective self-reliance and self-sustainment espoused in the LPA cannot be conceived as an isolated object. The experience of post-war Europe has clearly demonstrated the indispensability of an 'atmosphere of trust and peace' for economic recovery and technological advance, as this makes it possible for considerably fewer resources to be applied to military establishments or defence issues and considerably more cooperation on scientific research and exchange. In this regard, the OAU should be in a position to act effectively as a 'security community' [or something like the North Atlantic Treaty Organization—NATO] to deal with the internal and external forces which are threatening the peace and security of Africa. There exists, therefore, a definite need for positive action for a stronger OAU equipped politically and militarily to guarantee the security of the African continent.

Notes

1. Harold J. Laski, *The State in Theory and Practice*, Viking Press, New York, 1947, p. 4.
2. J.S. Nye, 'Collective Economic Security', *International Affairs*, vol.50, no.4, 1974, p. 585.
3. Organization of African Unity, *Lagos Plan of Action for the Economic Development of Africa, 1980-2000*, International Institute for Labour Studies, Geneva, 1981, para. 9.
4. See, for example, Elenga M'buyinga, *Pan-Africanism or Neo-Colonialism: The Bankruptcy of the OAU*, Zed Press, London, 1983.
5. See, for example, Berhanykun Andemichael, *Peaceful Settlement Among African States: Roles of the United Nations and the Organization of African Unity* UNITAR PS, no.5, New York, 1972 and Zdenek Cervenka, *The Unfinished Quest for Unity: Africa and the OAU*, Julian Friedmann, London, 1977.
6. Yashpal Tandon, 'The Organization of African Unity: A Forum for African International Relations', *Round Table*, Issue no.246, 1972, p. 221.
7. Julius Gould and William L. Kolb, (eds), *A Dictionary of the Social Sciences*, Tavistock, London, 1964, p. 489.
8. Paul Streeten, *The Frontiers of Development Studies*, Macmillan, London, 1972, p. 30.
9. Lynn K. Mytelka, *Regional Development in a Global Economy: The Multinational Corporation, Technology, and Andean Integration*, Yale University Press, New Haven and London, 1979, p. xiv.
10. See Arnold Wolfers, *Discord and Collaboration*, Johns Hopkins, Baltimore and Oxford University Press, London, 1962, p. 150.
11. For details see S.N. MacFarlane, 'Intervention and Security in Africa',

International Affairs, vol.60, no.1, 1984, p. 54.

12. In this context, the National Security Study Memorandum (NSSM) 39 objective of 'stabilizing Southern Africa' has been referred to as no more than a euphemism for 'continued US presence'. See A. Isaacman and J. Davis, 'US policy towards Mozambique, 1946-1976', in Rene Lemarchand (ed.), *American Policy in Southern Africa: The stakes and the Stances*, University Press of America, Washington, DC, 1981, p. 35 and S.M. Makinda, 'Conflict and the superpowers in the Horn of Africa', *Third World Quarterly*, vol.4, no.1, 1982, p. 93.

13. See D. Volsky, 'Local Conflict and International Security', *New Times*, no.5, 1983, pp. 5—7 and A. Gromyko, 'Soviet foreign policy and Africa', *International Affairs*, Moscow, no.2, 1982, pp. 30—33.

14. Water Lippman, *US Foreign Policy: Shield of the Republic*, Little Brown, Boston, 1943, p. 51.

15. Nye, 1974, p. 585.

16. For further discussion see Mohamed Ayoob, 'Security in the Third World: The worm about to turn?', *International Affairs*, vol.60, no.1, 1984, pp. 41—51 and Talukder Maniruzzaman, *The Security of Small States in the Third World*, Canberra papers on Strategy and Defence No. 25, Strategic and Defence Studies Centre, Australian National University, Canberra, 1982, p. 15.

17. Bruce E. Arlinghaus, introduction in Bruce E. Arlinghaus (ed.), *Africa Security Issues: Sovereignty, Stability, and Solidarity*, Westview Press, Boulder, CO, 1984, p. 2.

18. See Dean Pittman, 'The OAU and Chad', in Yassin El-Ayouty and I. William Zartman, (eds), *The OAU after twenty years*, Praeger, New York, 1984, pp. 297—325.

19. See John Damis, 'The OAU and Western Saharah', in El-Ayouty and Zartman, 1984, pp. 273—96.

20. Edmond Kwam Kouassi, 'The OAU and International Law,' in El-Ayouty and Zartman, 1984, p. 49.

21. David Meyers, 'Intraregional Conflict Management by the Organization of African Unity', *International Organization*, vol.28, no.3, 1974, p. 369.

22. For the OAU role in the Uganda-Tanzania war see P. Godfrey Okoth, 'The OAU and the Uganda-Tanzania War', paper presented at the 27th Annual Conference of the African Studies Association, 25-28 October 1984, Los Angeles, California and Amadu Sesay *et al., The OAU After Twenty Years*, Westview Press, Boulder, CO, pp. 50—2.

23. For details see S.K.B. Asante, 'OAU at Twenty: Descent into Immobility', *West Africa*, 23 May 1983, pp. 1225-7.

Amadu Sesay, 'The OAU and Continental Order', in T.M. Shaw and Sola Ojo, (eds), *Africa and the International Political System*, University Press of America, Washington, DC, 1982, pp. 172—97.

25. S.K.B. Asante, 'The Birth of the OAU: The Early Years', *Legon Observer*, vol.viii, no.10, 1973, pp. 218—23 and K. Mathews, 'The Organization of African Unity', in Domenico Mazzeo (ed.), *African Regional Organizations*, Cambridge University Press, Cambridge, 1984, pp. 49—84.

26. Meyers, 1974, p. 350.

27. Sesay, 1982, pp. 43—6.

28. *Special memorandum by the ECA Conference of Ministers on Africa's Economic and Social Crisis*, E/ECA/Cm. 10/37/Rev.2, Addis Ababa, 28 May 1984.

29. John Ravenhill, 'The OAU and Economic Cooperation: Irresolute Resolutions', in El-Ayouty and Zartman, 1984, p. 176.

30. For details see S.K.B. Asante, 'Pan-Africanism and Regional Integration', in vol.VIII of UNESCO, *General History of Africa: Africa Since 1935*, (forthcoming).

31. For details see Adebayo Adedeji, 'Development and Economic Growth in Africa to the Year 2000: Alternative Projections and Policies', in Timothy M. Shaw, (ed.), *Alternative Futures for Africa*, Westview Press, Boulder, CO, 1982, pp. 279—304.

32. Ibid.

33. Justin B. Zulu and Saley M. Nsouli, 'Adjustment Programs in Africa', *Finance and Development*, vol.21, no.1, 1984, p. 5.

34. World Bank, *Accelerated Development in Sub-Saharan Africa: An Agenda for Action*, Washington, DC, 1981, p. 3.

35. A. Adedeji, 'The Monrovia Strategy and the Lagos Plan of Action: Five Years After', in Adebayo Adedeji and Timothy M. Shaw (eds), *Economic Crisis in Africa: African Perspectives on Development Problems and Potentials*, Lynne Rienner, Boulder, CO, 1985, Chapter 1.

36. See ACP Council, ACP/365/77.

37. Adedeji, 1985.

38. The Plan covers a wide spectrum of issues which are of topical concern to Africa as it approaches the 21st Century. Among these are food and agriculture, industry, trade, science and technology, women and development.

39. Adedeji, 1985.

40. R.S. Browne and R.J. Cummings, *The Lagos Plan of Action vs. The Berg Report: Contemporary Issues in African Economic Development*, Brunswick, Lawrenceville, 1984.

41. Adedeji, 1985.

42. Ravenhill, 1984, p. 187.

43. See ECA, *Critical Analysis of the Country Presentations of African Least Developed Countries in the Light of the Lagos Plan of Action and the Final Act of Lagos*, Doc. no. ST/ECA/PSD. 2/31, Addis Ababa, 1982.

44. Adebayo Adedeji, 'Intra-African Economic Penetration, Co-operation and Integration: Progress, Problems and Perspectives in the Light of the Final Act of Lagos', paper presented at the ECA/Dalhousie University Conference on the Lagos Plan of Action and Africa's Future International Relations, Halifax, Nova Scotia, Canada, 2-4 November 1984.

45. See S.K.B. Asante, 'Development and Regional Integration Since 1980, in Adedeji and Shaw, 1985, Chapter 5.

46. OAU Doc., *Declaration on the Critical Economic Situation in Africa*, AHGH/DECL.2 (XX), November 1984.

47. For details see Adebayo Adedeji, 'The African Economic and Social Crisis: An Agenda for Action by Africa and the International Community', text of statements delivered during the General Debate and the Special Debate on the Critical Economic Situation in Africa at the 1984 Second Regular Session of the Economic and Social Council of the United Nations, Geneva, 10 and 12 July 1984.

48. World Bank, *Toward Sustained Development in Sub-Saharan Africa*, Washington, DC, 1984, p. 6.

49. Timothy M. Shaw, 'From Dependence to Self-reliance: Africa's Prospects for the Next Twenty Years', *International Journal*, vol.XXXV, no.4, 1980, pp. 836—7.

50. S.K.B. Asante, 'Africa and Europe: Collective Dependence or Interdependence?' in Amadu Sesay, (ed.), *Africa and Europe: From Partition to Interdependence*, (forthcoming) and 'The Lomé Conventions: Towards Perpetuation of Dependence or Promotion of Interdependence?', *Third World Quarterly*, vol.3, no.4, 1981, pp. 658—72.

51. OAU, November 1984.

52. For a recent analysis of the crisis see *Briefing*, no.6, February 1983, published by North-South Institute, Ottawa, Canada.

53. For details of the agreement see K. Venkata Raman, 'The Achievement of Specific NIEO Objectives by Means of Regional Approaches: Access to Markets, International Trade and Industrialization', in Davidson Nicol *et al.*, (eds), *Regionalism and the New International Economic Order*, Pergamon, New York, 1981, p. 273.

54. Ali A. Mazrui, *The African Condition: A Political Diagnosis*, Cambridge Unitersity Press, London, 1983, p. 82.

55. For details see Benno Engels, 'The Global Approach to South-South Cooperation', *Development and Cooperation*, (Bonn), 1, 1984, pp. 14—16 and Elvin Laszlo, *RCDC Regional Cooperation Among Developing Countries*, Pergamon Press, New York, 1981.

56. Adebayo Adedeji, 'Africa and the South: Forging Truly Interdependent Economic and Technical Links', *Africa Quarterly*, vol.XX, no.142, p. 13.

· 57. See *Developing Local Technical and Managerial capabilities for Dealing with Transnational Corporations in Africa*, ST/ECA/CTNC/3, July 1981.

58. George C. Abangwu, 'Systems Approach to Regional Integration in West Africa', *Journal of Common Market Studies*, vol.XIII, nos.1 and 2, 1975, p. 133.

59. ECA, *ECA and Africa's Development 1983-2008: A Preliminary Perspective Study*, Addis Ababa, 1983, pp. 17—18.

60. For details see *South*, no.51, 1985, p. 8 and D. Katete Orwa, 'National Security: An African perspective', in Arlinghaus, 1984, p. 208.

61. Celestine Bassey, 'Collective Amnesia or Perpetual Debate? The African Security Agenda', in David F. Luke and Timothy M. Shaw, (eds), *Continental Crisis: The Lagos Plan of Action and Africa's Future*, University Press of America, Lanham, NY, 1984, p. 107.

62. John M. Ostheimer, 'Cooperation Among African States', in Arlinghaus 1984, p. 161.

63. Ibid., p. 160.

64. Berhanykun Andemicael and Davidson Nicol, 'The OAU: Primacy in Seeking African Solutions Within the UN Charter', in El-Ayouty and Zartman, 1984, pp. 101—53.

8. The Economic Commission for Africa and African Development

Emmanuel Hansen

It is not often realized that the Economic Commission for Africa (ECA) was the first continent-wide Pan-African organization to be set up. It was established in 1958, and owes its origins to Resolution 67 A (XXV) of the Economic and Social Council of the UN, which designated Addis Ababa as its headquarters.[1] Five years later the headquarters of the Organization of African Unity (OAU) was also to be located in the Ethiopian capital. The ECA was the fourth of the United Nations regional commissions to be set up. The first two were the Economic Commission of Europe (ECE) and the Economic and Social Commission for Asia and the Pacific (ESCAP). Later the Economic Commission for Latin America (ECLA) was also set up. The present younger generation of Africans are apt to take the existence of the ECA for granted; but senior officials of the ECA and the older generation of African political leaders recall the fierce battles which had to be waged by the then few African and Third World members of the UN before the way could be cleared for its establishment.[2] Although the ECA was set up on the same lines as the other regional organizations, it differed from them in terms of its terms of reference. The ECE and the ESCAP had much narrower terms of reference. They were set up to respond specifically to the reconstruction problems of the war in Europe and Asia. By the time the ECA came to be formed the basic terms of reference of the regional commissions have been widened to include issues of economic development in the respective regions.[3]

The ECA's main terms of reference, as laid down by the Economic and Social Council, are to seek and promote economic development on the continent. In doing this it was also to concern itself with social aspects of economic development and the inter-relationship between economic and social factors. Its terms of reference allow it to make recommendations on any matter within its area of competence to the governments of the region and to specialized agencies. Its relations with its member nations are voluntary and it cannot undertake any action with respect to any country without the prior consent of that country.[4]

Structure and Organization

The ECA, like other regional commissions, operates under the general supervision of the Economic and Social Council and of the General Assembly. At its inception in 1958 the then existing independent African states were admitted into full membership. Initially, membership also included the colonial powers in Africa such as France, Britain, Belgium, Portugal and Spain. With the granting of independence to the specific countries under their rule and the consequent assumption of full membership of the Commission, the colonial powers ceased to be members. South Africa was a member until 1963 when it was suspended because of its apartheid policies. In the same year Portugal was expelled for non-compliance with the resolutions of the Commission and the General Assembly. [5] Dependent territories could become associate members and at one time there were a number of associate members; but as each African country became independent it assumed full membership of the Commission. At present Namibia is the only associate member. Since all independent African members states of the UN are automatically full members of the Commission, membership is more or less the same as for the Organization of African Unity. African liberation movements have observer status and may submit proposals which can be voted on at the request of any member of the Commission. Currently, the African National Congress (ANC), the Pan-Africanist Congress (PAC) and the South-West African People's Organization (SWAPO) enjoy observer status. [6]

From its humble beginnings in 1958 the Commission has now grown into a huge bureaucratic organization with a staff of almost a thousand. This is not surprising considering that its functions have multiplied over the years. The ECA currently functions through three main structures: the Conference of Ministers, the sectoral ministerial conferences and the specialized subsidiary bodies.

The Conference of Ministers

This is the main legislative organ of the Commission. It was first established in 1969 and it initially met biannually, but now it meets annually. It is made up of ministers of economic affairs, planning and development of member states, and its main functions are to 1) consider matters of policy and the priorities to be assigned to the programmes and activities of the Commission; 2) consider intra-African and international economic policy issues and make recommendations on such issues to member states; 3) consider questions relating to the representation of the African region on international and inter-governmental bodies dealing with economic and social matters; and 4) consider and endorse for consideration of the Economic and Social Council and the General Assembly proposals emanating from the sectoral ministerial conferences. [7]

The Sectoral Ministerial Conference

This is composed of ministers responsible for the development of that particular sector. Its main task is to 1) review issues and problems relating to their particular sector; 2) formulate regional policies, strategies and priorities with regard to that particular sector; 3) identify areas for multinational cooperation and integration and 4) formulate sectoral work programmes and priorities.[8] At the present moment there are sectoral conferences on industry, trade, social affairs, transport and communications, human resources, planning, development and utilization. There is also the Regional Conference on the Integration of Women in Development and the Councils of Ministers of the Multinational Programming and Operational Centres (MULPOC) and the Conference of Ministers of Africa's Least Developed Countries.

The Specialized Subsidiary Bodies
At the moment there are three such bodies in existence: one is the Joint Conference of African Planners, Statisticians and Demographers. This meets every two years and its main function is to advise the Executive Secretary of the ECA and the African Institute for Economic Development and Planning (IDEP) on annual programmes of work and research on economic development and planning. It also has the job of reviewing the statistical work programme of the ECA and the work of the secretariat in the field of population. The Inter-governmental Committee of Experts for Science and Technology Development has as its main function the reviewing on a periodic basis of the African strategy for science and technology development. It also reviews on a regular basis the work of the secretariat in connection with the implementation of the African Regional Plan for the Application of Science and Technology to Development. The third body is the Joint Inter-governmental Regional Committee on Human Settlements and Environment. Its functions include the formulation of policies, priorities and strategies for regional, sub-regional and transnational environmental management in the African region, the promotion and exchange of information and experience on national environmental policies, legislations, programmes and problems, the promotion of programmes on environmental education for the public and the promotion of close cooperation on environmental matters between the Commission and the UN Environmental Programme and all other United Nations inter-governmental and non-governmental organizations working within and outside the African region.[9]

In addition to these the Commission also runs sub-regional offices in each of the five sub-regions which the ECA has devised for its purposes. The main point of this is to decentralize the activities of the Commission, thereby making its influence more strongly felt on the ground and improving its general efficiency. At present there are sub-regional offices in Lusaka for Eastern and Southern Africa. Tangier for the North African countries, Niamey for the West African countries, Gisenyi for the Economic Community of the Great Lakes Countries and Yaounde for the countries of the Central African sub-region. The sub-regional bodies are actively involved not only in conducting studies and rendering technical advice but also with the identification of, and the design and implementation of projects.[10] They are also meant to be effective instruments of economic cooperation and integration at the sub-regional level. Their main instrumental mechanism is the Multinational Programming and Operational Centres (MULPOCs).

To make MULPOC more integrated into the decision-making machinery of governments, and reflect the priorities of governments both individually and collectively, a device has now been effected to enable them to be supervised by an inter-governmental policy organ at both ministerial and official levels. The ministerial body will be a Council of Ministers made up of all the ministers of planning within the particular sub-region served by that particular MULPOC. It will act on behalf of the ECA Council of Ministers and be the supreme policy-making organ for the MULPOC of that particular sub-region. This sub-regional Council of Ministers is assisted by a subsidiary committee made up of officials and bureaucrats dealing with development planning in their respective countries. Although it is far too early to assess fully the effects of this organizational structure, in the eyes of the Commission the establishment of the MULPOCs constitutes an important step in turning the ECA into an operational institution. 'It emphasized the practical and operational role which the ECA intends to play in promoting subregional co-operation and integration as a step towards regional integration'.[11]

The Secretariat

This is the executive organ of the Commission. It is headed by an executive secretary appointed by the Secretary-General of the UN. The present holder of the position, Dr. Adebayo Adedeji, a former Nigerian academic, is only the third person to hold the position. The first was a Sudanese diplomat, Mekki Abbas and the second a Ghanaian civil servant, Robert Gardiner. The professional staff of the Commission forms part of the UN secretariat. One remarkable thing has been the fast growth in the number of the staff of the secretariat. Thus, from its humble beginning with a staff of 52 in 1959, its staff has now grown to an impressive figure of just under a thousand.[12] This is a reflection of the growth of its responsibilities. Although its beginnings were hampered by the shortage of trained and highly skilled Africans (as this was the time of approaching independence and the few that were available were needed by their national governments) the staff has now grown to the extent that the Commission can boast of over 80% of its professional staff being African.[13]

The Commission is made up of a number of divisions each responsible for a particular aspect of its work. At the moment the following divisions exist: International Trade and Finance, Joint ECA/FAO Agricultural Unit, Joint ECA/UNIDO Industrial Development Unit, Social Development, Natural Resources, Transport, Communications and Tourism. The Commission is largely funded from the resources of the United Nations. Here also from a humble beginning of $US 500,000 in 1959 the Commission's budget has now reached $13 million a year. Its biannual budget for the 1982-3 fiscal year is almost $36 million.[14]

Functions and Activities

As we have said above, the main function and *raison d'etre* for the establishment of the ECA is to provide for the economic and social development of the continent. In the pursuit of this major objective it performs a number of functions. These are research, collection, systematization and analysis of data related to the economic and social conditions in Africa, advice to African governments on social and economic matters and assistance in the implementation of economic and social development programmes, the building of institutions to promote economic and social development and regional cooperation, facilitation of programmes of economic cooperation and regional integration in Africa, and the training of African personnel in economic development programmes and social planning. We shall now see how it has carried out these activities.

Research and Publications

The ECA has an active programme of collection, systematization and analysis of data relating to the economic and social development of the continent. It also disseminates such information to member states and other interested parties. To this end the ECA puts out four different types of publications: periodicals, year books, annual surveys or reports and specialized studies. It publishes two different types of periodicals. One is semi-popular, non-technical and directed to a general readership and the other is more technical and professionally oriented. It produces two of the first type: *Rural Progress* which comes out quarterly and *Transnational Focus* which is published by the Joint ECA/UNCTC Unit on transnational corporations and comes out once a year. *Transnational Focus*, as the title implies, features articles on the activities of transnational corporations in Africa and is published in pursuit of the ECA's aim of providing information on the social, economic, legal and political implications of the activities of transnational corporations in Africa to member states. The professional or scholarly publications in this area are *The Economic Bulletin for Africa, Investment Africa* and *Agricultural Economic Bulletin for Africa* which comes out twice a year. In the area of surveys and reports the Commission publishes the annual *Survey of Economic and Social Conditions in Africa*, the *African Economic Indicators* and the *Annual Report* as well as the *Biennial Report*. The ECA also publishes *African Statistical Year Book* and *Foreign Trade Statistics for Africa*. These publications contain useful and professionally written accounts of the profile and performance of the African economies. The third type of publications are specialist studies. These are undertaken at the request of a member or member states or at the ECA's own initiative. They are sometimes reports submitted to the Conference of Ministers. These now form a large body of material and only a few of them can be mentioned here: *External Indebtedness of African Countries, The Situation of Food and Agriculture in Africa, Feasibility Study for a Subregional Maize Research Programme for Eastern and Southern Africa*.

Training

Another function performed by the ECA in pursuit of its objective of promoting economic and social development in Africa and fostering regional cooperation is the training of African personnel in specific areas of economic development and planning, for which purpose it has set up a number of institutions; one of the first was the African Institute for Economic Development and Planning (IDEP). This was established during the formative years of the ECA to train African planners to think and conceptualize problems within the African context and to propose solutions in response to the specific needs of Africa. It is based in Dakar and owes much of its initial reputation to the fame of its first director, Samir Amin, a distinguished African political economist whose international stature brought the Institute much respect. Other ECA training centres established along the same lines are the Regional Centre for Training in Aerial Survey at Ile Ife, Nigeria, the African Institute for Higher Technical Research in Nairobi and the Arusha-based Eastern and Southern Africa Management Institute. In addition to these the ECA also assists in the training of demographers at the Regional Institute for Population Studies, located on the campus of the University of Ghana at Legon and at the Institut de formation et de recherche demographique (IFORD) in Yaounde, Cameroon. There is also the African Training and Research Centre for Women and the African Centre for Applied Research and Training in Social Development (ACARTSOD) based in Tripoli, Libya to provide training of high-level personnel for research and development programmes.

Institutions of Economic and Social Development

In addition to research and training the ECA has also established institutions specifically to foster economic and social development, of which the African Development Bank (ADB) is perhaps the most important. This is based in Abidjan, and was established in 1963 and started operations in 1966. Its main purpose is to mobilize capital for the economic and social development of Africa. It was also to free African countries from institutions such as the IMF and the World Bank whose conditions for lending many African countries find difficult to accept because of their priorities for social development and perceived obligations to the mass of the people of their own countries. Membership was initially restricted to African countries for fear that since African countries could, on the whole, command only small capital the Bank could easily be dominated by non-Africans, which would defeat the main purpose of its establishment. However, in 1978, with the decision of the Board of Governors to increase its capital stock, the contingent decision to extend membership to non-Africans was taken. Today the non-African members make up 31% of the membership. The non-African members were admitted on the basis of nine principles aimed at maintaining the African character of the Bank.

The ADB has five associated institutions through which private and public capital is channelled. These are: the African Development Fund, Nigeria Trust

Fund, the African Reinsurance Corporation, Societé International Financiaire pour les Investissements et le Development en Afrique (SIFIDA) and the Association of African Development Finance Institutions.

The Bank started operations with authorized capital stock of $250 million. It now commands a capital stock of over $6 billion with a permitted loan disbursement of a little over $5 million.[15] As a development bank its lending is mostly for development projects. This is reflected in its loan disbursements. For the 1982-3 fiscal year its disbursements were as follows: agriculture, 25.31%; transport, 25.95%; public utilities, 26.69%; industry and banks, 14.81%; social sector, 7.24%. As a development bank it is not surprising that social services attracted the lowest funding. The Bank has, either on its own or in association with other institutions such as the World Bank the IMF or the EEC, financed or co-financed many development and investment projects in Africa. By the end of 1983 the Bank had invested close to $1.38 billion in ECOWAS countries and $1.4 billion in the countries of the PTA region.[16] At the present the ADB has an important presence in Ghana where it has been financing projects in agriculture, industry, telecommunications and electrical power and transport as well as water resources.

There is no doubt that the Bank has been doing very useful work in mobilizing capital for economic and social development. It is also a good example of some of the positive effects of regional cooperation. However, the fact that African countries still find it necessary to go to the IMF and the World Bank, with their strict terms of conditionality, means that important though its work is, it has not replaced these organizations as sources of funding for African countries.

The ECA also established in 1968 the Association of African Central Banks. This was set up to promote cooperation in the monetary, fiscal and banking spheres of Africa. Nearly all African countries are affiliated to it and over the years it has been able to establish its own subsidiaries such as the African Centre for Monetary Studies, the West African Clearing House and the Central African Clearing House.[17] These organizations are all cooperating in their various ways towards the economic development of Africa and the promotion of regional cooperation in Africa. It is hoped that by the year 2000 Africa will have achieved the final act of Lagos—the establishment of an African Economic Community.

Other Activities

The ECA has also aided in the establishment of other regional and sub-regional organizations. The ECA has provided advisory services and prepared the protocols for the establishment of the Economic Community of West African States (ECOWAS). It earlier played an active part in the establishment of the now defunct East African Community and in the decision to establish a Preferential Trade Area for Eastern and Southern Africa. It prepared the draft protocols and took a leading part in the negotiations which brought the PTA into being. It was no surprise that the PTA chose Bax Nomvette, one of the senior officials of the ECA closely connected with the setting up of the PTA, as its first secretary-general. The ECA is now involved in a similar exercise establishing of the Economic Community of Central African States consisting of 11 member countries in the sub-region. Perhaps one of the most important acts of the Commission to date has been the preparation of the Lagos Plan of Action which is not only a clear statement of Africa's developmental options but also its collective response to the position of finance capital contained in the World Bank Report, *Accelerated Development in Sub-Saharan Africa: Agenda For Action*. The Commission has also been playing its part in assisting the implementation of the Lagos Plan of Action. Its latest action in this field has been the commendable assistance it gave the OAU in the preparation of Africa's Priority Programme for Economic Recovery 1986-1990 and its participation in the initiatives undertaken in arranging a Special Session of the UN General Assembly in May 1986 to discuss the current economic crisis in Africa.

In 1975 the ECA established the African Training and Research Centre for Women. It is based in Addis Ababa at the offices of the Secretariat. Its main purpose is to involve women more fully in the development of Africa. This it does through the promotion of work for food and nutrition programmes, and the encouragement of small-scale enterprises, family service management, income-generating projects and the improvement of the conditions for women in wage employment. It also organizes the African Women's Task Force, a volunteer corps of skilled women serving in development projects in countries other than their own. The ECA also provides assistance to member states in the formulation and implementation of economic strategies for development. It is particularly active in the area of population studies and demography. It has also been providing assistance to member states in negotiations with international finance and world organizations such as the International Monetary Fund, (IMF), General Agreement on Tariffs and Trade (GATT), United Nations Conference on Trade and Development (UNCTAD) and the World Bank. The ECA has also been working hand in hand with UNIDO in order to promote industrialization projects on the continent. The Commission has been participating, too, in the five African highway projects: the Trans-Saharan Highway (Algiers-Lagos), the Trans-African Highway (Mombasa-Lagos), the Trans-Sahelian Highway (Dakar-N'Djemena-Djibouti), the Trans-Coastal Highway (Lagos-Nouakchott-Tangier) and the Trans-African Highway (Cairo-Gaborone).

One area in which the ECA has also been particularly active is in the promotion of regional cooperation among African countries. It has been particularly concerned with the promotion of intra-African trade. We have already referred to its work with regard to the establishment of the PTA for Eastern and Southern Africa. Mention must also be made of its activities with regard to the Southern African Development Coordination Conference (SADCC). In West Africa it has provided assistance for programmes meant to help harmonize trade relations among the ECOWAS states, the *Communauté économique de l'Afrique de l'Ouest* (CEAO) and the Mano River Union. Towards the promotion of intra-African trade the ECA has been in the forefront of the drive for the establishment of an African Regional Federation of Chambers of Commerce which had its first general assembly in 1983. The Commission is also working actively for the creation of an African Monetary Fund.

It is clear from the above that the ECA has indeed been active in the field of economic and social development in Africa and in promoting regional cooperation. It could, however, be argued that whereas it has achieved a certain modicum of success and has established itself as an institution of repute as far as the collection, systematization and analysis of data on the profile and performance of the African economies is concerned, it has not acquired leadership in generating new economic thinking which can be regarded as the specifically African response to the problems of underdevelopment and dependency. Its writings exhibit an eclectic mixture of underdevelopment and dependency theories and neo-classical economic analysis. In other words, it has not been able to provide economic leadership in the area of theory formulation in the sense in which ECLA came out with *dependencia* theory. But this is unfair to the Commission. After all it was set up to respond to the concrete economic and social problems of the continent, not to establish economic theories; and it has been in existence for far too short a time for one to expect it to do more than it currently is. Since it concentrates mostly on economic and social matters, its work is a useful complement to the other Pan-African organization, the OAU, which concentrates on political issues and with which, after a rather frosty beginning, it has now succeeded in working out a pattern of meaningful co-existence for the general betterment of the continent.

Notes

1. United Nations *25 Years of Service to African Development and Integration*, 1983, p. 8.
2. Interview with Dr Adebayo Adedeji, Executive Secretary of the ECA. See *West Africa*, 25 April 1983. A similar remark was made by Robert Gardiner, former Executive Secretary of the ECA in a discussion with the author in April 1983.
3. *United Nations*, op cit., 1983, p. 8.
4. Ibid., p. 9.
5. E/CN.14/111/Rev.8 quoted in ibid., p. 9.
6. Ibid., p. 10.
7. Ibid., p. 12.
8. Ibid., p. 13.
9. Ibid., p. 15.
10. Ibid., p. 16.
11. Ibid.
12. Ibid., p. 17.
13. Ibid.
14. Ibid., p. 19.

15. *West Africa* 10 September 1984.
16. Ibid., p. 1842.
United Nations, 1983, p. 53.

9. Dependence and Economic Cooperation: The Case of SADCC

Thandika Mkandawire

By the end of 1974, only one of the several post-colonial schemes of regional cooperation was still alive. Many observers saw this as evidence of the futility of regional cooperation in Africa. Yet in the following decade, African heads of state were to unanimously adopt the Lagos Plan of Action (LPA) calling for the establishment of an African Common Market by the year 2000; the Economic Community of West African States (ECOWAS) was to be formed; countries of Southern and Eastern Africa were to join in the creation of the Preferential Trading Area (PTA); and in Southern Africa the Southern African Development Cooperation Conference (SADCC) was to be created. Looking back at Africa's experience over the preceding two decades, these new schemes must surely appear as examples of the triumph of hope over experience. The proliferation of such schemes raises a number of questions: what has been the basis of this new hope? What has changed in Africa? Why should SADCC succeed in Southern Africa where so many others had failed? Are there new arguments for regional cooperation or is it simply that the major actors on the African scene have become more receptive to the call for unity so indefatigably made by Kwame Nkrumah? Although the major focus of this paper is SADCC, I shall preface it with a look at the broader questions posed above.

If we compare the arguments advanced in the official document of the Government of Ghana to the first OAU conference two decades ago and the Lagos Plan of Action of 1980 there are few new arguments, except perhaps that the latter document is squarely based on the acceptance of regional schemes as the building blocks for a continental common market. The Ghana approach called for an immediate creation of continental structures and was opposed to regional organizations, thus sparking the famous confrontation between Nkrumah and Nyerere over the East African Community and its compatibility with Pan-Africanism.

The first and basic argument is still that a vast number of economic activities can only be profitably carried out at a regional level because of the economies of scale that can be reaped through cooperation and coordination. Africa has the necessary natural resources to sustain a major industrialization programme. However, as long as the continent continues to be balkanized these resources will be foreign-controlled and will be used only to meet foreign demand. It is only through cooperation that a convergence between Africa's great needs and its vast resources can be attained. Furthermore, regional integration, by removing the monocultural base of individual member states' economies, reduces risk by diversifying their collective export base. Lastly, since the political economy of resource use is not only determined by supply and demand but by such extra-economic factors as nationalism, diplomatic pressure and even military force, regional cooperation would shield African economies from exploitation and safeguard their sovereignty by enhancing their collective bargaining power. This highly telegraphic presentation of the case for African unity does not do full justice to the whole argument. I believe, however, that it captures the essentials and, in substance, the argument has not changed since the days of Nkrumah. Consequently, if all the regional schemes and meetings are no more than political charades, the current flurry of activities around regional cooperation must depend more on greater receptivity to the idea among policy-makers than the emergence of new arguments for cooperation. It is, therefore, necessary to examine the reasons for this greater receptivity.

In the following section I shall discuss some of the more plausible reasons for the new optimism about regional cooperation. For each argument I shall consider which factors, in the SADCC case, modify, weaken, reinforce or distort the thrust of each of these arguments. To the best of my knowledge, these arguments have never been presented together in a coherent manner. Most of them are only implicit in some of the academic and official documents reviewing past failures and future prospects for regional cooperation. Some are extensions to the regional context of the debate on the process of national development given the nature of class forces in Africa, the articulation of national and transnational actors and the overall impact of the international environment on accumulation.

The Current Economic Crisis and Regional Integration

The economic crisis argument states that the present economic crisis has dramatically exposed the futility of many of the go-it-alone attempts at development. The preamble to the Lagos Plan of Action would seem to confirm the force of this argument since in it the collective of African heads of states admit that after two decades of independence Africa is in a shambles. Various SADCC documents give the current economic crisis faced by member states as one more reason for cooperation. In the words of SADCC's first Executive Secretary, the late Mr Blumeris,

> if you look at the indicators of development something is wrong with the individual national approach. The advantages and wisdom of collective co-operation in the regional context must be developed and expanded economically. [1]

To the extent that African countries have pursued different development strategies and have thus reached the present crisis by different paths, we can expect that different states will have different expectations about what regional cooperation can do for their beleaguered economies. We shall therefore briefly look at the major strategies pursued by SADCC countries. These are: the export-oriented strategy; the import substitution strategy; and resource-based industrialization.

Of course no country pursues any of these strategies in its pure form. However, we can, for convenience sake, identify the salient features of a country's policies and then relate a particular country's attitudes towards integration and the trade exigencies and economic outcomes—successful or unsuccessful—of its particular strategy.

Let us first take the case of the export-oriented strategy which, in the SADCC group, has been pursued most clearly by Malawi and Swaziland. In these countries this strategy has meant export of primary commodities in unprocessed or semi-processed form. The export sector has been seen as the engine of growth; whatever industrialization has taken place has been dependent upon the rate and scope of accumulation in and the impulse derived from the export sector. A country pursuing such a strategy is unlikely to be interested in regional cooperation beyond such elementary forms as in transport and communication. Neighbouring economies are of little interest for the simple reason that they may be producing identical products or may not be significant consumers of the country's export goods. Interest in neighbours is bound to be even lower during periods of commodity price booms when the outward-looking strategy seems to be yielding high returns. The collapse of commodity prices will, conversely, reduce the euphoria about distant markets and may make the argument for regional cooperation sound less far-fetched than during boom time. The current recession may thus have given impetus to some of the present interest in various forms of regional cooperation by otherwise export-oriented countries. As these countries seek to diversify their exports to include non-traditional goods (e.g. simple manufactures) it may dawn on them that their neighbours are likely to be major buyers, especially if some preferential trade arrangement can be made and if the protectionism of the advanced countries continues.

The resource-based strategy is one in which the raw materials export sector is the handmaiden of the industrialization process. Increased processing of the country's export commodities and a deliberate channelling of export revenues towards a highly protected industry producing for the domestic market are the cornerstones of this strategy. In the SADCC region Zambia and pre-independence Zimbabwe have most consistently pursued such a strategy, the former by choice and the latter by force of circumstance. The global recession and the decline in demand for the major exports will basically have the same impact on attitudes towards regional markets as was the case with the export-oriented strategy. However, given the preponderance of highly protected and uncompetitive industries such countries will tend to favour a planned allocation of industry within the region or the extension of the protective measures to the region as a whole, especially if the countries concerned happen to be the most industrialized in the region.

The case of the import-substitution strategy is slightly different from that of the other two strategies because in its case a crisis will tend to be internally generated. In the initial phases of its industrialization a country may enjoy rapid rates of growth as it establishes a range of industries whose demand has already been revealed by the historical pattern of imports. In general, these are light consumer goods industries—food and beverages, textiles and simple household utensils. During the easy phase of such industrialization, the national market may be large enough to permit the establishment of a substantial number of light industries producing for domestic consumption. Once this phase is exhausted (and for some SADCC countries the threshold for such industry is low), further deepening of the industrialization process calls for the widening of the market either by moving towards an export-oriented strategy or seeking regional cooperation. Countries such as Taiwan and South Korea successfully moved from one strategy to another and have enjoyed legendary rates of industrialization.[2] Neo-classical ideologues have interpreted the performance of these countries as underscoring the supremacy of export-oriented strategies and the validity of setting prices right.[3] They have accordingly blamed the present economic crisis in African countries on import-substitution policies and the price distortions arising from these strategies. The so-called Berg Report is the main text of this doctrine as repackaged for the African context.[4] Overlooked in the studies is the importance of the preceding import substitution strategy and the unusually favourable international economic conditions then prevailing—which may not be easily replicable.

To move African economies from their present distorted forms to presumably more efficient export-oriented ones, a number of measures are recommended. These generally include the following ingredients of the standard IMF package: devaluation of the national currency, reduction of government expenditure especially on social services and subsidies to the poor and wage-earners; a freeze on domestic credit, especially to the state; liberalization of the trade and capital accounts of the balance of payments accounts and general reliance on market forces.[5] I shall discuss the effects of IMF-style stabilization programmes on regional integration in a later section.

Another way out of the impasse is regional integration in order to widen the market and remove the size constraint on the establishment of more complex industrial structures. Such a strategy is often based on export pessimism about the ability to penetrate the markets of the advanced capitalist countries. The present recession and the growing protectionism in precisely those labour-intensive industries in which underdeveloped countries are supposed to enjoy comparative advantages may lend credence to the pessimism and make regional cooperation a more attractive option. This may explain the liking of African policy-makers for preferential trade areas and the idea of an African Common Market enshrined in the Lagos Plan of Action.

On balance then, it would seem that the impasse faced by virtually all go-it-alone strategies of the past opens up room for serious consideration of the regional cooperation option. However, althouth SADCC documents refer to the crisis afflicting the member states, its economic measures do not in any way address themselves to these central issues. Indeed we could argue that the current low-cost strategy adopted by SADCC is failing to make use of what may be favourable conditions. We may, of course, wonder whether the resultant cooperation may be stable in the long run. In other words, can a conjuncturally induced need for regional cooperation be turned into a structural and developmental process of regional cooperation? Or would the end of the present crisis or improvements in terms of trade for member states' export commodities once again make the countries outward-looking so that they lose interest in regional cooperation schemes as fissiparous pressures from the uneven integration of African economies into the world market reassert themselves? Experience in Latin America suggests that temporary export bonanzas have tended to erode the 'integration vocation of Latin American countries'.[6] It is not far-fetched to assume that the same may happen in the SADCC region. This, however, is not the expressed fear of SADCC and its foreign advisers. Its failure to exploit or explore any such opportunities seems based on a decision to eschew any politically loaded decision in the name of pragmatism. We discuss some of the sources of this minimalist stance in a later section of the paper.

Stabilization Programmes and Regional Cooperation

The most potent threat that the present crisis poses to regional cooperation stems from the domestic process of adjustment to the crisis. As a result of the devastating impact of the current recession, a number of SADCC states have had to turn to the IMF for financial assistance and undergo stabilization or structural adjustment programmes. Despite IMF claims to the contrary, its package has invariably consisted of the same ingredients, some of which are listed above. Although much has been written on the implications of this standard policy package for the domestic economy, little, if any, has been said about its impact on efforts at regional cooperation. Although preferential trade arrangements are not yet on the agenda for SADCC, one expectation is that trade will be promoted among member states initially through bilateral arrangements. It is, therefore, worthwhile considering the impact of IMF conditionality on prospects for increased regional trade.

Often implicit, but sometimes explicit, in IMF conditionality is that a country's trade should be liberalized and non-discriminatory towards all countries. Consequently, regional cooperation, to the extent that it entails preferential margins for, or exclusive bilateral arrangements with, some country or group of countries, runs counter to the spirit, if not the letter, of IMF programmes. Not surprisingly, the IMF has not shown particular enthusiasm about regional cooperation schemes and the preferential trade arrangements implicit or explicit in these schemes. Nevertheless, the IMF has, in response to requests for advice in the establishment of Clearing Houses, suggested that properly priced currencies would obviate the need for such houses and lead to greater trade among African countries by enhancing convertibility of national currencies.[7] In other words, integration is encouraged if it encourages free trade. *A fortiori*, the removal of all trade barriers, and therefore, all preferential arrangements, would promote more trade and a more efficient allocation of resources.

The outward-looking strategies that the IMF is now imposing on the crisis-ridden economies of SADCC probably go further than any external intervention in the region to undermine aspirations towards greater economic integration. Regional cooperation in the Third World always calls for some kind of regionally-oriented import-substitution programme and leads to trade diversion. It is, by its very nature, inward-looking, not in the sense that investments are national or regional but that the regional market is the centre of focus of major investment programmes. The current wave of IMF stabilization programmes are, in sharp contrast, outward-looking, stressing the continued export of primary products.

Political Will, the State and Regional Cooperation

What we have so far discussed are the structural and conjunctural hindrances to or imperatives towards regional cooperation. We have not discussed the crucial issue of whether or not the hegemonic groups in the nations of the region will respond logically to the arguments developed above. Our presentation has thus failed to take into account the central fact that economic integration in particular, and economic policy in general, are social practices situated in concrete social formations. Since the costs and benefits of integration are unevenly distributed among different social classes within member states, the reactions of these social classes will condition the nature and stability of the integration.

In a seminal survey of the crisis of regional integration in Latin America, Vaitsos notes that there has seldom been a systematic analysis of the economic and political actors whose interests are served by regional economic cooperation.[8] He further argues that in a theory of integration it is fundamental to analyse not only the instruments or policies used but to ask who integrates and for whose benefit.

> The mechanism and instruments of the integration process correspond to the interests, ideology and conception that is attributed to economic development by the social groups which stand to derive the major advantages from that process. The evolution of integration becomes modified as new classes and groups participate in the system of economic integration.

Studies on SADCC are singularly devoid of the kind of analysis that Vaitsos is calling for. We shall, in the following section briefly review the activities, expectations and influences of some of the major actors—domestic and foreign

—in SADCC countries. (The exercise is tentative and to a large extent conjectural and needs to be backed by more systematic analyses to delineate the positions of various social forces involved in the integration exercise.)

It has often been argued that one source of weakness of integration efforts among underdeveloped countries is lack of political will; consequently little or no weight is attached to the political reasons for integration. In the words of Tironi, 'there is no analogy in developing countries to the EEC's drive for integration to strengthen Europe against communism.'[9] We may of course question the validity of the importance attached to the spectre of communism in the birth of the EEC. Others have argued that it was the political war weariness of a whole new generation of Eurocrats that provided the necessary political impulse to the integration drive. Be that as it may, the importance of political will cannot be denied, although, as we shall argue, such will must not be seen in purely subjective and voluntaristic terms.

SADCC seems to have started off well in this political respect, having emerged directly out of the frontline states' cooperation and support to the liberation forces of Zimbabwe and Namibia. Further impetus to SADCC was provided by the imminence of Zimbabwe's independence. Lurking behind most of the early declarations on SADCC was the political commitment to the liberation struggle and resistance to South Africa's strategy to further intensify its dominance through a constellation of Southern African states. It was on the basis of a common enemy—apartheid South Africa—that much of the optimism on SADCC's prospects was based.[10] Some observers have attributed the brightness of SADCC's prospects to the personal and political commitment of its leaders.[11] This seems also to be the nature of the region's leaders own self-perception. The vice-president of Botswana is, for instance, quoted as saying, 'The critical factor is that SADCC commands the political will of our leaders. In our short experience a strong will is a sine qua non for any regional grouping.'[12]

If all this was true of SADCC in its formative years, surprisingly much of the political thrust has been lost in a rather short span of time. Under the guise of pragmatism there is a growing tendency to keep politics out of SADCC affairs and to increasingly technocratize the dealings among SADCC states. And donors have time and again been impressed by the depoliticization of SADCC and have, in a rather paternalistic way, praised SADCC for this pragmatism. They have also not hesitated to voice their concern over bringing politics in SADCC matters whenever they felt this was the case.

Yet if experience elsewhere is anything to go by, this technocratization of the process of regional cooperation and its subsequent depoliticization may spell doom or, at least, the emasculation of SADCC. By its very nature the economic problem of underdevelopment contains a highly charged political element and calls for high government priority, regardless of the dominant ideology. The consequence for integration of this close bond between politics and economics is a drastic reduction of the arena of action for the technicians.[13] Experience elsewhere in the Third World demonstrates the rapid contraction of the non-political arena and premature appearance of problems requiring political action at the highest government level. Reinforcing this premature politization of issues is the severity of problems of redistribution which are in turn aggravated by the scarcity of resources for redistribution. The pragmatism that constitutes so much of the SADCC's leaders' own self-image and for which they are so lauded by aid donors may be illusory and self-defeating. It would be wiser for the leaders to insist, as they did from the beginning, upon the political nature of the integration endeavour and the distribution of its costs and benefits and thus upon the primacy of politics. If no such awareness is present, SADCC will be restricted to an extremely narrow range of purely technical issues and will be deprived of its major asset—the political will to delink SADCC economics from a politically abhorrent system of apartheid and to assist in the liberation of Namibia and South Africa itself.

Talk of political will smacks of voluntarism. To go beyond this, we have to examine the nature of the state in the sub-region for it is this which mediates the process of regional integration by defining it and allocating to it the necessary resources—people, finance and political capital—for its achievement. If we start with the world systems approach of Wallerstein, Frank and others, which characterizes the state as dependent and basically unable to initiate and carry out projects autonomously of accumulation nationally or with other peripheral states, we will tend to interpret regional cooperation schemes as mere variants of the international division of labour, determined by demands of capital accumulation on a world scale. Whatever logic there is to such schemes is not locally generated but merely a reflection of the global needs of capital. Consequently, SADCC, with its rather extensive involvement of metropolitan capital, is seen as nothing but the affirmation of this thesis.

In sharp contrast to this perspective we have the Third Worldist view that sees Third World governments as generally engaged in a bitter struggle for autonomy and development. Regional cooperation schemes such as SADCC are here viewed as attempts to collective self-reliance on a regional level. This is the favoured self-image of the Third World leadership. The assertion that regional cooperation is aimed at collectively strengthening the sovereignty of each member state is thus one of the common denominators of African regional schemes. Accordingly, the first summit conference of SADCC stated quite categorically that the organization would seek to reduce economic dependence 'particularly, but not only on the Republic of South Africa'.[14]

Behind these rather broad and overly simplified views are questions of the existence and nature of a national bourgeoisie, its links with foreign capital and its position in the state apparatus. The world system approach tends to exclude any possibility of the emergence of a national bourgeoisie in the present historical epoch. At best, the local governing class will be a comprador one, closely linked to imperialism and serving as the conduit through which imperialist interests are transmitted. Such a class has, by definition, no particular need for regional cooperation schemes largely because it has no interest in the kinds of import-substitution industrialization strategies that are the *raison d'etre* for regional schemes. If it does accede to any schemes of regional cooperation it will be at the behest of imperial capital which may want such regional schemes for broader global or systemic reasons.

The national bourgeoisie is, by contrast, interested in the national market. The defence of such a national market against incursions of foreign metropolitan capital may compel such a class to seek cooperation with classes facing similar extra-regional threats and competition in neighbouring countries. It should, however, be noted that given the lilliputian capital available to the nascent national bourgeoisie, the national market may be more than enough, especially if the national bourgeoisie is able to induce the state to protect this market and more so if the domestic market is of medium size. In this case, there will simply be no compulsion towards regional integration as the national bourgeoisie wallows in the comfort of its puny but highly protected domestic market. This may explain the general passivity of the indigenous capitalist class towards regional schemes; they see their major constraint not as the size of the market but the lack of investable surplus to capture the economies of scale guaranteed by modern technology. In cases where the national bourgeoisie takes the form of a state bureaucracy, the impulse towards regional cooperation is even further circumscribed. State bureaucracies are never under great compulsion to find new markets unless strong extra-economic pressures are imposed or personal material gain is indicated.

Geographical size and level of development play an important role in all this. It has been observed, for instance, that the bourgeoisie of small countries will generally favour greater regional planning, although the same elements may be ideologically and congenitally opposed to planning at the local level. The reason for their seemingly schizophrenic behaviour is that in a free market situation industry will tend to locate itself in the more advanced regions largely because of the prosaic capitalist principle that nothing succeeds like success or because of the disequilibrating process of cumulative causation. the bourgeoisie of the more advanced countries whose larger market allows them greater efficiency will tend to favour free intra-regional trade and a weak supra-national structure with no power to propose or initiate common policies but strong enough to protect the regional market. Such measures as planned allocation of projects among member states or sectoral programmes will be anathema. For instance, the preoccupation of Zimbabwean industrialists with SADCC as a market and their lack of interest in any coordination may be indicative of this rather logical, albeit myopic, response.

What our rather sketchy discussion suggests is that whether or not SADCC has support at the national level will depend on the nature of the state, the character and interests of the hegemonic social forces (domestic or external) in the state apparatus and the compatibility or non-compatibility of their interests with regional cooperation. The expression and perception of their interests will also depend on the economic situation. This is an area which needs extensive research. None the less, the fact remains that we can only understand SADCC's current progress (or lack of it) by a clear analysis of the configuration of the social forces at the national level and their perception of the problems and prospects of regional cooperation.

Transnationals and Regional Co-operation

No scheme of regional cooperation can escape the ever-watchful eye of transnational corporations (TNCs). As Vaitsos has emphasized, TNCs are one of the strongest actors in regional cooperation: 'They influence policies, participate in or even dominate policy implementation and can become critical integrating or disintegrating forces in the pursuit of their corporate objectives.'[15]

Thus far TNCs and private business in general have not been prominent in SADCC affairs, with perhaps the exception of the Confederation of Zimbabwe Industries which seems to be actively consulted by the government. Yet there is a *prima facie* case for expecting TNCs to be interested in, if not ecstatic about, regional cooperation since the scale at which they generally operate and the organizational capacity they possess could be more optimally used in larger markets. In other words, we would expect that regional cooperation, by widening the market and rationalizing the regional economic space (through better communications, standardization and so on), would be supported by TNCs. But, as Vaitsos argues, contrary to these commonsense expectations, TNCs do not (or do not wish to) promote effective economic integration among developing countries if the latter have a medium or large size market and some (even minimal) industrial capacity.[16] Vaitsos' proviso is crucial. Medium size refers to economies such as those of Ecuador and Peru whose GDP in 1980 was US$1.3 billion and $1.9 billion respectively—levels that are much higher than for any state in SADCC. Indeed, SADCC's total GNP is close to Peru's (Table 8.1). Vaitsos adds that TNCs generally promote particular types of integration among LDCs only if the latter's markets are quite small and if TNCs were not involved through parallel foreign investment

Table 8.1
SADCC Countries GDP Per Capita and GDP in 1981

Country	GDP/CAP	GDP (US$million)
Angola	470	820
Botswana.	1,010	820
Lesotho	540	730
Malawi	200	1,630
Mozambique	360	2,700
Swaziland	740	450
Tanzania	280	5,840
Zambia	600	3,140
Zimbabwe	870	6,390
Total		21,700

Source: OECD, *Development Cooperation Review*, 1981; World Bank, *World Bank Report*, Washington, DC, 1982.

in these countries before regional cooperation. On both counts SADCC would seem to be acceptable to TNCs. Although TNCs are present in SADCC, their total investments are relatively small (see Table 8.2). The estimated total stock of foreign investment of US$1,311 billion is smaller than that for Liberia (US$1,230 billion) and Zaire (US$1,250 billion).[17] Most of this investment is, in any case, in mineral production for export to extra-regional markets; trade liberalization would therefore not be as costly as in cases where parallel investment in substitutional structures for local markets is well established and where liberalization would involve competition among subsidiaries or costly rationalization achieved by closing down some plants.

Table 8.2
Foreign Direct Investment (FDI) in SADCC Countries

Country	Stock of FDI (end-1978)	FDI as percentage of Domestic Investment
Angola	100	4.9
Botswana	57	0.5
Lesotho	4	—
Malawi	100	0.8
Mozambique	100	1.2
Swaziland	50	2.6
Tanzania	170	0.6
Zambia	330	5.2
Zimbabwe	400	8.6
Total	1,311	

Source: UNCTAD, *Transnational Corporations in World Development: A Survey*, United Nations, New York, 1983.

Even where the above conditions—smallness of market and absence of previous parallel investment—are not fulfilled TNCs may not be enthusiastic about regional cooperation if, as Vaitsos argues, it incudes:

(a) increased production and input links with the home country of their parent firms in ways which are economically much more than the market interconnections established among the members of the corresponding regional groups;
(b) exclusive preference for intra-regional free trade of goods while maintaining a high external protection for the subsidiaries;
(c) an aversion to any form of host government intervention in the field of industrial planning or in establishing common policies on foreign flows (i.e. tariffs on extra-regional inputs, common foreign investment policies *à la* Andean Pact).

The reticence of TNCs on SADCC may be a reflection of their uncertainty about SADCC intentions in these matters. However, it could well be that they are waiting for the groundwork to be done by their home governments who are actively involved in the organization of infrastructure. Some TNCs may be conveniently placed in South Africa to serve the SADCC region from there, fully confident that SADCC pragmatism will not affect their South African subsidiaries' access to SADCC markets.

Foreign Aid and SADCC

There is probably no regional scheme in Africa which has received so much attention, finance and effusive accolades from erstwhile colonial masters and aid donors as SADCC. And in no other African regional organization is the involvement of aid donors as intimate and as far reaching as in SADCC. The acceptance today by the imperialist powers of regional cooperation is, of course, not exclusive to Southern Africa. Only a decade or so ago the characteristic attitude of the imperialist powers, or at least the erstwhile colonial masters, was summarized by the age-old slogan 'divide and rule'. Imperial rivalry reflected itself through deliberate and systematic attempts to maintain linguistic and geographical division bequeathed to Africa by its colonial masters. The French were particularly conspicuous in their attempts to keep francophone Africa to themselves.

One of the grounds for optimism about regional integration in Africa is that today much of this has changed. Inter-imperialist rivalry seems to have partially given way to fighting the spectre of communism and the desire for collective maintenance of law and order in the periphery (not that the rivalry has completely disappeared). Tensions do occur from time to time (increasingly between the USA and Western Europe) but these are subordinate to the larger task of the systemic maintenance of stability. Furthermore, the presence in this hegemonic structure of such countries as the USA, Japan and West Germany has undermined the exclusive claims of former colonial powers to any parts of Africa. Hence policies towards Africa are increasingly defined by such supranational organizations as the World Bank, OECD and EEC. These organizations hold no special brief for the colonially created boundaries of Africa. Indeed it can be argued that with increased transnationalization of African economies, the colonial spatial delineations make less and less sense. Hence there is no built in objection to regional cooperation across former colonial lines. Furthermore, the great strides in communication and the enhanced organizational capacity of the imperial powers make 'regroup and dominate' more efficacious than the earlier 'divide and rule'. The acceptance of some kind of regrouping of countries is clearly spelt out in the 1981 Review of the Development Assistance Committee (DAC) of the OECD. The review sketches out a possible scenario in which interested groups of donors and recipients would experiment with various arrangements, preferably at a sub-regional level. John Lewis, Chairman of the DAC until 1981, gives the following reason for the preference of the sub-regional over the regional approach:

The subregional mode allows subsets of donors and recipients who are disposed towards some integration to get on with experimentation without being blocked by the rule of universality; in so doing this mode can scarcely fail to reduce the degree of disjuncture in the situation.[18]

More germane to SADCC is that the EEC, which has so far given more than US$400 million dollars to SADCC, seems to like sub-regional groupings. Stevens indeed argues that 'the most tangible feature of EEC policy that can be reasonably characterized as _communautaire_ is its predilection for regional groupings.' He adds, however, that 'the unity fostered by the EEC is of a very partial and idiosyncratic variety. Europe selects regional groups with which it deals on the basis of perceptions of its self-interest'.[19]

It will be recalled that the first Arusha Declaration clearly stated that economic independence would be sought not only from South Africa but also from any other nation or group of other nations. Experience so far suggests that whether by design or not, SADCC countries have been exclusively concerned with the South Africa connection while deepening their dependence on Western powers. This is done presumably on the basis of pragmatism since it cannot have escaped SADCC leadership that the same countries that are aiding SADCC are deeply involved in supporting the prosperity and military might of South Africa.

Lacking access to confidential discussions on SADCC we can only surmise SADCC attitudes towards aid by examining official documents that are accessible to the public. Several things about these are striking. Most outstanding is the absence of agreement on the type and conditionality of aid each member state may receive for purportedly SADCC projects. In addition, there seems to be the assumption that all SADCC projects will be financed largely by foreign aid. Take the example of SADCC industrial development projects. More than 80% of the expected finance is foreign (Table 8.3). All pre-feasibility studies (most of which cost US$10,000) were to be foreign-funded. The same is true of other regional activities in transport and communication. The share of foreign funding at SADCC level is much higher than that at national level where, in general, domestic savings increasingly account for the largest share of capital accumulation. Comparing the patterns of investment at national and SADCC levels we get the impression that while member states have opted for increased national economic independence they have accepted collective dependence at the regional level. This attitude is in sharp contrast with usual African practice. Historically, African states, including the most neo-colonial, have insisted on the Africanness of their regional organizations. We have only to recall the fate of the OAU Secretary-General who was sacked after he entered into an agreement with Lonrho to oversee African oil supplies or the battle over the membership of non-Africans to the African Development Bank. It is as if African states were convinced that what they cannot resist nationally they ought to at least try to resist regionally. SADCC seems to hold to the opposite view.

Although the industrial projects are designated as SADCC projects, nearly all of them are national and could have been carried out—SADCC or no

Table 8.3
SADCC Development Projects—Estimated Investment Costs (US$million)

Percentage	Local	Foreign	Total	Foreign as proportion of total
Salt	11.50	18.10	29.60	61.01
Textiles (knitting, power-looms and polyester yarn projects)	34.90	81.67	116.57	70.01
Wool and Mohair	2.73	6.85	9.60	71.5
Textiles chemicals, pesticides and insecticides	4.00	3.50	7.50	47.0
Tractors and farm implements	22.47	38.75	61.21	63.40
Fertilizers	128.90	603.21	732.11	82.30
Pulp and Paper	67.97	457.13	525.10	87.00
Cement	10.25	26.75	37.00	73.00
Total	*282.72*	*1,235.97*	*1,518.69*	*81.30*

Source: SADCC Industrial Projects Workshop, Harare, Zimbabwe, 10-11 January 1984.

SADCC. In any case, nowhere is there evidence that they are a result of clearly sectoral programming by some supranational body. Each member state simply submits a list of projects which are then lumped together in a kind of regional shopping list for pledges from donors. There is no ranking of projects according to a regional social welfare function. What projects are ultimately implemented seem to depend on donors' preference and national commitment to them. Nowhere is there an indication as to which projects SADCC member states would collectively fund as a matter of priority even if aid donors were not interested.

Why have aid donors rallied to SADCC more than to any other African regional organization? The donors' own rhetoric is that they are helping the region in its stand against apartheid. They do not explain how this tallies with their deep economic and strategic involvement with the racist regime in South Africa. Other interpretations of donors' interests—especially the EEC's— are less kind. One view is that the aid is conscience money to assuage the troubled spirit of the donors for their complicity with apartheid. This, I believe, is too simplistic. States are rarely moved by such moral qualms. A more plausible set of arguments is based on the historical interests of imperialism in the region.

First, there is the danger of the radicalization of the region as the confrontation in South Africa spills over to the neighbours. It is important that Western presence in the region be clearly affirmed.[20] Second, to the extent that most of the investment is simply a rehabilitation or expansion of past patterns of transport and communication, they facilitate the continued accessibility of the region to foreign capital for markets and raw materials. Third, some measure of independence from South Africa is essential to the region if it is not to collapse as a result of strains caused by confrontation with South Africa. Fourth, SADCC is potentially a huge market. Aid has always served well as a key to new markets. So this may be one aspect of business as usual. We already noted that most of the so called SADCC projects are purely national in character. Their funding at regional donors conferences does not change their character as national, foreign and funded projects. Aid donors may thus be getting extra mileage by claiming that they are not helping only one nation but SADCC as a whole.

What does all this foreign presence entail for SADCC? We have already mentioned the contribution of foreign donors towards the depoliticization of the SADCC endeavour. This, as we suggest, will reduce SADCC cooperation to the least controversial projects of a technical nature and make it difficult for member states to embark on politically urgent and challenging developmental and distributional issues. Another effect has been the prominence of foreign experts in policy-making in SADCC institutions. The prominence of experts from donor countries who carry out virtually all the consultancies and studies has deprived the region of any autonomous technical character as a regional enterprise. We could argue that this is a logical outcome of the pragmatic decision to have a weak secretariat and to decentralize activities so as to avoid bureaucratization. Whatever the argument, one effect has been the reliance on expertise from outside the SADCC region. Ever since its inception, SADCC has had a group of expatriates as members of the London Steering Committee consisting of African diplomats in London and invited individuals in a position to provide specialist advice on assistance. The committee was later renamed the SADCC Liaison Committee; its primary function was 'following up requests for assistance'.[21] Indeed, there are probably more better organized teams of experts and bureaucrats in Europe who are fully occupied with SADCC matters than there are in Southern Africa. This may explain why aid donors seem so pleased with the weakness of the SADCC secretariat. In the absence of a strong supranational body, the foreign experts will hold sway in each speciality assigned to them with no corresponding regional expertise and institutional set-up to interfere with their work. But one sign of hope is that regional experts and officials are increasingly beginning to see the anomaly of the arrangement. Whether this awareness will translate itself into action is, of course, another matter.

Conclusion

Prognostication in social and political matters is a hazardous exercise and it is even more so in Southern Africa where all the scourges of Africa's history—racism, colonialism and underdevelopment—are still manifest. SADCC will survive at least in its present lethargic (or, if you like, pragmatic) form. Judging by the rather arrogant and self-congratulatory tone of the EEC's aid commissioner Mr Pisani at the recent donors' conference in Lusaka, foreign powers, and especially the EEC, will remain fully entrenched in SADCC affairs for many more years. Never have the countries of the sub-region been so collectively economically weak as they are today, with the world recession, the worst drought in years and South Africa's destabilization offensive. As a result, the economic policies they can pursue towards each other are circumscribed by the intentions of those who have so far come to their rescue. And these aid donors are not interested in anything more than the present SADCC format which does not facilitate the planned development of the region to meet the democratic demands of the people and create an ally for the forces of liberation in Namibia and South Africa.

Notes

1. *African Business*, no.53, January 1983, p. 16.
2. C. Hamilton, 'Capitalist Industrialisation in the Four Tigers of East Asia', in Limqueco and Macfarlane (eds), *Neo-Marxist Theories of Development*, Croom Helm, London, 1983 and Eddy Lee, *Export-Led Industrialisation and Development*, ILO Asian Employment Programme, Bangkok, 1981.
3. Ian Little *et al.*, *Industry and Trade in Some Developing Countries*, Oxford University Press, London 1970.
4. World Bank, *Towards Sustained Development in Sub-Saharan Africa: A Joint Programme of Action*, Washington, DC, 1984.
5. Tony Killick (ed.), *The IMF and Stabilisation: Developing Country Experiences*, Heinemann, London, 1984 and G. Williamson, *IMF Conditionality*, Institute for International Economics, Washington, DC, 1983.
6. A. Puyana, 'Economic Integration among Unequal Partners: The Case of the Andean Group', *Development and Peace*, vol.2, no.3, Autumn 1982.
7. Eken Anjara and Laker, 'Payments Arrangements and the Expansion of Trade in Eastern and Southern Africa', *IMF Occasional Paper*, no.11, IMF, Washington, DC, 1982.
8. C. Vaitsos, 'The Crisis in Regional Economic Cooperation (Integration) among Developing Countries: A Survey, *World Development*, vol.6, no.6, 1978.
9. R. Tironi, 'A Case Study of Latin America', in Dudley Seers (ed.), *Integration and Unequal Development: The Experience of the EEC*, Macmillan, London, 1980.
10. R.H. Green, 'Southern African Development Cooperation: From Dependence and Poverty Towards Economic Liberation', in C. Legum (ed.), *Africa Contemporary Record: 1981/82*, Africana Publishing Company, New York, 1981.
11. Douglas Anglin, 'Economic Liberation and Regional Cooperation in Southern Africa: SADCC and PTA', *International Organization*, vol.37, no.4, 1983.
12. Ibid.
13. Puyana, 1982.
14. Record of the Southern African Development Coordination Conference Summit Conference, Lusaka, 1980 (mimeo).

15. Vaitsos, 1978.

16. Ibid.

17. UNCTAD, *Transnational Corporations in World Developent: A Survey*, United Nations, New York, 1983.

18. John Lewis, 'Development Assistance in the 1980s', in R. Hansen (ed.), *US Foreign Policy and the Third World*, Overseas Development Council, Praeger, New York, 1982, pp. 123—4.

19. Christopher Stevens, 'Does Europe really have a Unique Role?', *IDS Bulletin*, vol.14, no.3, 1983.

20. Brown, 1982.

21. Anglin, 1983.

10. Regional Integration in West Africa: The Role of the Economic Community of West African States (ECOWAS)

Guy Martin

When in Lagos, Nigeria, on 28 May 1975 15 West African countries signed the Treaty establishing the Economic Community of West African States (ECOWAS),[1] hopes and expectations ran high among the African political and cultural elite, generally committed to the Pan-African ideal of regional and continental unity. In the first place, the sheer size of this vast economic grouping, with a total population of about 153 million and a combined Gross Domestic Product (GDP) of US$113.5 billion was impressive and augured well for the economic potential and future of the Community.[2] More significantly, ECOWAS was the first regional integration attempt ever to transcend the traditional historical and linguistic cleavage between French, English and Portuguese-speaking West African states. This was in keeping with the recommendations of the February 1979 OAU Monrovia Symposium on the future development prospects of Africa which, *inter alia*, called for 'the creation of an African common market based on progressive co-ordination and integration, which would evolve in the form of concentric circles reflecting the economic areas that currently exist on the continent'. ECOWAS was also consistent with the 1980 Lagos Plan of Action for the economic development of Africa, which proposed 'the eventual establishment of an African Common Market leading to an African Economic Community', optimistically by the year 2000.[3]

As the organization is about to celebrate its tenth anniversary, this seems an appropriate time to evaluate its achievements. A global analysis and evaluation of the nature, purpose, objectives and activities of ECOWAS will, of necessity, have to take into account both political and economic factors. Furthermore, such an undertaking implies the examination of a variety of related problems and questions: what is the significance and impact of the ECOWAS experiment in terms of the theory and practice of regional integration in Africa? How does ECOWAS relate to other intra- and extra-regional cooperative ventures in West Africa? What are some of the major problems and obstacles encountered by this experiment and how could they be overcome? Obviously, such wide-ranging and penetrating questions can only be adequately answered within the framework of existing or future full-scale studies of ECOWAS.[4] Within the limited scope of this paper, the present author can do no more than attempt to give some tentative and partial answers to these fundamental questions on the basis of a brief analysis of the institution's objectives and achievements.

The Theoretical Basis of Economic Integration in Africa

Economic integration is one of several strategies open to African states in their efforts to achieve economic growth and development. According to conventional neo-classical theory, economic integration is a means of expanding economic opportunities through specialization based on comparative advantage and economies of scale. Stated briefly, the main contention of this theory is that a customs union will be beneficial if on balance it is trade-creating and it will be harmful if it is trade-diverting. The core of the argument for integration is that so long as there are economies of scale to be obtained or so long as there are possibilities for specialization between countries on the lines of comparative advantage, industrialization to serve the wider regional market will be more efficient than industrialization within the confines of each national market.[5] Furthermore, neo-classical theory views economic integration as a gradual process evolving through successive stages. From its lowest to its highest forms, integration is said to progress through the freeing of barriers to trade (trade integration), the liberalization of factor movements (factor integration), the harmonization of national economic policies (policy integration) and the complete unification of these policies (total integration).[6]

In its classical form the theory seems to be of little or no relevance to Third World countries. Since trade diversion will obviously prevail over trade creation in Third World customs unions as the members shift from low-cost producers in the developed world to high-cost producers among their neighbours, there seems to be no rational economic basis for the creation of customs unions among developing countries.

This approach has been criticized on various grounds. First, it relies heavily on a number of neo-classical assumptions such as full employment, perfect competition, constant returns to scale, perfect internal mobility of factors of production and equality of private and social costs. These assumptions do not obtain even in developed countries, much less in developing countries. Second, the neo-classical analysis of economic integration is set within a purely static framework. In evaluating the desirability of economic integration among developing countries, the emphasis should be placed on dynamic rather than static effects. As Asante rightly points out, 'we should be concerned with the dynamics of economic growth and stress positive effects in the creation of regional markets on the developmental pace of member countries.'[7] Thus, 'while there could not be sufficient justification on a "purely static analysis basis" for the creation of a West African customs union, the contrary is the case on dynamic grounds.'[8] It is therefore obvious that Western theories of integration are inadequate for studying integration processes in Africa. Indeed, as Rothchild and Curry correctly observe, 'The Euro-based intellectual concepts and integration schemes, when strictly applied, have not proved to be adequate bases on which to construct integration in Africa.'[9]

As a partial answer to this kind of criticism, some socialist economists have tried to develop more universal concepts of economic integration. Thus the Hungarian economist Imre Vajda, discussing trade integration, introduces an important distinction between market integration and production and development integration. The former is defined as 'the guarantee of unhindered sale of each other's products within the framework of the social system of participating countries', while the latter is said to involve 'raising to an international level and programming the production of those branches of industry which... cannot be developed to an optimum size within national boundaries'.[10] We should keep these concepts in mind when discussing the objectives and achievements of ECOWAS.

ECOWAS: Goals, Objectives and Achievements

According to the terms of its treaty, ECOWAS' major goal is

> to promote co-operation and development in all fields of economic activity... for the purpose of raising the standard of living of its peoples, increasing and maintaining economic stability, of fostering closer relations among its members and of contributing to the progress and development of the African continent.[11]

This goal is to be realized by gradually achieving the following specific objectives:

1) trade liberalization and harmonization, notably the elimination of all tariff and non-tariff restrictions on trade among the member states and the establishment of a common customs tariff and a common commercial policy towards third countries;

2) the abolition of all obstacles to the free movement of persons, services and capital between member states; and

3) the harmonization of the agricultural, infrastructural, industrial, monetary and economic policies of the member states.[12]

As can be seen, this strategy is consistent with the neo-classical theory of economic integration, since integration is to progress through trade integration and factor integration to attain the ultimate aim of policy integration.

Five protocols were subsequently appended to the original Treaty. These protocols, signed at Lomé in November 1976, covered budgetary contributions, a fund for cooperation, compensation and development, the re-export of goods, rules of origin, and the assessment of revenue effects of trade liberalization. Still other protocols on non-aggression (April 1978) and the free movement of persons (July 1980) were later added.

In the area of trade, an eight-year liberalization programme, designed to achieve a free trade zone in West Africa by 1989, was approved in May 1980 and officially started on 28 May 1981 (the period May 1979 to May 1981 being considered as a customs consolidation period). Studies on regional telecommunications and currency convertibility have been commissioned and programmes on postal, industrial and agricultural cooperation have been devised. A common defence pact has also been drafted.

Inevitably, ECOWAS was initially 'preoccupied with staffing, undertaking studies and carrying out "rule-carrying decisions" necessary for its institutionalisation', as Ralph Onwuka reported in 1980. [13] Such a description remains valid today. Indeed, as Daniel Bach rightly observes, 'it is increasingly unlikely that the institutional development achieved by ECOWAS amounts to much more than the self-proliferation of bureaucracy in the face of the repeatedly delayed implementation of Community policies.' [14] Up to the end of 1984 no significant progress had been made in the priority area of trade liberalization. The other areas of Community policy are at a standstill and seem to be caught in the quicksands of proliferating and never ending studies. Thus, of the several studies commissioned by ECOWAS mentioned above, only one had reached the implementation stage by mid-1983, namely the $35 million PANAFTEL telecommunications project.

It has by now become clear that ECOWAS has achieved none of its short- and medium-term objectives, not to speak of its long-term goals. In view of such a dismal record, we are led to wonder whether the organization has actually moved beyond the planning stage: is it not merely a paper organization? Before assessing the potential for survival of this institution, it seems necessary to examine the reasons, both economic and political, for its failure to realize even its minimal objectives.

ECOWAS: Political and Economic Problems and Difficulties

While economic and political problems will be treated separately for the purposes of analysis, both categories overlap to a considerable extent and should be used concurrently in any comprehensive analysis of ECOWAS' predicament.

Economic Difficulties

Assuming that we accept the premises on which the neo-classical theory of economic integration are based and supposing that maximal integration is achieved, the fact remains that member states will necessarily differ in size and capabilities. Thus, they will demonstrate dissimilar abilities to take advantage of specialization, economies of scale, augmentation of factor input and opportunities to improve market structures. Economic integration, then tends to yield unequal benefits. Consequently, deliberate policies designed to distribute more evenly whatever net benefits might accrue to the partner states must be devised. [15] The ECOWAS Fund for cooperation, compensation and development, which was established for precisely that purpose, did not start operating until 1980. Even then, it could not properly discharge its duties because of delays in the payment of contributions by member states and institutional malfunctions.

Other economic difficulties result from the colonial legacy. Although these are well known, they are worth reiterating. First, there is the problem of extroverted, rather than introverted, communication and telecommunication links. It is common knowledge that transport and communication links in West Africa are predominantly geared towards the former metropolis rather than towards the neighbouring countries. Similarly, seven of the member states of ECOWAS belong to the franc zone and, as such, are structurally linked to the French economy, via the French franc, whereas all other member states have their own, national currencies. This accounts to a large extent for the persistence of former colonial trade and economic relations, particularly among the francophone member states of ECOWAS.[16] In general, ECOWAS member states are still very much economically dependent on the metropolitan powers. It is clear, therefore, that 'external dependence... constitutes one of the main obstacles to the creation of a West African regional economy through laissez-faire approaches to integration and the operation of effective corrective measures.'[17]

Problems relating to the equitable distribution of the benefits of economic integration should also be considered. Who, we should ask, are the ultimate beneficiaries of economic integration in West Africa? In the absence of deliberate restrictive policies, ECOWAS has apparently stimulated flows of foreign capital and technology by transnational corporations.[18] The latter are thus among the primary beneficiaries of economic integration in the sub-region as they are in a better position to reap the benefits from the specialization, economies of scale and enlarged markets protected by common external tariffs. Foreign business interests are linked with various interest groups within West Africa such as private businessmen and the bureaucratic elite in charge of the national economy. These groups also benefit, though to a lesser extent, from the windfalls of economic integration within ECOWAS. Ultimately, the major beneficiaries of ECOWAS seem to be the foreign businessmen and the West African comprador bourgeoisie; the net losers are the bulk of the population in the member states in whose name and to whose benefit integration is supposed to be realized. Assuming, therefore, that ECOWAS were functioning as planned (which, as we have seen, is not the case), its operation would actually result in increased economic and social inequalities within the sub-region. A further problem arises from multiple institutional membership, and thus divided loyalties among ECOWAS member states, to the extent that six of them also belong to CEAO and all of them are party to the Lomé convention.

The Economic Community of West Africa (*Communauté économique de l'Afrique de l'Ouest*/CEAO) was created in April 1973 by six francophone countries—the Ivory Coast, Senegal, Niger, Burkina Faso, Mali and Mauritania—with the active support of France. The idea was to revive the defunct French West Africa Federation under a new guise by encouraging economic relations among the member states. On the basis of the apparent institutional successes and economic achievements of CEAO, its members

175

proclaimed their willingness to preserve their identity and supposed acquired advantages (*les acquis*) within the wider and much looser ECOWAS economic framework. They also aserted their determination not to be swallowed up by the Nigerian economic giant.[19] To the extent that CEAO and ECOWAS have similar objectives, multiple membership raises the issue of primary allegiance and conflicting loyalties. Contrary to Bach's argument, there does not seem to be any rational economic basis for the continued existence of CEAO within the sub-region.[20] Indeed, it has been demonstrated that trade relations among member states remain extremely marginal (around 7% of total trade) while trade relations between CEAO and the EEC and France remain at a high level (around 40% of total trade).[21] This seems to provide grist to the mill of those who argue that CEAO is a purely neo-colonial institution which should be scrapped in order to allow ECOWAS to be fully operational.[22]

All ECOWAS member states are also party to the Lomé II convention of 31 October 1979. These states are among the 64 African, Caribbean and Pacific states linked to the European Economic Community (EEC) through contractual arrangements on trade and aid cooperation. The problem of potential conflict of interests arises in this context, too. Reasoning within the framework of conventional economic integration theory, Sam Olofin convincingly argues that the trade liberalization provisions of the two treaties are a possible area of conflict; this has implications for the static welfare effects of the two arrangements. While acknowledging the fact that such static gains may be limited in the short run within ECOWAS, given the existing trade structure of member countries, Olofin shows that the trade liberalization provision in the Lomé convention would further limit the scope for realizing such gains.

> On the trade-creating side, ECOWAS countries as associate members of EEC for example may find it cheaper to import from the EEC what they could produce at higher costs within ECOWAS or vice-versa. On the trade-diverting side the EEC countries are bound to increase their imports from associate ACP members including ECOWAS countries or vice-versa, at the expense of the minimal trade that may have been taking place between Anglophone-Francophone ECOWAS countries. Both ways, the trade-creating and trade-diverting effects of Lomé are likely to stifle and hamper the realisation of similar effects within ECOWAS.[23]

Indeed, it does not seem that the creation of ECOWAS has resulted in any significant increase in intra-regional trade so far. Intra-ECOWAS trade represented only 2.1% of total ECOWAS exports in 1970, 3.1% in 1976, 3.8% in 1979 and 4.6% of such exports in 1981.[24] At the same time, trade between ECOWAS and the EEC has remained significant, averaging around 50% of total ECOWAS trade (exports and imports) during the period 1976 to 1980.[25] More fundamentally, ECOWAS and the Lomé convention differ widely in their approach to economic cooperation and development. Whereas the Lomé convention aims at promoting a close and permanent relationship based on cooperation, complementarity and interdependence, ECOWAS pursues a strategy of political autonomy and economic independence. The Lomé convention haŝ been shown to constitute a purely neo-colonial arrangement designed to institutionalize Africa's dependency, to strictly control its development and to better organize its exploitation. [26] As such, it is basically at variance with the ECOWAS strategy of collective self-reliance. [27] In view of the fundamental incompatibility of the two sets of cooperative arrangements, ECOWAS member states will at some point be faced with a problem of choice and will have to decide whether they want to give priority to intra-regional or to extra-regional economic relations.

Political Problems

Although there is a general consensus among the African political elite on the need and desirability of economic and political integration and African unity, serious disagreement exists on various points such as the level and strategy of unification, the scope of cooperation and the period of transition to, and conditions and consequenses of, unification. A more fundamental area of disagreement has to do with the political philosophy underlying unification strategies, i.e. whether they should lead to capitalism or socialism. [28] Indeed, the variety of political ideologies and related development strategies to be found in West Africa might account for the clear trend towards the disintegration or stagnation of regional integration in the sub-region. In this respect, ECOWAS is no exception, with political regimes ranging from the militant and vocal socialism of (pre-1984) Guinea, Burkina Faso and Benin to the self-proclaimed capitalist haven of Ivory Coast, via the puritanical Islamic state of Mauritania. It is certainly one of the organizations's greatest challenges to attempt to create some sense of common ideal and purpose out of such a great variety of political ideologies.

It is generally argued that one of the main preconditions of economic development in the Third World (be it in a national or regional context) is political stability. Such stability usually results from a strong, authoritarian political leadership based on a firm and sound institutional basis and sanctioned by popular elections held at regular intervals in order to give the regime a democratic label. Once they have established their credentials as stable and democratic political systems, Third World regimes will presumably be in a position to attract the flows of (mostly Western) foreign public aid and private investment necessary to their economic growth and development.

Viewed against this background the West African political landscape is chaotic. During the 22 years (1963-85), the sub-region witnessed 30 military coups which left eleven of sixteen ECOWAS member states with military governments. This progressive militarization of ECOWAS is an additional source of instability in the sub-region; military regimes are generally insecure (because of the permanent threat of possible counter-coups and because they create a potentially dangerous civilian/military cleavage among the various states of the area. [29] This negatively affects the chances of success of any regional integration scheme in West Africa.

Another potential area of conflict arises from what we can refer to as the Nigerian factor. With a population of 87.6 million and a GDP of US$70.8 billion (representing 57.2% of the total population and 62.3% of the combined GDP of ECOWAS), [30] Nigeria emerges as the dominant economic and political power in the sub-region and within the organization. This power is reflected in the fact that Nigeria contributes up to 32.8% of the total budget of ECOWAS. This has led to suspicion and charges that Nigeria is wielding its power within ECOWAS to promote its own national, economic and political interests to the detriment of community interests. According to this line of argument, Nigeria views ECOWAS essentially as a protected market for the manufactured products of its industrial sector. Consequently, it views with hostility economic relations between francophone West Africa and the EEC or France to the extent that these relations distort trade patterns within the community to the detriment of Nigeria's economy. [31]

While there is undoubtedly an element of truth in this argument, we should beware of the persistent tendency on the part of Western (and particularly French) press and media to use it in order to perpetuate the Nigeria/francophone West Africa cleavage in typical, divide-and-rule neo-colonial fashion. It is true that Nigeria's dramatic expulsion of over one million 'illegally' established ECOWAS immigrants in January 1983 did not help to promote its image in the sub-region and did create a serious human, moral and political crisis within ECOWAS (to say the least). This distasteful and regrettable episode notwithstanding, it could be argued that Nigeria is to some extent capable of assuming political and economic leadership within the sub-region: 'A sound financial economic situation realized in Nigeria could thus be a guarantee to the viability, credibility, and effectiveness of ECOWAS.' [32] Assuming that such a leadership would be acceptable to a majority of West African states, it is clear that, for the moment at least, its economic, social and political preconditions are far from being realized.

Equally divisive, from the point of view of the internal cohesion of ECOWAS, is the play of extra-regional power politics. France's continuing economic and political dominance over its former colonies in the sub-region is a permanent irritant and a major obstacle to the progress of economic and political integration in West Africa. Such institutions as CEAO, engineered and supported by France, may have to be scrapped before any progress towards integration with ECOWAS can be realized. In addition to its unimpressive economic record, this organization is showing clear signs of institutional decay: its top-level administrative staff are currently under investigation for alleged mismanagement and fraudulent budgetary and financial practices. [33] Similarly, ECOWAS member states' economic and political links with the EEC within the Lomé convention have been shown to be incompatible with intra-ECOWAS cooperation and integration. This is because the Lomé convention tends to perpetuate and institutionalize dependent, neo-colonial North–South links to the detriment of the collective self-reliance and South–South strategy of ECOWAS. In this respect, the extension of the Lomé convention into the 1985-90 quinquennium (Lomé III) would undoubtedly damage the chances of progress toward unification within ECOWAS.

Finally, we should consider the question of the extent and degree of political commitment to and support of ECOWAS on the part of the ruling elite in the member states. While such commitment is not lacking at the purely official and declamatory levels, it does seem to be somewhat wanting when it comes to concrete decisions and actions, as ECOWAS' poor record amply demonstrates. Indeed, we could take a pessimistic view of the situation and ask whether there is any future for this organization. A more realistic and practical approach would be to suggest ways and means of giving substance and meaning to the goals and objectives of ECOWAS. In other words, we should try to see what could and should be done in order to make ECOWAS an effective and efficient institution.

Conclusion: What Future for ECOWAS?

In view of the obvious failure of the laissez-faire approach to integration, we could argue that the only way out of the West African states' neo-colonial predicament—with its attendant problems of underdevelopment and dependency—would be through the setting up of a federation of socialist states. This would make possible the adoption of production and development (as opposed to market) integration and create the necessary economic and political preconditions for a genuinely self-reliant, independent strategy of development.

While this would certainly be a most desirable outcome, it is an extremely unlikely one under the prevailing circumstances given the economic and political forces at work in the sub-regional, regional and international environments. At the regional level, hopes of expanding ECOWAS to include other states from Central Africa have been momentarily dampened by the creation in Libreville (Gabon) on 18 October 1983 of an Economic Community of Central African States (*Communauté économique des Etats de l'Afrique centrale (CEEAC)* which includes ten mostly French-speaking Central African states under a joint Cameroon/Zaire leadership.[34] Possible cooperation between ECOWAS and CEEAC is predicated upon the actual progress toward integration realized within each organization. Were CEEAC to remain a purely paper organization, ECOWAS could try to persuade some of its member states to join the West African grouping, provided it demonstrates more dynamism and shows more tangible achievements than has been the case so far.

Another way for ECOWAS to become more efficient would be to increase cooperation in non-controversial, social, economic, scientific and technical areas, in typical neo-functional fashion. It could thus concentrate, as is presently the case, on cooperation in postal, transport, communication and telecommunication infrastructure. This could possibly be extended to what Domenico Mazzeo calls the service sector, namely training and research, control of foreign investment and transfer, adaptation and development of technology.[35] More specifically, special attention should be given to the

179

regulation of direct foreign investment and technology transfer by multinational corporations within ECOWAS. In this respect, the broad and far-reaching Decision 24 on the Common Treatment for Foreign Capital, Trademarks, Patents, Licensing Agreements and Royalties adopted on 31 December 1970 by the Andean Group could serve as a model law. [36]

Whatever options are considered, the ultimate beneficiaries of integration should be the majority of the population in the member states, not sectional or private interests. In the final analysis, any real progress towards greater economic and political integration in West Africa—and hence the survival and success of ECOWAS—is predicated upon the emergence of an able, honest and dedicated political leadership truly committed to the ideals of Pan-Africanism and African unity and able and willing to translate these into concrete decisions and actions for the benefit of their people.

Notes

1. The 15 original signatory states were Benin, Gambia, Ghana, Guinea, Guinea-Bissau, Ivory Coast, Liberia, Mali, Mauritania, Niger, Nigeria, Senegal, Sierra Leone, Togo and Burkina Faso. Cape Verde became the 16th member state in July 1977.

2. World Bank, *World Development Report 1983*, Oxford University Press, New York 1983, pp. 148, 152; *L'Etat du Monde*, La Découverte, Paris, 1984, pp. 302—3.

3. OAU, *What kind of Africa by the year 2000*? International Institute for Labour Studies (IILS) Geneva, 1979, p. 18; OAU, *Lagos Plan of Action for the Economic Development of Africa 1980-2000*, IILS, Geneva, 1981, p. 6.

4. Recent full-length studies of ECOWAS include Uka Ezenwe, *ECOWAS and the Economic Integration of West Africa*, C. Hurst and Co., London, 1983 and S.K.B. Asante, *The Political Economy of Regionalism in Africa; A Decade of ECOWAS*, Praeger, New York, 1986.

5. The classic exposé of the theory is Jacob Viner, *The Customs Union Issue*, Carnegie Endowment for International Peace, New York 1950. For an extension of the theory to the case of developing (and specifically African) countries, see Arthur Hazlewood, *Economic Integration: The East African Experience*, Heinemann, London, 1975, Chapter 2, pp. 10—20. Trade creation is considered beneficial as the elimination of protection for domestic production *vis-à-vis* producers in the partner countries permits the replacement of high-cost domestic products with lower-cost partner-country products. In turn, trade diversion may be detrimental both to member and to non-member countries.

6. See Bela Balassa, 'Types of Economic Integration,' in Fritz Machlup (ed.), *Economic Integration: Worldwide, Regional, Sectoral*, John Wiley, London, 1976, p. 17.

7. S.K.B. Asante, 'ECOWAS, the EEC and the Lomé Convention', in Domenico Mazzeo (ed.), *African Regional Organizations*, Cambridge University Press, Cambridge, 1984, p. 176.

8. S.K.B. Asante, 'Economic Integration in West Africa: Some Critical Issues', *Africa development*, vol.V, no.2, 1980, p. 69.

9. Donald Rothchild and Robert L. Curry Jr., *Scarcity, Choice, and Public Policy in Middle Africa*, University of California Press, Berkeley and Los Angeles, 1978, p. 199.

10. Imre Vajda, 'Integration, Economic Union, and the National State', in I. Vajda and M. Simai (eds), *Foreign Trade in a Planned Economy*, Cambridge University Press, Cambridge, 1971, p. 35.

11. *Treaty of the Economic Community of West African States* signed in Lagos on May 28 1975, Article 2 (1).

12. Ibid., Article 2 (2).

13. Ralphh Onwuka, 'The ECOWAS Treaty: inching towards implementation', *The World Today*, vol.XXXVI, no.2, 1980, p. 58.

14. Daniel C. Bach, 'The Politics of West African Economic Co-operation: CEAO and ECOWAS', *Journal of Modern African Studies*, vol.XXI, no.4, 1983, p. 613.

15. On this point, see Rothchild and Curry, 1978, pp. 200—4.

16. For a more detailed discussion of this problem, see Guy Martin, 'Les Fodements historiques, économiques et politiques de la Politique africaine de la France; du colonialisme au Néo-coloniamisme', *Genève-Afrique*, vol.XXI, no.2, 1983, pp. 49—56.

17. S.K.B. Asante, 1980, p. 72.

18. This is the argument developed, somewhat inadequately in our opinion, by Ely Fall, 'L'Intégration économique de l'Afrique de l'Ouest confrontée aux solides liens de dépendance des états africains de l'extérieur', *Africa Development*, vol.IX, no.1, 1984, pp. 40—55.

19. Indeed, Daniel Bach argues that CEAO was created as a deliberate attempt to counterbalance Nigerian influence within West Africa (1983), p. 605.

20. Ibid., pp. 617—21.

21. H. Kouvahé Amoko, *La Promotion des Echanges Commerciaux au sein de la CEAO*, graduate thesis, Yaounde 1981, pp. 173—4.

22. At a recent ECOWAS summit meeting (Cotonou, Bénin, 28-29 May 1982), President Houpouët-Boigny of the Ivory Coast acknowledged that CEAO would one day have to disappear (*Africa Contemporary Record 1982/83*, Africana Publishing Company, New York, p. C33).

23. Sam Olofin, 'ECOWAS and the Lomé Convention: an Experiment in Complementary or Conflicting Customs Union Arrangements?', *Journal of Common Market Studies*, vol.XVI, no.1, 1977, pp. 69—70.

24. UNCTAD, *Handbook of International Trade and Development Statistics 1983*, New York, 1983, Table 1.14, p. 51.

25. Guy Martin, *The Political Economy of African-European Relations from Yaoundé I to Lomé II, 1963-1980* (unpublished PhD dissertation, Indiana University, 1982, p. 493.

26. Ibid.; Guy Martin, 'Africa and the Ideology of Euro-Africa: Neo-colonialism or Pan-Africanism?', *Journal of Modern African Studies*, vol.XX, no.2, 1982, pp. 221—38.

27. S.K.B. Asante, 1984.

28. Abdul-Aziz Jalloh, Regional Integration in Africa: Lessons from the Past and Prospects for the Future', *Africa Development*, vol.I, no.2, 1976, p. 45.

29. The five remainign civilian regimes in ECOWAS are those of Cape Verde, Gambia, Ivory Coast, Senegal and Sierra Leone. The traditional distrust of civilian regimes, such as that of Ivory Coast's Houphouët-Boigny, *vis-à-vis* their military

counterparts, is well known.

30. World Bank, 1983, pp. 148, 152.

31. Such an argument is put forward, *inter alia*, by Daniel Bach, 1983, p. 610.

32. Aguibou Y. Yansané, *Decolonization in West African States with French Colonial Legacy*, Schenkman, Cambridge, MA, 1984, p. 401.

33. On these developments, see *Jeune Afrique* no.1244, 7 November 1984, pp. 34—6; *Jeune Afrique* no.1245, 14 November 1984, pp. 46—53.

34. CEEAC member states are Burundi, Cameroon, Central African Republic, Chad, Congo, Gabon, Equatorial Guinea, Rwanda, Sao Tomé et Principe, and Zaire. Equatorial Guinea (Spanish-speaking) and Sao Tomé et Principe (Portuguese-speaking) are the only non-French-speaking countries of this organization.

35. Domenico Mazzeo, 'Conclusion: Problems and Prospects of intra-African cooperation, in D. Mazzeo (ed.), *African Regional Organizations*, Cambridge University Press, Cambridge, 1984, pp. 237—8.

36. On this question, see Lynn K. Mytelka, 'Regulating Direct Foreign Investment and Technology Transfer in the Andean Group', *Journal of Peace Research*, vol.XIV, no.2, 1977, pp. 155—84 and 'Multinational Corporations and Regional Integration in the Andean Group and the CMEA', *Development & Peace*, vol.III, no.1, 1982, pp. 77—95.

11. Food for Security and Peace in the SADCC Region

Archie Mafeje

Southern Africa Coordination Conference (SADCC) and Regional Food Security*

The problems of military and political insecurity in Southern Africa are well-known, as is the threat to regional and international peace posed by South Africa. However, peace and security for any people includes a wide range of social conditions necessary for existence. In the SADCC region food security ranks high among these. Since the late 1970s, because of a combination of natural and social factors, the food situation has deteriorated to an alarming extent. Chronic food shortages not only threaten the internal security of each country but have added a new dimension to the economic dependence of the SADCC countries on South Africa. It was in recognition of the implicit dangers of such dependence that SADCC was formed in 1980 and a common regional strategy was adopted.

The SADCC countries are committed to freeing themselves from the legacy of colonial economic structures that make it difficult for them to meet their national and regional food requirements. In agriculture one of these structures is the existence of relatively few, capital-intensive commercial farms or estates producing high-value crops for external markets alongside a multitude of small, undercapitalized farms which produce chiefly for immediate subsistence with little or no marketable surplus. While the former have adequate access to markets and necessary inputs, the latter often have little or no access to these vital inputs. Thus those producing cash or export crops have incentives, while those who are able to produce only enough to feed themselves—although they make up the majority of the population and have the ability to feed the rest—are unfortunately without the incentive or means to do so.

Consequently, the importing of basic foods is increasing, resulting in a loss of foreign exchange that could otherwise be better employed. In general this has meant low levels of internal economic activity; incomes and employment have remained lower and undernutrition higher than they would otherwise be.

*This essay is based largely on *SADCC Agriculture Towards 2000*, Rome, 1984 which the author prepared for FAO as a consultant. We are grateful to FAO for allowing us to include it in our collection.—Editor

The necessity to import food has resulted in dependence on external sources of supply. This runs contrary to any notion of economic independence or self-reliance.

Dependence on South Africa

The Republic of South Africa has been the principal source of supply of imported food for some of the countries of the region. However, this dependence has opened the door for South Africa to penetrate further the economies of the region, so that it has become economically dominant—especially in those countries which are its immediate neighbours—through investment and direct or indirect participation in many worthwhile economic activities.

The level of dependence varies from country to country. The economic links are especially strong in the case of Botswana, Lesotho and Swaziland (the BLS countries) which are members of the Southern African Customs Union of 1910. This agreement provides for the free movement of goods from South Africa to member countries and greatly influences industrial and agricultural production, prices and wage levels as well as patterns of trade. Consequently, trade, particularly imports, between the BLS countries and South Africa is more important than with the other countries of the region. Total imports from South Africa amounted to 97% of Lesotho's total in 1979, 91% of Botswana's in 1981 and 90% of Swaziland's during 1980 and 1981. Imports from South Africa by the other countries of the region are considerably smaller, e.g. 15% in the case of Zambia.

With regard to exports from the region to South Africa, in terms of value Zimbabwe is the most important country with more than 21% of its total exports going to South Africa in 1981. Two-way trade between South Africa and all African countries totalled US$1.5 billion in 1981, almost 75% of which consisted of exports from South Africa whose most important African trading partner is Zimbabwe.

Economic Liberation

To meet head on the challenge of South Africa in their internal affairs and to obtain long overdue economic liberation, the heads of state of nine countries of Southern Africa met in April 1980 in Lusaka, Zambia, to formally establish the Southern African Development Coordination Conference (SADCC). The nine states were Angola, Botswana, Lesotho, Malawi, Mozambique, Swaziland, Tanzania, Zambia and Zimbabwe. At this same summit meeting the Lusaka Declaration, commonly referred to as 'Southern Africa Towards Economic Liberation', was issued calling, *inter alia*, for a reduction of external dependence, especially on South Africa, and the mobilization of resources to carry out national, inter-state and regional policies designed to promote regional cooperation.

At present, the SADCC countries have far closer economic ties with the outside world than with one another. This situation arises from a variety of reasons—historically determined—such as inadequate transport and other physical infrastructure, lack of a regional market and inconvertible currencies. The volume of trade between the SADCC countries is minimal, amounting to about US$290 million in 1981, representing only 5.1% of total exports and 3.9% of total imports by member countries. Zimbabwe, owing to its central location and diversified production, was by far the most important intra-regional exporter accounting for 45% of the total. Next in order of importance were Zambia, Botswana, Mozambique and Malawi, each accounting for from 15 to 11% of intra-regional exports. Last are Swaziland, Tanzania, Lesotho and Angola, which together account for only 6% of the intra-regional exports and 7% of the imports. Table 11.1 shows intra-regional trade within SADCC.

However, unlike the export composition outside the region which consists of a few basic commodities, the product mix in intra-regional trade is more diversified. This would suggest that intra-regional trade has a promising potential to diversify and expand.

The economies of the SADCC states are exceptionally vulnerable to external or natural factors over which they have no control, such as recurrent drought and torrential rains. Since 1978 each of the SADCC countries has suffered from abnormally severe weather conditions for one or more years. The agricultural years since 1981-2 have been extremely dry as a result of one of the worst droughts of the century which has resulted in sharp declines in production and a consequent increased demand for food imports. Being dependent on primary commodity exports, the SADCC countries have suffered considerably from the world recession, high interest rates and fluctuations in international commodity prices.

By international standards SADCC countries are small producers of export crops. They are therefore unable to influence international prices; instead they are price-takers. As a result, the amount of foreign exchange they are able to earn can fluctuate sharply from year to year, often culminating in negative balances of trade as well as of payments. Without exception, the balance of payments for all nine SADCC countries was negative in 1981.

Angola's traditional surplus in its balance of payments came to an end in 1981 owing to war and low prices for its three major export commodities—coffee, petroleum and diamonds. In 1982, the situation in Botswana was similar owing to the low prices and sales of diamonds, its most important commodity.[1] Malawi was not much different because of low prices for tobacco, sugar and tea; in Swaziland it was sugar-cane and cotton, in Zambia, copper and cobalt, in Zimbabwe, tobacco, cotton and sugar-cane and in Tanzania, coffee and cotton.

Yet the role of agriculture in the region is, and will continue to be, important for achieving both food self-sufficiency and earning foreign exchange for investment in economic development. Agriculture, including livestock, is the base of the regional economy and provides the livelihood for 60% of the population. For the foreseeable future much industrial development

Table 11.1
Trade Within SADCC Region 1981 (US$ millions)

Destination / Origin	Angola	Botswana	Lesotho	Swaziland	Mali	Mozambique	Tanzania	Zambia	Zimbabwe	Total Exports
Angola	—	NA	—	—	—	0.05	—	—	—	0.05
Botswana	8.94	—	0.03	0.01	0.10	6.60	0.01	1.21	21.74	38.64
Lesotho	—	0.02	NA	—	—	0.11	—	—	0.01	0.14
Swaziland	—	0.07	—	NA	—	5.10	0.11	—	4.34	9.62
Malawi	—	0.57	—	—	NA	1.58	0.05	4.22	22.11	28.53
Mozambique	0.79	0.01	—	—	3.05	NA	3.98	—	24.49	32.32
Tanzania	—	0.01	—	0.34	0.17	3.99	NA	1.88	0.26	6.65
Zambia	—	0.52	—	—	5.01	0.08	3.39	NA	35.57	44.57
Zimbabwe	1.16	40.25	1.74	2.02	20.81	10.23	1.54	51.04	NA	128.79
Total imports	10.89	41.45	1.77	2.37	29.14	27.74	9.08	58.35	108.52	289.31

Note: — indicates no trade: NA indicates figures not available.

Source: FAO, *SADCC Agriculture Toward 2000*, 1984.

will be in agro-industries or processing local agricultural products.

With few exceptions, the post-colonial period has been one of national reconstruction and consolidation within the individual countries of the region; emphasis has been laid on promoting agricultural and agro-industrial exports in order to earn foreign exchange for development. Such a policy has in general been at the expense of the traditional agricultural sector and subsistence producers. In recent years there has been a marked regional decline in the growth rate of both food and export crops. The annual growth rate of the former declined from 2.4% (characteristic of the 1960s) to 1.7% in the 1970s; while the latter declined even more from 0.4% in the late 1960s to −4% in the 1970s. Yet, regardless of which of the two sub-sectors declined by the greater amount, the sombre fact remains that the growth rate of food production has progressively lagged behind that of the population, which is in excess of 3% annually. In other words, SADCC countries are increasingly less able to feed themselves and rely progressively more on food imports.

By the end of this century the population of SADCC countries will be more than 107 million, as compared with the present figure of 60 million. If catastrophe is to be averted the agricultural sector must produce the food needed for this expanding population. Double the present amount of food will have to be grown by the year 2000 to meet minimum requirements, not only for the larger population but for improved basic nutritional levels and the increased demands arising from higher incomes. To plan and execute such an ambitious programme governments will have to give the problem greater priority than before if the objectives are to be met on time.

By tackling this problem on a regional basis, SADCC will exercise a central role in the struggle for economic independence so necessary to complement and strengthen the economic independence of its nine member countries. SADCC is fully aware of the magnitude of the task ahead and has clearly defined its food strategy for which Zimbabwe has been given special responsibility under the Lusaka Declaration of 1980. The Lusaka Declaration calls for the mobilization of domestic and regional resources to carry out national and regional policies aimed at reducing external dependence and building regional cooperation. Three implications of the Lusaka Declaration will be examined specifically for food and agriculture. The performance of the agricultural sector has been unsatisfactory in the past and is untenable for the future. But it is feasible, from an agronomic and economic point of view, to improve agricultural performance and to increase production. National resource mobilization and regional cooperation are required to promote the goal of increasing agricultural self-sufficiency and reduce external dependence in the SADCC region. The purpose of this section is to demonstrate why this is both necessary and feasible for the future.

The Present Food Crisis

The food security of the SADCC countries is precarious. The needs of survival alone have increased food imports to the extent that external dependence has become onerous for most of the countries of SADCC. This situation has developed against the backdrop of deteriorating terms of trade, long-term neglect of the agricultural sector, the more recent phenomenon of a world recession and the worst drought of the century. The present situation is one of crisis. Continuation of recent trends portends disaster.

The total annual cereal production of the SADCC countries was estimated by the FAO at 9.3 million tonnes in 1981—a good year. Owing to drought, however, which has affected all SADCC countries (with the exception of Malawi) for the last three years, the aggregate production of cereals fell in 1982 by more than one million tonnes to 8.2 million tonnes, and in 1983 by almost that much again to 7.3 million tonnes.

Future prospects are gloomy. At present all the SADCC countries, with the exception of Malawi, are on FAO's list of 24 African countries facing a major food crisis.

The cereal import requirements of the region are estimated to have risen to 2.1 million tonnes in 1983-4—the highest level ever—or about 700,000 tonnes more than the actual imports of the preceding year and over one million tonnes more than the annual cereal imports for 1976-7-1978-9. Several countries have been unable to increase their commercial cereal imports owing to a deterioration in their balance of payments; food aid pledges have not risen sufficiently to meet the gap. Hence, severe food shortages affect the region.

Despite critical needs, food aid shipments of 522,000 tonnes in 1982-3 had declined from deliveries of 765,000 tonnes in 1981-2. Since last year, the overall deficit of the region in cereals has increased further, with food aid requirements likely to increase to over one million tonnes in 1983-4. So far, total food aid pledges recorded by FAO total 920,000 tonnes, leaving unfilled food aid requirements of about 100,000 tonnes. Even if this gap is closed by last minute emergency arrangements and additional food aid becomes available to minimize human suffering, it will at best be a temporary solution since food aid alone will not insulate the region from recurrent food shortages.

At the same time, the effects of the drought on SADCC economies, still strained by the world recession and the low prices of export commodities, are potentially disastrous. SADCC has estimated the cost of direct agricultural losses and of diverting limited financial resources to fund extra food imports at close to US$ one billion for the six worst-hit countries. Longer-term costs in lost output and exports and in rehabilitating agricultural schemes in progress are incalculable.

But SADCC's need is not only for short-term relief. It is above all for funds and assistance to initiate action on wider focused food security programmes and strategies to ensure that the region is not so badly affected the next time the rains fail to materialize. The current food crisis must be considered within the framework of long-term trends and prospects in the agricultural sector.

The Recent Past

Even before the present food crisis, the average person in the SADCC region had considerably less access to food than ten years before and average dietary intakes were below nutritional requirements. Though food production in the region grew at a respectable average annual rate of 2.0% over the period 1966-81 (Table 11.2) compared with a 1.1% growth in the region's total agricultural outputs, the population of the region increased in the 1970s at an average annual rate of 3.4%, one of the highest growth rates in the world.

Table 11.2
Annual Growth Rates of Agricultural and Food Production, 1966-81 (percentages)

Country	Agricultural Production Total	Per Capita	Food Production Total	Per Capita
Angola	-3.8	-5.9	0.8	-1.4
Botswana	1.4	-1.1	1.4	-1.1
Lesotho	0.6	-1.7	0.6	-1.7
Malawi	2.9	-0.2	1.9	-1.1
Mozambique	-0.1	-2.6	0.3	-2.1
Swaziland	4.7	2.1	4.2	1.7
Tanzania	1.9	-1.1	2.5	-0.4
Zambia	2.7	-0.3	2.8	-0.3
Zimbabwe	3.5	0.1	2.2	-0.1
Total SADCC	*1.1*	*-1.7*	*2.0*	*-0.8*

Source: FAO, *SADCC Agriculture Toward 2000*, Rome, 1984.

The increase in population growth has nullified gains in production, with the result that on a per capita basis regional food production has declined at an annual rate of 0.8%, while agricultural output has fallen by 1.7% per year. Only Swaziland and Zimbabwe have registered gains in per capita agricultural production.

Where production has increased, it has been because of an expansion of the area under cultivation; yields per hectare have on the whole stagnated or declined. With the exception of Zimbabwe, yields in the SADCC region average about half of those in Asia and Latin America for cereals and are 30% lower for roots and pulses.

Partly as a reflection of the deteriorating production pattern and partly as a result of the high rate of urbanization (and also because of the overvalued exchange rates favouring imported cereals) food imports to the region soared even before the latest crisis caused by drought and recession. Large cereal imports, especially of wheat and rice, reflect and simultaneously stimulate the longer-term changes taking place in the food consumption pattern of the region away from traditional staples. Where wheat is concerned, the trend keeps pace with that of urbanization, reflecting emulation of the dietary habits of urban dwellers and abetted by food aid. The shift gives rise to concern because it involves cereals that either cannot be grown economically or are more costly to produce than millet, sorghum and maize.

The food security implications of longer-term agricultural trends must also be seen in light of external constraints, reflecting international trade problems in general and the problems of agricultural trade in particular. In spite of the fact that some countries of the region (e.g. Zambia) depend on non-agricultural exports (i.e. copper), while others (e.g. Malawi) depend on agricultural exports for over 90% of their merchandise export receipts, there are a number of common problems.

In terms of current values, the total merchandise exports of the SADCC countries grew at 8.3% per year and agricultural exports at 6.7% per year for the period 1970-82. However, in real terms, the overall volume of exports declined at an average rate of 0.6% per year while agricultural exports fell by 2.1% for the same period, notwithstanding the comparatively favourable access of most SADCC countries to the EEC market. At the same time the current value of total merchandise imports grew much faster, at an annual growth rate of over 11%, while in real terms the volume of total merchandise imports declined by 1.3%. Partly as a result of the worldwide recession, the region's terms of trade have deteriorated and, according to the World Bank, the terms of trade of most of the agricultural export commodities of the region are likely to further deteriorate in the near future, with inevitable effects on the region's foreign exchange earnings.

SADCC countries have attempted to suppress imports (with the exception of food grains); their success is evidenced by the negative rates of growth of imports in real terms over the period 1970-82. Even so, the overall trade balance of the region shows a major shift from surplus to deficit, while its current account deficit grew almost sixfold during the 1970s. As a share of GDP, the current account deficit of the SADCC region increased from about 3% in 1972 to more than 8% in 1979, resulting in the virtual exhaustion of foreign exchange reserves, growing indebtedness and continuing difficulties in obtaining credit. Consequently, governments have been forced to rely heavily on ad hoc external assistance to fulfil basic needs.

In the case of food needs, a heavy and growing dependence on food aid (amounting to almost half the cereal import requirements for 1983-4) has been the major outcome. Even in the pre-drought years, food aid for the region accounted for about one-third of the total food imports in the late 1970s, compared with only 10% for developing countries as a whole. Food aid for the SADCC region grew from 20,000 to 40,000 tonnes of cereals in the early 1970s, to an estimated record level of about one million tonnes in 1983-4. Maize accounted for approximately 50% of the total.

The current food crisis in Southern Africa is part of a wider agricultural crisis—basically a production crisis—reflecting a variety of causes of both internal and external origin. As will be shown later, the continuation of past trends in demand and production could lead to a staggering fivefold increase in the net cereal import requirements of the region by the year 2000. A deficit of this dimension would clearly be beyond the capacity of the region to finance. But even a high-performance scenario, implying major policy and financial efforts to step up food production above the present trend, might not bring about the desired food self-sufficiency at the regional level, at least not by the end of the century (the cereal import gap remaining at just above two million tonnes). It would, however, produce essential improvements in the agricultural production base and reverse a decline in per capita output.

While the deterioration in the international trading climate of the SADCC countries is unlikely to be corrected substantially during the 1980s, a still more determined effort for agricultural reform is necessary by the governments of the region. The issue is not just one of a priority to supply food versus a priority to export agriculture, since both are equally necessary and urgent, but of absolute priority to the agricultural sector as a whole as a *sine qua non* of regional food security.

Present and Future Trends

The preceding review highlights the need for policy action to turn round the situation in the agricultural sector. This need can be quantified further by extending the trend scenario (T scenario) to the year 2000. On the other hand, two other counterfactual scenarios are presented to suggest that the continuation of present trends is not immutable. Instead, it is perfectly feasible to improve agricultural performance sufficiently to handle most of the problems likely to occur in the absence of corrective measures.

The FAO, using certain major driving forces in the economy such as population and income growth (Table 11.3), has constructed three hypothetical future scenarios. The T scenario is based on a simple extrapolation of past performance and has disastrous implications for the SADCC countries in terms of food security and external dependence. It serves to highlight the proposition that an unchanged policy in the agricultural sector is untenable. The T scenario serves also as a benchmark for the other two scenarios of the study, the Improved Performance (IP) scenario and the High Performance (HP) scenario. The IP scenario begins with relatively modest rates of overall GDP growth, assumes a gradual recovery from past disruptive trends and implies a considerable effort by national governments to strengthen the agricultural sector. It emphasizes the fact that even after significant progress has been made in improving agriculture in the SADCC region, the problem of food security and external dependence will not have gone away by the end of the century.

In contrast, the HP scenario solves most of the problems of the agricultural sector but it also assumes that concerted action will be taken by national governments favouring agriculture under conditions of a generally vigorous rate of growth for the economy as a whole. The HP scenario amounts to a description of the conditions to be fulfilled in individual countries to reach a

Table 11.3
SADCC Population and GDP

	1970	1980	1990	2000
Population (m)	43	60	81	107

	Annual Growth (%)			
	1970-80	1980-90	1990-2000	1980-2000
Population	3.4	2.9	2.9	2.9
GDP				
Improved Performance	(1.9)	3.6	4.5	4.0
High performance		4.8	7.0	5.9

Source: FAO, *SADCC Agriculture Toward 2000*, Rome 1984.

high, but technically feasible, level of self-sufficiency and self-reliance by the end of the century. It assumes optimistic gains in productivity, taking into account limits in land and water resources; but at the same time it assumes a massive concentration of human, financial and capital resources on agricultural development. In this sense, the HP scenario quantifies the requirements of a costly, but certainly feasible, restructuring of the agricultural sector in SADCC countries to solve the vital problem of food security and external dependence in agricultural trade. On the other hand, the IP scenario is a second-best alternative in the event that all the favourable conditions assumed in the HP scenario cannot be fulfilled simultaneously.

The quantitative results of the T scenario summarize, with a few main variables, the situation to 2000 if recent trends, coupled with population growth (but unencumbered by further exogenous shocks such as wars and unusual weather conditions), continue.

Demand and Production

Fuelled by high population growth, total agricultural demand has grown rapidly in the past decade and a half. An annual rate of 2.9% amounts to a 50% growth in total demand during the period (Table 11.4). Production growth, on the other hand, was sluggish at 1.1% amounting to a total increase of 20% during the fifteen-year period. While per capita production declined by 1.7% annually, demand grew by 1.1%, signalling an increased dependence on agricultural imports.

Projection of these trends into the future is unsettling. Demand will grow to the end of the century at an annual rate of 3.5%, doubling base-year demand levels. Production will grow slightly faster than the historical levels, at 1.4% per year. The total increase in production to 2000 is 30% above the base year, thus meeting only one-third of the total increase in demand. In per capita terms, this results in a 1.5% annual decline in production as compared with a

0.6% increase in demand, thus further widening the gap to be filled by agricultural imports.

Table 11.4
Trends in Agriculture: Total and by Commodity Group

| | Annual Growth Rates (%) | | | |
| | Demand | | Production | |
	1966-81	*1979-81 to 2000*	*1966-81*	*1979-81 to 2000*
Total Agriculture	2.9	3.5	1.1	1.4
Per Capita	0.1	0.6	−1.7	−1.5
Cereals	3.1	3.4	1.6	1.0
Basic food	2.7	3.5	1.7	1.8
Livestock products	3.3	4.3	2.3	1.7
Other food	2.7	3.1	2.1	1.5
Total Food	*2.9*	*3.5*	*2.0*	*1.5*

Source: FAO, *SADCC Agriculture* 2000, Rome 1984.

Self-Sufficiency and Trade

The disparity between the growth of demand and production as projected would inevitably result in a drastic deterioration in self-sufficiency and in catastrophic trade balances. As Table 11.5 shows, from a net exporter of agricultural commodities (1979-81), the SADCC region would become a net importer in the aggregate and for almost all commodities, with rapidly deteriorating self-sufficiency. Only half of all cereals demanded would be produced domestically. Net cereal imports would increase more than fivefold from 1.5 million tonnes in 1979-81 to over 8 million tonnes in 2000.

Only one of the five exporting countries in 1980, Zimbabwe, would remain a net exporter by the year 2000 and at the same time be self-sufficient in basic foods. Other indicators tell an analogous story: total agricultural imports are projected to increase by over 10% annually, while agricultural exports would virtually stagnate at a 1% annual growth. In financial terms, the trend projections entail an unsustainable drain of resources: in 2000 almost US$4 billion (at 1980 prices) would be needed for net agricultural imports. This is equivalent to 40% of the gross value of agricultural production in 2000. By contrast, net exports in 1969-71 equalled 22% and in 1979-81, 9% of the gross value of agricultural production.

Table 11.5
Trends in Self-Sufficiency (percentages)

	1969-71	*1979-81*	*1990*	*2000*
Total Agriculture	131	108	89	72
Cereals	96	80	64	52
Basic food	97	89	73	62
Livestock products	106	94	75	74
Other food	110	102	89	57
Total Food	*106*	*95*	*80*	*64*

Source: FAO, *SADCC Agriculture 2000*, Rome 1984.

Food Consumption and Nutrition

There has been considerable variation in the average calorie intake in the SADCC countries over the last decade. Estimates of the 1979-81 per capita calorie supply range from 1,796 kcal per day in Mozambique to 2,548 kcal per day in Swaziland. For the region as a whole nutritional intake has remained nearly constant at levels below the average nutritional requirements. It is estimated that at present about a quarter of the SADCC population is at risk of undernutrition. Under the T scenario, the prospects for nutrition for the remainder of the century are predictable from the increasing gap between production and demand. Undernutrition will increase dramatically unless substantial increases in food imports take place. For basic foods (cereals, roots, tubers and pulses) which provide over two-thirds of the calorie intake, the trend increase in imports over the period 1980-2000 is dramatic. The estimated increase in cereal imports alone is fivefold. Should SADCC countries be able to finance such massive imports the likely outcome is a negligible net increase in average calorie intake. It remains almost 10% below requirement (on average) and by 2000 about a quarter of the population would still be afflicted by undernutrition. Should SADCC countries be unable to finance imports, the results are too grave to contemplate.

Alternatives to the doomsday trend scenario exist if the appropriate policy actions are taken promptly. This section presents in tabular form a comparison of the three scenarios, the T, IP nd HP, prepared by the FAO. The discussion centres on the IP and HP scenarios—not because either is likely to happen in a pure form, but to emphasize that feasible and acceptable outcomes lie somewhere in between. The growth in total food demand is derived from population growth and the growth of per capita food demand. The latter is determined by such factors as changes in dietary habits, food prices and individual purchasing power. The change in income becomes the main variable component determining changes in demand under alternative scenarios (see below).

Table 11.6
Alternative Scenarios: Annual Growth Rates, 1979-81 to 2000 (percentages)

	Demand			Production		
	T	IP	HP	T	IP	HP
Total Agriculture	3.5	4.0	5.0	1.4	3.2	4.8
Per capita	0.6	1.1	2.1	-1.5	0.3	1.9
Cereals	3.4	4.2	4.8	1.0	3.9	5.6
Basic food	3.5	3.6	4.2	1.8	3.3	4.5
Livestock products	4.3	4.5	6.4	1.7	3.9	5.6
Other food	3.1	3.5	4.3	1.5	3.2	4.4
Total Food	*3.5*	*3.9*	*5.0*	*1.5*	*3.5*	*5.0*

Source: FAO, *SADCC Agriculture 2000*, Rome 1984.

The IP scenario shows a growth in total agricultural demand of 4% per year and in per capita demand of 1.1% per year, 0.5% higher than for the T scenario. By commodity groupings, the growth rates are higher for livestock products than for basic foodstuffs. This entails a shift in the direct versus indirect use of cereals. Under the HP scenario, the direct use of cereals for food would fall from 81% in 1979-81 (or 125 kg per capita per year) to 75% by 1000 (or 145 kg per capita), while the use of cereals for animal feed would have increased to 13% of the total cereal demand (or 25 kg per capita), as compared with 7% in 1979-81 (or 11 kg per capita). This reflects the improvement in diet resulting from an increase in per capita income.

The improvement in the patterns of demand growth is reflected in all SADCC countries. The past and projected growth rates of demand for each SADCC country are above the average levels of growth for all Africa. While the growth in demand under the IP scenario is relatively modest (compared with the T scenario), the growth in production is dramatic: 3.2% per year as compared with 1.4%, which almost amounts to a doubling of production over 1979-81 levels. Such production growth would nearly match the growth in demand, implying that the gaps between the two would shrink in relative terms and be brought back to manageable proportions.

The strong increase in production takes place in all SADCC countries and for all commodity groups (Figure 11.1). A sustained growth in agricultural production of 3.2% per year is high and calls for major efforts in mobilizing resources and re-orienting policies. This is certainly feasible. Agriculture in most SADCC countries is still at a relatively low level of development and in several countries ample resources still remain to be developed. The how of this development will be explored later.

Figure 11.1

PRODUCTION INDICES FOR SADCC REGION BY 2000
(1976-81 = 100)

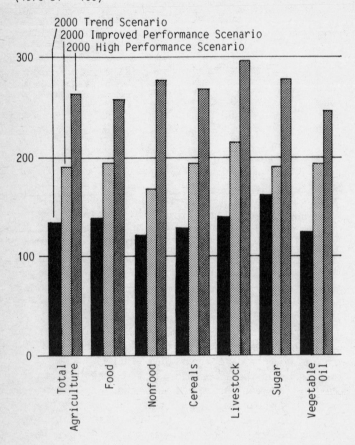

Self-Reliance

Although no alternative scenario leads to full self-sufficiency in food for the region by 2000, the IP scenario will enable the SADCC region to remain almost self-reliant in the agricultural sector as a whole and to check the dramatic drop in the self-sufficiency ratio projected in the continuation of trends. Self-sufficiency in total agriculture reaches 96% and in total food 88% (Table 11.7). While the imports of most commodities would increase (Figure 11.2)—with net imports of cereals rising from 1.5 million tonnes in 1980 to 5.0 million tonnes in 2000—the impact will be partly offset by an increased export availability of non-food commodities.

Table 11.7
Alternative Scenarios: Self-Sufficiency Ratios

	1979-81	1990			2000		
		T	IP	HP	T	IP	HP
Total Agriculture	108	89	102	110	72	96	107
Cereals	80	64	76	84	52	75	91
Basic food	89	73	85	91	62	84	95
Livestock products	94	75	91	95	74	84	81
Other food	102	89	101	106	57	97	104
Total Food	*95*	*80*	*92*	*97*	*64*	*88*	*94*

Figure 11.2

NET AGRICULTURAL TRADE OF SADCC REGION UNDER ALTERNATIVE SCENARIOS
(US $ billions, 1980)

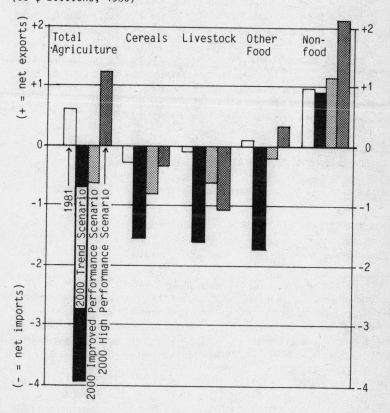

While net agricultural imports would increase at 6.8% per year (against 5.6% for 1966-81), agricultural exports would increase at 2.4% per year (5.4% under the HP scenario). Consequently, the SADCC region would become a net agricultural importing region of about US$0.6 billion by 2000 (at 1980 prices), mainly owing to increased food imports with a slight improvement in the export availability of non-food commodities. Under the HP scenario, the SADCC region would remain a net exporter of agricultural commodities with a doubling of the export availability of non-food commodities and with manageable imports in the food sector (e.g. two million tonnes of net cereal imports).

Diet

The increase in demand projected in the alternative scenarios reflects the nutritional requirements of the increased population and a component available to improve per capita food consumption over base-year intake levels. Population growth claims over 70% of the increase in demand under the IP scenario. The balance would be available to raise the average per capita calorie intake level in the SADCC region by 15%, from 2,109 calories in 1979-81 to 2,435 calories in the year 2000 (Table 11.8). The year 2000 average calorie intake would be 4% above average requirements, but undernutrition would not be eradicated since the distribution of calorie intake would be likely to continue to be unequal (which governments would be ill-advised to ignore).

Table 11.8
Alternative Scenarios: Nutritional Indicators

Average Calorie Supply	*Improved Performance*			*High Performance*	
	1979-81	*1990*	*2000*	*1990*	*2000*
Kcal/person/day	2,109	2,312	2,435	2,412	2,744
Percent of average requirements	90	99	104	103	118

Dietary composition would change slightly in favour of high value crops and commodities; the share of basic foodstuffs (cereals, roots, tubers and pulses) in calorie supply would decline from 73% in 1979-81 to 67% in 2000, the balance being taken up by the share of sugar, oil-seeds, vegetable oil and livestock products whose portion of the calorie supply would increase in 2000 to 26% from 20% in 1979-81. The latter is in line with the pattern seen for Africa as a whole.

Food Aid

As mentioned, the importance of food aid has been growing in Southern Africa, along with a rising dependence on cereal imports. Dependence has risen from near self-sufficiency fifteen years ago to about 80% self-sufficiency in 1980. Currently, about a fifth of the region's consumption is supplied from imports (1.5 million tonnes on average in 1979-81), one-third of which is in the form of food aid. As net cereal imports increased in the aftermath of the drought, so did food aid, amounting at present to over 40% (or 920,000 tonnes) of total imports.

Cereal self-sufficiency could well decline further by the end of the century. While under the T scenario only 52% of cereal requirements would be met from domestic production, the self-sufficiency ratio would rise to 75% under the IP scenario, with five million tonnes of cereals being imported, and to 91% under the HP scenario, with cereal imports of two million tonnes. The SADCC pre-feasibility study of regional food aid puts the region's food aid requirements in cereals at 1.9 million tonnes in 1995, reduceable under certain assumptions to 1.5 million tonnes.[2] Year 2000 food aid requirements under the IP scenario could rise to over 3.5 million tonnes if the indicated high demand growth materializes and export earnings are insufficient to raise commercial imports of food grains.

One way or another, the region will continue to depend on food aid for part of its cereal requirements for some years to come, though under the HP scenario estimated food aid requirements in 2000 of about 400,000 tonnes would be lower than the 1979-81 average. This is consistent with the situation that could also develop under favourable production circumstances in other parts of the world.

There are two major policy implications of the large and growing size of food aid in the SADCC region. First, food aid in the form currently provided carries a risk (although no conclusive evidence is available) of encouraging an undesirable shift in consumption from basic staples to crops with a high technological content (such as wheat and rice) which are more common food aid commodities. Through these induced changes in dietary preferences, food aid may be a disincentive to local food production in the long run.

Second, food aid—whether as emergency aid or to assist economic development—has never been meant as a permanent means of offsetting structural food deficits in recipient countries. Yet food aid to the SADCC region has been systematically meeting the region's growing deficit in cereals. The alternative would have been mass hunger and starvation. But the fact remains that food aid has unacceptable implications for developing countries.

Need for Restructuring Agriculture

The agricultural sector will have to undergo profound changes in order to arrest trends and work toward the IP scenario. Such changes are quantified in this section in terms of major agricultural inputs.

The near doubling of production between 1980 and 2000 in the IP scenario results by three-fifths from an increase in yield levels and a quarter from the expansion of arable land, with the balance coming from increases in cropping intensity. This pattern is contrary to current experience in the SADCC region, where most production increases have resulted from area expansion. The limits of economical land expansion are fast being reached and, as a result, the area under cultivation will expand by only 16%, from 33.1 million hectares to 38.4 million hectares (Table 11.9). Along with an expansion inland, average

Table 11.9
Inputs to Crop and Livestock Sectors

	IP 1980	HP 2000	2000	IP 1980 to	Annual Growth Rate (%) HP 2000
Arable land (million ha)	33.1	38.4	43.3	0.8	1.4
Harvested land (million ha)	17.3	23.0	27.2	1.5	2.3
Cropping intensity	0.5	0.6	0.6	—	—
Arable irrigated land (000 ha)	385.0	595.0	735.0	2.3	3.3
Fertilizer (000 tonnes)	356	1,277	1,720	6.6	8.2
Total power (person-day equivalent, million)	2,224	3,243	4,102	1.9	3.1
Tractors (000)	67	128	232	3.4	6.2
Draught animals (000)	2,464	2,817	2,817	0.7	0.7
Gross Investment (1980 US$billion)					
Crops		1.2	2.0	2.4	4.1
Livestock		1.0	1.6	3.7	4.6
Storage and marketing		0.2	0.4	3.2	5.6
Total of OECD/DAC narrow definition of agriculture[a]		2.4	4.0	3.0	4.4
Transport and first-stage processing		1.0	1.4	3.9	5.6
Total		*3.4*	*5.4*	*3.2*	*4.7*

[a] Excludes assistance for forestry, rural development, rural infrastructure, agro-industry, fertilizer production and regional and river projects.

cropping intensity will have to increase by 15% from 0.52 to 0.60.[3] The major change in the IP scenario is in improvements in yields. The average crop yield per harvested hectare would rise by 40% by 2000. More specifically, the average cereal yield is expected to increase from 0.9 tonnes per harvested hectare in 1980 to 1.3 tonnes in 2000. Likewise, maize yields would rise from 1.0 to 1.4 tonnes and groundnut yields from 0.6 to 1.0 tonnes per hectare.

These are major, but not impossible, improvements requiring substantial additions to current and capital inputs. The use of non-agricultural inputs would have to increase almost fourfold with fertilizer use growing at a rate of at least 6% and mechanization by over 3% per year. This growth in mechanization, while increasing tractor density from one tractor per 494 arable hectares in 1980 to one for every 297 hectares in 2000, would not be at the expense of labour but would rather compensate for the small increase in the number of available draught animals.

In fact the share of labour in total person-days required in crop production would remain constant at about 85%, and the person-day equivalent for tractors would account for only 5% of the total person-day equivalent supplied in 2000. With a projected increase in the agricultural labour force of 1.5% per year (from 15.7 million in 1980 to 21.4 million in 2000) and an estimated growth of 2.0% per year in person-days needed in crop production, the average utilization rate of labour in crop production would rise from 110 days per year in 1980 to 130 days per year in 2000. Considering the seasonal distribution of labour requirements in agriculture, seasonal labour shortages are likely to persist in certain countries, despite the overall low average number of labour days involved.

Massive investment would be needed for land development and the modernization of the crop and livestock sectors in general. By 2000, gross annual investment requirements would reach about US$1.2 billion for the crop sector and US$1.0 billion for the livestock sector in constant 1980 dollars (Table 11.9). The replacement of obsolete capital stock would account for approximately a quarter of that amount. Year 2000 gross investment in primary agriculture would represent about 14% of the estimated agricultural GDP in 2000.

External Resource Flows to Agriculture

Like most developing countries, SADCC members rely on both private and official external resources to supplement domestic savings in financing their investment programmes and to close emergency consumption gaps. Individually, the SADCC countries have borrowed considerably over the last ten years from both private international capital markets and official sources, with the result that their total debt (disbursed and undisbursed) increased at current prices by 17% per year in the period 1973-82, amounting to about US$11 billion at the end of 1982. About one-third of the total debt is owed to private creditors (from supplier credits and loans from financial markets). The share of private creditors in the total debt varies from 5% for Swaziland to 72% for Zimbabwe and accurately indicates the relative capacity of the various countries to borrow on commercial terms.

Although this debt level is not excessive in relation to the development and growth potential of SADCC economies, some countries are currently facing serious problems in meeting repayment and service charges, owing both to internal and external factors. As a result, the creditworthiness of several SADCC countries has suffered. This increases reliance on official external resource flows to meet both short-term needs, such as food aid, and longer-term development finance requirements.

Development Assistance

The commitments of official development assistance (ODA) for capital investment in narrowly defined agriculture have grown rapidly since the 1970s,[4] amounting to US$322 million by 1982 or an increase at current prices of more than 60% over 1980 (Table 11.10). Over 90% of this assistance is provided on concessional terms, of which 45% is in the form of grants of total ODA

Table 11.10
Capital Commitments of Development Assistance to Agriculture, Narrow Definition (US$ millions)

Donor	1980	1981	1982	Average 1980-82
Total concessional and non-concessional commitments	*200.0*	*309.0*	*322.1*	*277.2*
Bilateral	124.2	146.2	205.6	158.6
DAC/EEC	124.2	142.3	188.0	151.5
OPEC	—	3.9	17.6	7.1
Multilateral	75.8	163.3	116.5	118.6
World Bank	40.6	102.6	59.6	67.6
African Development Bank	29.0	40.2	16.7	28.7
International Fund for Agricultural Development	6.2	10.5	40.2	19.0
OPEC Multilateral	—	10.0	—	3.3
Concessional commitments (ODA)	*182.9*	*272.4*	*311.4*	*255.5*
Bilateral	117.4	140.9	204.2	154.2
DAC/EEC	117.4	137.0	186.6	147.0
OPEC	—	3.9	17.6	7.2
Multilateral	65.5	131.4	107.2	101.3
World Bank	40.6	90.6	59.6	63.6
African Development Bank	18.7	30.3	7.4	18.8
International Fund for Agricultural Development	6.2	10.5	40.2	18.9
OPEC Multilateral	—	—	—	—

commitments for all sectors of the economy; the share of agriculture (narrow definition) is about 10%.

The distribution of capital commitments for development assistance within the agricultural sector is given in Table 11.11. Activities included in the narrow definition of agriculture absorb just over one-half of the total capital commitments to agriculture broadly defined. A substantial share, about 45% of the total over the 1980-82 period, goes to activities indirectly linked to agricultural production, such as forestry and rural development and infrastructure. As compared to the rest of Africa, this share is relatively high, primarily because of the needs of the SADCC countries to build a rural development infrastructure.

Table 11.11
Distribution of Capital, Commitments of Assistance within Agriculture, 1980-82 (percentages)

Activity	1980	1981	1982	Average 1980-82
Land and water	4	a	2	2
Research, training and extension	6	3	5	5
Current inputs	7	14	3	8
Agricultural services	7	14	8	10
Crop production	14	12	6	11
Livestock production	2	1	1	1
Fisheries	3	8	4	5
Agriculture unallocated	12	11	20	14
Agriculture, narrow definition	*55*	*63*	*49*	*56*
Forestry	1	1	4	2
Manufacturing inputs	a	0	1	a
Agro-industries	10	14	6	10
Rural development and infrastructure	31	22	37	30
Regional and river development	3	0	3	2
Agriculture, broad definition	*100*	*100*	*100*	*100*

a Indicates a level of less than 0.5%

It is more difficult to place a value on technical cooperation from external sources. It is estimated, however, that the planned expenditure for 1980 for technical cooperation by both multilateral and bilateral donor agencies was US$130 million.[5] Such assistance is generally provided on concessional terms in the form of grants. The level of expenditure on technical cooperation in agriculture is high compared to the expenditure on capital assistance. This is another indication of the extent of the existing needs of the SADCC community to improve its technical and managerial capacity in agriculture.

It is expected that the reliance of the region on external capital assistance will remain high. This is the result of the substantial capital requirements for overall development and specifically for restructuring the agricultural sector. Gross investment in agriculture (narrow definition) is projected to reach an annual level of US$2.4 billion in the year 2000 under the IP scenario and calls for greater resource mobilization efforts than in the past. Within this framework, development assistance will play an important role in helping SADCC countries restructure their agriculture along conventional lines. But the implicit indebtedness and dependence constitutes a political and economic handicap which the SADCC countries can ill afford in the long run.

International Trade Agreements

Food security in SADCC countries, both individually and collectively, could be greatly strengthened through international trade arrangements designed to ensure that adequate food supplies are available in world markets. This would reduce the effects of production instability in global markets and facilitate access by importers to the supplies they require. Unfortunately, the economic and political climate required for multilateral action of this nature is unfavourable at present.

An international grains arrangement, with the traditional objectives of stabilizing commercial markets and assuring access to supplies, could make an indirect but significant contribution to food security. However, despite the urgings of UNCTAD, there are no signs that the chief participants in the cereals trade are prepared to envisage such arrangements, following the collapse of negotiations in 1979 and the expiry in 1986 of the present International Wheat Agreement.

For most SADCC countries, food security depends largely on their ability to earn enough foreign exchange to finance food imports. Once again, the prospects for improving the export capacity of developing countries through international trade arrangements are not promising. The results obtained at UNCTAD VI in 1983 were poor and little progress has been made in GATT toward trade liberalization in agricultural products. Global negotiations on North-South issues have not made any progress.

Finally, existing international arrangements for meeting emergency needs remain unsatisfactory. Various improvements to the current system were suggested by FAO recently, including the strengthening of the International Emergency Food Reserve (IEFR), the pre-positioning of stocks at strategic points to speed up the provision of emergency relief and the adaptation of earlier recommendations on standby arrangements for meeting large-scale food shortages.

Regional Cooperation: Scope and Limitations

The standard case for economic cooperation at the regional level rests on several general conditions being met partly or fully, including: strong political affinities among neighbouring countries, a complementarity of resources, geography and productive structures and a smallness of local markets. In addition, regional cooperation is increasingly regarded as at least a partial answer to the lack of progress on a number of global issues that bear on relations between developed and developing countries. Food security considerations add another dimension to the standard arguments for economic regionalism; the developing countries increasingly emphasize the need for closer ties between themselves as a means of enhancing their collective food security.

Apart from these standard arguments, there are special reasons for SADCC cooperation. First and foremost, one of the basic goals of SADCC is the reduction of external economic dependence in general and on South Africa in particular. This can only be accomplished by intensifying intra-regional trade and cooperation. Second, the outside world has begun to look at Southern Africa as a region and as a negotiating partner, developing special policies toward it—as witnessed by EEC interest (with six SADCC countries already members of the Lomé Convention) and other European states. To match such external policies and attitudes, it is essential that SADCC develop regional strategies and a common negotiating position.

Notwithstanding considerable *a priori* benefits, regional cooperation is not always easy in practice. It requires complex negotiations and the striking of a delicate balance between conflicting regional and national interests. The conflict usually revolves around the problem of the equitable distribution of costs and benefits in joint undertakings. Many past attempts at regional cooperation have foundered on this obstacle. For example, it was a conflict of interest over the distribution of net benefits that led to the breakdown of the East African Community in 1970.

So far the SADCC approach to regional cooperation has been to try and avoid the pitfalls of confrontation by concentrating on projects and programmes that are national in character and by setting aside potentially divisive issues. In fact, the name SADCC indicates a flexible form of cooperation, since coordination implies only a little more than operating in harmony—rather than separately—for mutual benefit. SADCC has distinguished itself from all other regional ventures by delegating functional responsibilities for specific programmes and projects to designated countries and by concentrating on projects that do not involve governments in making priority choices between regional and national interests.

Whether this original approach to regional cooperation can be sustained indefinitely under the present political organization of SADCC and in the absence of an overall development plan strategy for the region as a whole remains to be seen. Beyond a certain point, basic issues are difficult to avoid and regional cooperation becomes a formidable task, especially if it involves economic integration and policy harmonization, the creation of new regional structures and regional orientations or establishing inter-sectoral links that cut across national borders.

There is no doubt, however, that a good deal of progress can be made on food security matters in a manner consistent with the preferred, pragmatic approach. The essence of the food security problem facing SADCC is how to strengthen the food security of its member states by stimulating the production of basic foods without undermining their export potential and balance-of-payments position. Objectives have to be achieved while trying simultaneously to reduce dependence on the outside world. The task may appear daunting; but it is essential and urgent, especially in the face of the current food crisis which poses a growing threat to millions of people in Southern Africa who are exposed to hunger and malnutrition.

Regional Cooperation for Food Security

SADCC's food strategy has the following objectives:[6]

● To satisfy the basic needs for food of the whole population of the region and to improve food supplies to the people progressively, irrespective of the specific economic situation of each person or their position in society.

● To achieve national self-sufficiency in food supply in order to free the region from the constraints imposed by the present situation of external dependence.

● To eliminate the periodic food crises that affect areas or countries in the region and which, besides having catastrophic social consequences, reinforce dependence and underdevelopment.

The first stage of a comprehensive programme for the region to attain these objectives has been elaborated by the government of Zimbabwe, the country entrusted with the responsibility of coordinating SADCC activities in food security. The following ten feasibility and pre-feasibility projects have been identified for execution by different bodies, of which several have already been implemented:

Technical Assistance for Coordination on Agrarian Issues
Early Warning System for Regional Food Security
Regional Resources Information Systems
Inventory of Agricultural Resource Base
Regional Food Reserve
Regional Food Aid
Regional Food Marketing
Post-harvest Food-Loss Reductions
Food-Processing Technology
Recruitment and Retention of Professional and Technical Staff in Agricultural Ministeries in the Region

While indicating major problems and possible approaches to their solution, these topics raise other questions. Even though additional studies and information can be useful, especially in technical fields, the basic problems of sub-Saharan Africa, including Southern Africa, have been extensively analysed over the years and discussed in numerous publications and reports by FAO, the World Bank and other agencies. It is not a lack of knowledge of basic facts and remedies that constitutes a constraint to food production in the region. Rather, it is the agricultural policies adopted by the various governments.

SADCC has identified several study topics other than those listed above that are equally relevant to the central issue of food security. These topics include: animal disease control and agricultural research (both delegated to Botswana for coordination); soil and water conservation and land utilization (delegated to Lesotho); fisheries and forestry (Malawi); transport and communications (Mozambique); energy (Angola); and trade (not yet allocated).

Even though SADCC has established a system for technical consultation among member states covering some areas of agrarian concern, major uncertainties still remain at this stage. Who is to coordinate additional studies with those commissioned under the food security heading? What is the operational value of the studies already completed? How soon will others be available? How will the studies interact, particularly regarding the food security issue? How will they be evaluated? And, above all, what will be their follow-up at national and regional levels? Finally, it is essential that the various projects be integrated eventually into an overall regional policy for food security.

Once the first stage of the programme for the region has begun, the scope of regional food security can be significantly expanded through SADCC cooperation, especially in the production and flow of supplies. There are certain production problems (e.g. pest control) which cannot be solved without cooperation at the regional level. Unused food production capacity could be activated if another country in the region provided a guaranteed market. It might be easier to use production incentives that have already been successfully adopted elsewhere in the region. Agricultural practices vary from country to country, but certain lessons about the use of new technology, the effectiveness of an extension system, the success in using new seeds, the reduction of post-harvest losses and the suitability of certain pesticides or biological pest control measures can be drawn on and adapted to advantage in other areas of the region. Experimentation and agricultural research on a regional basis may prove particularly rewarding.

Where the flow of supplies is concerned, the scope of regional cooperation expands greatly. Through joint regional efforts a maximum stability of supplies and markets can be assured, both with respect to fluctuations in domestic food production and periodic gluts and shortfalls in world markets. More specifically, concerted regional action can provide early warning of the advent of drought, crop failure or plant disease; can help deficit countries to obtain imports more quickly from surplus countries within the region; result in economies in procurement and the movement of supplies within the region; improve the bargaining position of developing countries in international markets and provide easier and more reliable access to food reserves within the region at times of shortages.

The establishment of national stocks providing full insurance against domestic crop failures may not be feasible in all countries because of the high costs of setting up and maintaining food stocks. However, relatively modest national stocks of a size required to meet minimum consumption requirements temporarily can be secured through commercial imports or food aid. Such minimum stocks are an essential element of a sensible supply stability policy at the country level and should be established, together with an effective early warning system capable of alerting policy-makers to potential changes in the national food supply situation.

Regional cooperation in the field of food security should be built from modest beginnings. Most of the regional food security arrangements currently in operation are still at an early stage with little experience to draw upon. Apart from this, the scarcity of necessary infrastructure, qualified personnel and expertise is another reason for proceeding slowly. The scarcity of financial resources hinders national action and is a major constraint to regional efforts.

In due course it would be useful for the SADCC region to establish direct links and mutual arrangements with other regional schemes for collective self-reliance in food security, such as Caribbean Community (CARICOM); Permanent Inter-State Committee on Drought Control in the Sahel (CILSS); Association of South-East Asian Nations (ASEAN); Latin American Economic System (SELA); or the Arab Organization for Agricultural Development. Such links could initially include an exchange of practical experience gained in formulating and implementing various regional food security schemes and the operational problems encountered.

Regional Cooperation and Intra-regional Trade

Another important area for regional cooperation is intra-regional trade. The present level of trade among SADCC countries is minimal, amounting to about US$290 million in 1981, representing only 5.1% of total exports and 3.9% of total imports. Zimbabwe, owing to its central location and diversified production structure, is by far the most important exporter by the region. In 1981 it accounted for 45% of exports. Next in importance were Zambia, Mozambique, Botswana and Malawi, with between 11% and 15%, while Swaziland, Tanzania, Lesotho and Angola were collectively responsible for 6% of intra-regional exports and 7% of imports. Unlike the composition of exports outside of the region, intra-regional trade is quite diversified, suggesting that it has potential for further development.

There are at present many obstacles to increasing intra-regional trade. The lack of exchangable currencies and existing demand and supply structures tends to militate against the exchange of merchandise across the borders of member states. In contrast to Western Europe, where market forces reinforce and integrate traditional complementarities of production structures through commodity trade and capital movements across national frontiers, in Southern Africa market forces do not themselves create processes of exchange and integration.

While the process of constructing basic demand and supply structures is a long-term proposition, it is a worthwhile task. With an area of approximately 15 million km², a population of over 50 million and with vast agricultural, fishery and mineral resources, Southern Africa has great potential for intra-regional specialization and exchange. Moreover, much can be done within the framework of SADCC to eliminate some of the obstacles to intra-regional trade. The recently established preferential trade area (PTA) for East and Southern African states with proposed tariff preferences of 10 to 70% on a common list of imports, may help to some extent. On the whole, however, efforts should first be concentrated on production, rather than on trade liberalization, with trade following rather than leading new production patterns. New patterns of production could be fostered through negotiated agreements on medium-term import-demand and export-supply guarantees and on pricing formulas.

There is a definite trade-off between increasing intra-regional trade and reducing the external dependence of the region. As has been pointed out, by the year 2000 the SADCC region could become a net importer of agricultural commodities. There is no need, however, for assumed imports to add to external dependence, since negative trade balances in agriculture for some countries can be met by pushing agricultural production in others above the limits of the IP scenario and closer to the HP scenario limits. Given the largely differing endowments among SADCC countries in land and water resources, this can be done easily with certain countries and for several commodities.

The scale of regional trade possibilities varies according to the time horizon. In the short term, Zimbabwe has the greatest potential, particularly for maize and wheat, although Malawi should be able to continue to compensate for at least part of the region's maize deficit. Until 2000 Zimbabwe is likely to remain the dominant surplus producer of maize, though in the very long term Angola and Mozambique could also contribute to regional needs. However, regional self-sufficiency in maize is not possible given present and projected demand patterns, but there are several options for reducing the size of the deficit, which has important implications for intra-regional trade. Part of the demand for maize could be replaced by encouraging rice consumption. In the short to medium term, Malawi and Zambia could supply part of any increased regional demand for rice. While in the longer term, though possibly not until beyond 2000, Angola could meet the deficits of the whole region. Similarly, substitution possibilities exist for using maize as livestock feed. Zambia and Angola, for example, have substantial potential for expanding cassava production, which could replace at least part of the feed demand for maize—as well as sorghum.

The trade situation for wheat is similar to that for maize. Zimbabwe is the only surplus producer of wheat, but would find it impossible to compensate for the whole of the region's present or projected deficit. However, the size of this deficit could be reduced by encouraging and expanding the use of composite flour. Cassava, maize, rice and soya flours can all be used to replace part of the wheat flour for bread. Such action could open new regional trade possibilities for these substitute flours.

In contrast to cereals, the sugar production potential exceeds likely regional demand. Botswana and Lesotho will continue to be in deficit and could be readily supplied by other members, such as Swaziland and Zimbabwe. Angola is also likely to remain in deficit, but again its neighbouring SADCC countries should be able to meet its needs.

Regional trade possibilities also exist for fruits and vegetables, but except in the case of dry pulses, such trade will be inhibited by poor road and rail links and the lack of specialized transport and storage. Consequently, such trade is likely to be a long-term, rather than a short- to medium-term feature.

The prospects for trade in livestock products, as with cereals, vary with the time horizon. At present, trade is primarily restricted to flows of beef from Botswana and Zimbabwe to Angola and Zambia. In the longer term, the former are likely to remain the dominant suppliers, but their surplus may decline because of increasing domestic demand. Relative to beef, all other trade flows in livestock products are likely to be small and restricted primarily to poultry, eggs and fish.

Examples of regional trade possibilities could be multiplied. Rationalization could create additional complementarities of production structures, while preventing individual countries from having surpluses or deficits of the same products at the same time. There is no doubt that the potential long-term rewards of regional specialization and trade are substantial, but they can not be secured through individual national efforts alone and require substantial regional planning and coordination.

In the meantime, a study should be launched of the agricultural complementarities of the region, including the relevant demand and cost structures, with a view to identifying the scope and measures required to expand intra-regional trade. A regional system should also be considered for the collection and dissemination of information on selected food commodities of intra-regional interest. The system could include forecasts and market intelligence on production, trade and prices, as well as other background information on trading policies and practices. The regional trade and marketing centre for fish, to be set up in Africa and already operational in Latin America and Asia, could be a suitable model.

Conclusion

For the SADCC countries regional integration means a severe struggle on all fronts. South Africa is a powerful enemy and is well-connected. In the past one of its advantages was that it was able to deal with its neighbours piecemeal. Economically it was the centre into which the regional periphery was being integrated, or more precisely, being subordinated. This was made possible by its objectively greater productive capacity and lower dependence on the outside for its basic needs. Its weakness is that it has always been a captive black labour force which staffs most of its industries.

To counteract the economic impact of South Africa, the SADCC countries will have to go beyond mere exchange relations. Integration through *production* will have to be their principal objective. Positive involvement of their labouring masses in such an effort will give them a political advantage over South Africa. In the light of the struggles ahead mass mobilization should be seen as absolutely crucial. If people are still faced with the more primitive question of food to appease their hunger, the problems of economic liberation let alone security can hardly be raised. This might apply *ipso facto* to individual nations. Therefore, if a political sellout on grounds of economic expediency is to be avoided, collective self-reliance must be taken to mean, among other things, acceptance of responsibility for one another. In times of particularistic nationalism, it is hard to preach regional nationalism. But regional insecurity and the threat to peace dictates the necessity.

Notes

1. With good prices and sales of diamonds in 1983, Botswana now has a sizeable surplus of foreign exchange.
2. Prepared for the Ministry of Agriculture of Zimbabwe by Technosynesis, Spa., Rome, June 1983.
3. Ratio of area harvested annually to total arable area.
4. The narrow definition excludes assistance for purposes such as forestry, rural development, rural infrastructures, agro-industries, fertilizer production and regional and river projects, which are included under the broad definition.
5. This does not include assistance from non-official sources and centrally planned developed countries.
6. SADCC, Proceedings of the 1984 Annual Southern African Development Coordination Conference, Gaborone, Botswana, 1984.

Part 4: Peace, Development and Security: Agenda for Action

12. Realizing Peace, Development and Regional Security in Africa: A Plan for Action

Okwudiba Nnoli

Peace is an important human value. And it has been so ever since the history of humanity began. In fact, it is so basic a value that it is a prerequisite for the attainment of other values. It is most commonly defined as the absence of violence in the political life of a society. This violence is often seen in terms of acts committed directly by persons against others, taking the forms of war or torture and actions by the police or the army to repress street demonstrations against the government. The consequences are so dramatic and significant that the pacifist liberal view of violence is that it is inherently evil. This viewpoint deprecates all violence on the grounds that it begets violence and, therefore, is operationally futile in terms of its objectives; that there is always access to a whole range of non-violent options which should first be exhausted in any dispute.

This pacific outlook, by absolutizing the concept of violence and war, provides aggressive circles within and outside Africa with a weapon with which to mystify and obscure the essence of the problem. By clearly avoiding the necessary distinction between aggressor and victim such a view loses all practical meaning as well as moral force. Frantz Fanon forcefully made this point when he extolled the violence of the colonized against the colonizer.

In reality, however, peace and violence are both forms of struggle. Political forces choose one or the other depending on what is necessary and possible in the light of the interests at stake. In other words, neither is an end in itself but each is governed by vital interests. Peace and violence are never in conflict as such. Only the vital interests of political forces are in conflict. And whether peace or violence will be used depends on the nature of that conflict, particularly whether it is unnecessary or impossible to use force to change or restore the balance between these interests.

Even a situation in which violence is absent may, in fact, be the result of dominance, initially by force but sustained later by propaganda, intimidation, blackmail, bribery and corruption. Under these circumstances structural violence prevails, usually visited on the powerless majority by the dominant minority. This form of violence is not direct. It is exerted through various channels that are not as immediately visible as war. At the external level structural violence may consist of the domination–dependency syndrome characteristic of imperialism in its various cultural, economic, political,

215

scientific, technological and other aspects. At the internal level it consists of all those systems which are characterized by the exploitation of people by people and, therefore, produce the alienation of the individual in the process of production. In such systems the social, economic, political and cultural processes also produce alienation because the individual is prevented from participating in the various processes of life that are necessary for integral development.

In other words, development is critical to overcoming structural violence which in turn may be crucial to eliminating direct violence. Structural violence is often based on a combination of exploitation and fragmentation of the majority, putting the latter at a disadvantage. Inevitably there are confrontations of the spokesmen of the majority with the authorities, including revolts, uprisings and civil wars which involve direct violence. Development is meant to raise the majority above the minimum conditions of existence and eliminate their disadvantages. By so doing it abolishes structural violence and the direct violence that emanates from it.

Development itself is first and foremost a phenomenon associated with humanity and creative energies. It is an unending improvement in the capacity of the individual and society to control the forces of nature as well as themselves and other individuals and societies for their own benefit and that of humanity at large. It is a process of actualizing people's inherent capacity to live a better and more rewarding life. It implies increasing skill and capacity, greater freedom, self-confidence, creativity, self-discipline, responsibility and material well-being. Since people extend and reproduce themselves socially through labour, development or qualitative self-improvement occurs when labour conditions improve. Through the cooperative use of such labour with others, people are able to transform their immediate physical and human environment. In normative terms, the concept of development may be formulated as the movement of the whole socio-economic and cultural system towards an ever larger measure of power to the people for conscious participation in building their own future, higher production for societal needs based upon non-exploitative relations of production and equitable principles of distribution and the maximum possible enjoyment by the producers in society of culture that is oriented towards their own reality, needs and aspirations in an aesthetically and ecologically sound environment.

If development is thus linked with peace, it is in another way linked to security, thereby linking peace with security. By the concept security we mean protection from both direct and structural violence. It may refer to the security of one state from another, one ruling class from another, the masses from its ruling class, the masses from a foreign ruling class or the masses from an alliance of the domestic and foreign ruling classes. That security which ignores the forces of change and development, which violates the aspirations of the great mass of the people cannot, in the long run, survive. On the other hand a developed society, as defined above, is the best guarantee against threats to the security of a people.

Such threats to the security of a country arise when another country decides to exploit its resources including the labour of its population; when two or more foreign countries struggle to dominate the exploitation of its resources; one or more foreign countries intervene in its local disputes; one or more foreign countries intervene in disputes with its neighbours and another country prevents it from obtaining some external resources that are vital to its survival. These threats to security may be adequately contained by a society whose development places maximum reliance on 1) the political power of the producer classes, the workers and peasants, concretized through every institutional means, formal and informal. In this respect, 'power to the people' is the prime mobilizing value for development; 2) a serve-the-people ethic; 3) self-reliance and autonomy in development; 4) social justice based on freedom from exploitation, with human relations of egalitarianism, cooperation and respect for work; 5) economic welfare for all in a society of abundance, with special attention to raising the level of life of marginalized groups (such as women and disadvantaged ethnic and social groups) and regions that have been resource-poor or historically oppressed; and 6) maximum cultural and aesthetic fulfilment, including full popular participation in the production of culture.

Thus the concepts peace, development and security form a web of interwoven relationships and processes. This is as it should be because they all address themselves to people's existence, happiness and liberation. In this web, peace as a value is a synthesis. It is the implementation of a number of inter-related values which advance the individual to a new and higher level of existence and security. It demands a measure of economic welfare, requires social justice, calls for participation and necessitates the creation of a harmonious relationship between people and nature, as well as between people and their own society and other societies. Peace presupposes the suppression of both direct and structural violence; but on the basis of a clear distinction between wars of aggression and wars of resistance and liberation.

The goal of achieving peace through development can only be a long-range one for many countries of the world, particularly those of Africa. In the short run, therefore, no contribution to peace is likely to emanate from a lofty even-handed condemnation of all wars and violence. This can only give aid and comfort to the subject of an aggressive war without deluding the victim of aggression. To condemn all wars without recognizing the need of victims of war and aggression to employ violence in pursuit of their liberation is unjust. Aggressive war is the beginning of all wars, and the most immediate way to discourage it is to defeat it. The logic is clear. If aggressive war is eliminated, how can there be defensive wars of liberation? Therefore, to eliminate war is essentially to eliminate aggressive war. To suggest that it can be done by eliminating liberation wars turns both human logic and human values upside down.

Direct Violence and Structural Violence: The State of the Continent

Imperialism of finance capital is the major purveyor of both direct and structural violence in Africa. It does so by sustaining an externally-oriented system of production, structurally linked to the advanced capitalist powers, which marginalizes the African economies and populations, by sustaining a minority petty bourgeois ruling class in power through foreign aid economically and military aid politically; this excludes the majority of the population from the benefits of production through political repression. The advanced capitalist powers intervene in African conflicts in support of forces oriented toward the maintenance of the imperialist structures of exploitation, albeit with minor and sometimes major reforms; this intensifies the violent aspects of these conflicts; they further offer all-round support for the violent and aggressive policies of the racist and apartheid regime in South Africa.

Economic Repression

Imperialism in the forms of colonialism and neo-colonialism created and has sustained in Africa dependent economies that are externally-oriented, dominated by foreign enterprises, have a high propensity to import and are therefore critically dependent on foreign exchange, subservient and passive in the international division of labour and encourage the export of funds from the African countries. Their dominant sectors, import-export business, wholesale trade, shipping, banking, insurance, mining and manufacturing industries do not address the domestic needs and habitual consumption patterns of Africa and do not primarily use local resources and skills in their production processes. The rural areas hardly benefit from developments in science and technology. And little indigenous science and technology is encouraged.

Such dependent economies do not permit the centralization of capital in the African country, the coordination of various enterprises by one centre within the nation or the elimination of the meaningless product differentiation that the domination of foreign enterprises generates. Consequently, they cannot provide the country with a full complement of skills, occupations and products or create a situation in which the benefits of the horizontal and vertical integration of a nation's economic activities by the headquarters of economic enterprises will accrue to the African country concerned. They are not geared to utilizing local resources to perform better and more easily the present economic tasks of the masses of the population. Hence they put no emphasis on food production, the provision of rural and urban housing, and the manufacture of drugs for such endemic diseases as malaria and gastro-enteritis or for childbirth and childcare or sanitation and preventive health services.

Thus the African masses are abandoned in the pit of ignorance, poverty, squalor and disease. They are crushed, degraded, disenchanted, blinded and divided by the inexorable power of imperial capital. They do not have enough to eat: the caloric content of their meals is usually below the minimum considered necessary by the UN. They cannot afford reasonable shelter for self and family. In the urban areas they usually pack themselves six to ten in one room. Associated with this urban living are high densities of building, over-crowding, lack of space for open-air living, the overspilling of domestic life, work and recreational activities into the streets, lack of light and ventilation, poor standards of building construction often connected with the use of non-durable materials, poor building maintenance, poor street lighting, if any, poor water supply, nightsoil and other waste removal and a lack of space for schools and other community and social facilities. Some people only find shelter in the manner of tramps and vagabonds in dugouts and under flyovers.

In the rural areas the masses live in windowless ramshackle mud huts which collapse with heavy rains. Most of them live from hand to mouth. Men, women and children have craggy skins, thin limbs and protuberant abdomens. They are certified victims of drought and preventable diseases which derive from malnutrition. Inside rural houses, men, women and children are herded together under conditions which defy the rules of hygiene, in conditions of life so poor that they prevent the realization of human potential. Some have little clothing or footwear and others have none at all.

The rural masses are destitute of medical services and good roads. Medical centres and hospitals are in short supply in the rural areas. Compounding this problem is the reluctance of medical personnel, especially doctors and nurses, to work in the villages. Consequently, the few such institutions that exist are staffed by those who have limited training but are frequently called upon to carry out unusually difficult tasks for which they are unqualified. Many times the rural poor are victims of patent medicine dealers, quasi-chemists, quack doctors and medicine-men. Leprosy afflicts them. There is a high maternal death-rate and high infant mortality.

The rural masses are compelled to use substandard transport. In the villages they must travel on foot and by bicycle most of the time because only footpaths and narrow roads are available. The few roads that exist are so bad that they can only be used during the dry season. Most of the goods transported within the villages are carried on the head from one location to another. And when the rural masses venture to the urban centres to sell some of their cash crops and handicrafts or buy some manufactured goods, they do so in 'mammy wagons' which carry both passengers and goods. There, they are crowded together like so many packs of sardines.

The poor majority in both the urban and rural areas live under conditions of permanent austerity which defy any sense of peace, justice and security. They have no savings and they lack access to credit facilities. Consequently, they cannot afford medical treatment. Primary education is largely inaccessible to their children because of the intolerable cost of clothes and books and the innumerable other financial burdens education generates. Education at the secondary level is only a very remote possibility.

Furthermore, the poor masses of Africa lack access to elementary social amenities and basic needs such as social security insurance, adequate provision for old age and simple recreational facilities for their children. Wives are often subjected to the most humiliating oppression and physical toil. We are talking here about the small and middle level subsistence farmers who inhabit the African villages and who constitute a high proportion of the total population, about rural-rural farm migrants, plantation workers, low-level salaried workers, day labourers, the unemployed, the underemployed such as street-hawkers, the petty artisans including roadside mechanics, motorcycle and bicycle repairers, blacksmiths, welders, masons, carpenters, nightsoilmen, petty traders, tramps, including touts at the airports and motor parks, beggars and lower class prostitutes.

Political Repression

Imperialism has sponsored some African social classes, particularly the petty, and comprador bourgeoisie, which have acquired vested interests in the system of national economic dependence and the consequent poverty and immiserization of the masses. They retain power by excluding the people from participation in the political and economic processes of their societies. The political tin gods, life presidents, political sit-tighters, ubiquitous one-party systems and military regimes, the muzzling of the press, arrest and detention without trial of political opponents, the disappearance of political dissenters soon afterwards—presumed dead—and the capricious desire to control what is read or taught in schools—singly or in various combinations. These characterize most African states and are an eloquent testimony to the exclusion of the masses from African politics.

Even where democratic participation by the masses in the election of their leaders is permitted, it soon becomes a farce. The political parties offer no structural transformation designed to overcome poverty and alleviate people's suffering. They have no objective interest in doing so. Such a transformation might abolish the basis of their power. They are content to muddle along with their strategy of import substitution, of which the present poverty of Africa is a result. All available evidence from other Third World countries with a longer history of neo-colonial development suggests that the import-substitution strategy of development inevitably reaches a dead end well before self-sustained economic growth has been achieved. Regional economic groupings such as ECOWAS, SADCC and EAC only delay the time of reaching the dead end; they do not provide the means to bypass it.

The almost religious adherence of the political parties to the strategy of import substitution, the obvious sterility of that strategy in the struggle against economic backwardness and their weakness or unwillingness to pursue the anti-imperialist struggle for economic liberation means that they must find appropriate methods of holding the population in check as their economic condition deteriorates. One of these means is the creation of political illusions. Today, African politicians are masters in the art of illusions. Experts of 'the more you look the less you see', they have converted all political campaigns into an intellectual fraud and a political illusion. They prevent the masses from coming to a true consciousness of themselves, of their position in society and of their own interests as people. Political campaigns in conjunction with government-owned mass media create a hypocritical situation in which the party in government hears only its own voice but surrenders to the illusion that it hears the voice of the people.

When the African political conjurer cannot fully count on the people's loyalty, he supplements illusions with intimidation, blackmail, bribery and election-rigging. Otherwise, he pours in money as an inducement. Still the politician does not fully trust the people—even after making them swear an oath to vote according to money received. Having spent so much money on bribery he is even more determined to win the elections, and probably plans to rig them. In Africa, political and electoral skills frequently boil down to the capacity to rig elections.

The truth of African politics, of course, is that the African petty bourgeois has no commitment to democracy and cannot tolerate political participation. Selfishness and inordinate ambition for power compel the petty bourgeois to view democratic values and institutions as luxuries which cannot be afforded. Arbitrariness in the exercise of power replaces respect for the people. Inevitably, the leader and the people drift apart under conditions of mutual mistrust. The leader trusts only himself, his blood relatives and a gang of petty bourgeois sycophants and philistines. Others become objects for control and manipulation. He abandons the search for legitimacy and relies on lies, intimidation, blackmail, bribery and naked force. Dissenters are crushed. Rivals are liquidated. The people dissolve into indifference and apathy. Any one who stands up for the truth and the masses is an enemy and must be bought or destroyed.

The leader arrogates to himself the mission of civilizing his people. For this he needs the skills, competence and fine distinctions of the expert, not the interference of the ignorant masses. The civil servants, technocrats and consultants now proceed to bury themselves in figures, diagrams, graphs and statistics rather than in the hearts of the people, as Fanon would say. The government assumes the task of supervising the masses. It becomes an administration, relying on the army and the police to control the people merely to exact loyalty and obedience from them. In this task the leader has the unambiguous support of the imperialist powers. The masses respond with occasional demonstrations, uprisings and revolts which are quickly and brutally suppressed. In the main, however, they behave like a flock of sheep and sing the praises of the regime. Their bitter disappointment, despair and anger only make themselves heard when the leader and the officials face the music of a military *coup d'etat*.

External Intervention

Prolonged foreign military intervention by the imperialist powers in the affairs of the African countries is the most important single threat to peace, development and security. It has included not only the open use of military force, as by France in Chad or the Central African Republic, but also various forms of covert military action such as the American funding of mercenaries to fight alongside FNLA and UNITA in Angola in 1975-6. It has occurred at two levels: with respect to conflicts involving internal parties in an African country and in conflicts between one African country and another. In both cases the ground has been prepared by the presence of the imperialist powers in the region, previously established as a result of colonialism and neo-colonialism. The goals are usually to avert a threat to Western investments and raw material supplies; to protect an indebted economy, whose default would disturb international financial markets; to shore up a client regime that is losing control because of a continuation of foreign dependence and its own internal corruption; to help this client regime to quell a popular uprising that threatens to sweep it away and to counter a perceived threat in a region from the socialist countries, particularly the Soviet Union.

The desire of the imperialist powers to continue to control activities in an African state, coupled with the complementary desire of the African ruling class to continue in power even at all costs explains external intervention in an internal conflict of an African state. Such interventions are made easier by domestic conditions of structural violence, conflict and instability which are caused by the mounting pressure for radical changes under conditions of multi-polar conflicts. The arbitrary nature of colonial boundaries has created horizontal cleavages within the African nations. These are usually based on ethnicity, race, religion, language and culture. In many cases these cleavages coincide with and reinforce each other in increasing the potential for conflict or the intensity of conflict. The crises that have characterized the post-colonial political histories of Nigeria, Zaire, Sudan and Uganda are illustrative. Foreign intenvention was a common feature of all of them.

The Shaba incidents of 1977-8 in Zaire are a particularly clear cut example of external intervention to protect the foreign economic interests of the imperialist powers. They took the form of joint military action by a number of NATO powers and African client states, together with attempts to restabilize the economy, with IMF experts seconded to the Zaire treasury. In Angola the Western powers have similarly intervened in an attempt to re-establish their economic domination of the country through UNITA and against the anti-imperialist regime of the MPLA. Similarly, external intervention in the current civil war in Mozambique is designed to force FRELIMO to make substantial concessions to foreign economic interests. And in Chad, the imperialist powers, spearheaded by French interventionary forces, are attempting to protect their interests in the area.

The external intervention in internal conflicts of African countries by the socialist countries is also real but of quite a different kind from that of the imperialist powers. It is usually in response to revolutionary processes as they unfold out of Africa's underdevelopment and external dependence. This does not mean that the motives of socialist countries are always pure The Soviet intervention in the Nigerian civil war on the side of the federal authorities was hardly motivated by consideration of revolutionary interests. Nevertheless, their intervention does not have the same kind of protective and preservative drive behind it as that of the West. It has tended to support causes with which the masses in Africa readily identify, especially in Southern Africa, and generally speaking it has respected the existing norms of the African inter-state system. As with the distinction between aggressive wars and wars of resistance, a distinction ought also to be made between external intervention against the masses of the people and external intervention in support of the masses. While the former is to be deprecated the latter is to be encouraged.

At the level of inter-state conflicts in Africa the Western powers have often intervened to support client states against more radical people-oriented regimes. On the other hand the socialist nations have supported the latter against the former. For example, the West has supported Morocco's attempt to annex Western Sahara against the wishes of the Polisario Front because of the former's pro-West role in relation to the Middle East and the radical character of the latter. In the Somalia–Ethiopia conflict over the Ogaden the USA has supported Somalia because of the latter's military facilities and proximity to the Persian Gulf as well as its recent anti-socialism, against Ethiopia's radical anti-imperialism, socialist orientation and friendship with the Soviet Union. In the conflict between Libya and Egypt, the USA has taken a hostile posture against Libyan radicalism and in favour of Egyptian moderation in the Middle East crisis. This posture has, in fact, been carried to the extent of direct US hostility against Libya which finally culminated in a US bombing raid against Libya in April 1985.

Apart from these conflicts that involve non-African intervention there have been others in which one African country has sought to intervene in the domestic affairs of another. Examples include the role of Ghana in the early 1960s and Libya at the present time in sharpening ideological differences within and between African states; the Ivory Coast's attempts to destabilize its radical neighbours in the 1960s; the consternation of some OAU members at the 1979 and 1980 coups from the lower ranks of the army in Ghana and Liberia; and the role of some of the conservative francophone African states in opposing the MPLA in Angola and supporting Mobutu in Zaire during the Shaba uprising. Tanzania participated in ousting Idi Amin from Uganda. Senegal intervened in Gambia. The arming of African states by external powers is becoming an important factor in such conflicts. African states are now acquiring the kinds of weapons that make war against other African states a feasible proposition.

External intervention disrupts the peace, development and security of the African continent. By introducing large-scale and sophisticated weapons of violence into Africa it widens the sphere of conflict. Second, by introducing weapons of mass destruction it leads to a greater loss of life and property in Africa. Third, by providing an almost inexhaustible source of arms supply it destroys the will to compromise thereby making large-scale violence inevitable and preventing violence from being brought to an end quickly. Fourth, it considerably weakens the country involved by diverting its attention away from other pressing problems, consuming its scarce resources of manpower and material and further reinforcing its dependence on foreign countries which adversely affects its economic emancipation. And fifth, it creates a culture of violence and repression which are destructive of morale, self-confidence and the creative potential of the majority of the population.

South African Aggression

The threat to peace, development and security in Africa posed by South Africa is both unique within Africa and part of the broader picture of external dependence and foreign intervention. South Africa is the only country in the modern history of Africa not only to perfect a monstrous system of structural violence but also to consciously and deliberately sanction it by law and to protect it by a conscious policy of military aggression against the neighbouring African states. It is unique in that there is a permanent threat to neighbouring African states from a state and military system physically located on the African continent itself. And it is part of the broader picture of dependence and external intervention because both the South African economy and military machine are to a large extent sustained by the imperialism of finance capital in return for gold and other valuable minerals from South Africa, the availability of cheap black labour and the latter's security value in controlling the Cape and South Atlantic sea routes. There is also the matter of Western tribalism which binds Europeans and Americans to their kith and kin in South Africa.

Apartheid, the cornerstone of the structural violence in South Africa, is a particularly vicious and dangerous form of human domination and oppression. Its central tenet, racism, is based on the false assumption that one person should rule another because of outwardly physical differences. More dangerous than colonialism, it thrives on group prejudice and therefore offers an easy escape from real life. It appeals to people's cowardice and prevents both the person who discriminates and the one discriminated against from living a full life or contributing to human progress.

The racist policies of South Africa are a daily affront to human dignity. The militant, consistent, unequivocal and intensely emotional opposition to these policies by African countries is a reflection of the latter's commitment to the principle of human dignity for blacks. Apartheid is highly provocative because it insults the dignity of Africans. Its existence is inimical to the internal security of African countries because it undermines their national efforts to achieve just, multiracial and multi-ethnic societies. By challenging an African nation's most fundamental principles of human equality and national self-determination apartheid poses a serious threat to law, order, and social stability in Africa.

Initially, Africa responded to apartheid by intense diplomatic pressure designed to isolate South Africa and shock it into a realization of the untenability of its policies and, therefore, cause it to make the necessary changes. Africans also sought to mobilize world opinion against apartheid and to pressure world leaders into applying arms embargoes and economic sanctions. The emphasis at the time was on avoiding bloodshed. But the apartheid war-machine continued its rapid expansion. Society became increasingly militarized. Although an arms embargo has been in force against South Africa, it has continued to acquire military technology, including nuclear technology, from the West. And that racist enclave is the only country on the continent with a substantial military production and a research and development capacity of its own. It soon became clear that only military confrontation could shake the racists out of their arrogant intransigence.

As guerrilla war inside the territory has increased and intensified, state repression against blacks has likewise intensified. The system of structural violence is being expanded. South Africa has been conducting an undeclared war against Mozambique and Angola in an attempt to browbeat them into abandoning support for the guerrilla war raging inside the citadel of apartheid and in Namibia. Raids carried out without compunction into these two neighbouring territories, and South African support for puppet guerrilla movements in both countries, are the major instruments in this war. The pressure has, however, been intense enough to compel Mozambique to sign the Nkomati Accords and Angola to seek some accommodation with the racist regime.

Agenda for Action I: Strategic Recommendations

Just as development is central to the problem of peace and security in Africa, only a development strategy that is fundamentally antagonistic to economic dependence and external control of African economic activities will usher in peace, development and regional security in Africa. Such a strategy can only come about from a consistent struggle for national economic independence. The major task here is to transform those structures of the economy that tend to reinforce the African nations external economic orientation, high propensity to import and a subservient and passive role in the international division of labour and focus production on domestic needs and habitual consumption patterns, so that these can be satisfied primarily by the use of local resources and skills.

The central aim of this structural reorganization of the economy will be to set up an economic system which will permit the centralization of capital in an African state, coordination of the various enterprises by one centre within the nation and the elimination of the meaningless production differentiation that domination by foreign enterprises generates. In time it will provide the country with a full complement of skills, occupations, and products and create a situation in which the benefits of the horizontal and vertical integration of the nation's economic activities will accrue to Africa.

Countries will then be able to control and coordinate the primary, secondary, and tertiary economic processes of their natural resources. This will stimulate an increased capacity to transform and adapt the structures of production to changing demands and conditions. African countries can then focus attention primarily, but not exclusively, on domestic resources and priorities for the accomplishment of national objectives. By so doing they will bring all their potential local resources into productive use and into the mainstream of economic life, enabling societies to maximize the benefits accruing from those of its resources where they enjoy a comparative advantage over others, including benefits from scientific and technological research, final products and their marketing.

It is under such conditions rather than those where the more advanced stages of the products, such as elaboration, production, marketing and research take place in foreign countries, that the economy can become flexible, dynamic and capable of adapting to changing conditions. Such an economy is essential in any programme to end permanent and temporary austerity. This is because the neo-colonial economies of the African states are rigid and inefficient structures which encourage the transfer of potential savings abroad. Flexibility coupled with efficiency of the production process leads to a high degree of scientific and technological capacity, as well as to a certain degree of economic specialization; these are powerful forces making for progressive transformation of the productive forces.

In order to be true to the objective of economic independence such a restructured economy must aim primarily to utilize local resources to satisfy the needs of the rural population. This will mean an emphasis on food production, the provision of rural housing and the manufacture of drugs for such endemic diseases as malaria and gastro-enteritis, as well as for childbirth, childcare, sanitation and preventive health services. All national resources must justify themselves in terms of their contribution to the success of this pattern of production rather than in terms of increases in foreign exchange, export production and abstract GDP. What is needed to make such a programme successful is a long-term view of production in which the rural areas become the social and institutional framework through which indigenous science and technology are developed and applied to agricultural and other forms of production.

In addition, the state must intervene to eliminate or, at least, ameliorate the effects of those forces which prevent the individual from contributing the maximum to production. Among them are poor health, ignorance and poverty. A sterile and self-serving argument is often put forward that social progress in these areas runs counter to economic progress because an attempt to divert funds from the rich to social services for the majority will reduce the potential accumulation fund. But the experience of the socialist countries explodes this myth. In fact, the bulk of the incomes of the rich in Africa, especially of the trading, usurious, finance, banking, contracting and even manufacturing elements, is utilized for non-productive consumption. This enables the rich to live in luxury at the level of ultra-modern Western standards. It is this pattern of life that sharply reduces the potential accumulation fund and also creates a home market unfavourable to economic growth.

Such social progress is possible, provided that the living standard of all segments of the population and the real wages of the working people do not as a rule increase, for any considerable time, faster than the increase in production and the productivity of labour. The standard of living must not run ahead of the expansion of production but must follow, keeping a certain distance behind it. Only the observance of this condition can ensure the harmony between the economic and social aspects of development which will turn social progress into a motive force for economic growth. Progressive legislation ensuring the maximum removal of non-productive incomes for the purpose of national development and shifting the burden of this development on to the propertied wealthy classes, is in line with principles of natural justice and as such does not represent the expropriation of property in productive capital.

There are several ways of putting into practice this policy of social progress. They include radical land reforms which release the tiller of the soil from the oppression of the big landowners, capitalist farmers and merchants, as well as usurious capital; the establishment and strengthening of a network of cooperatives capable of defending the ordinary producer from market anarchy and rapacious exploitation by traders, money lenders and the monopolies. Others include the implementation of progressive labour legislation, including measures that would assure full social insurance for the working people. Such insurance should include all wage-earners, as well as the rural and urban poor and must provide for all cases of disability such as illness, accidents, permanent disablement and old age; compensation of full earnings in case of disability and the full democratization of social security. The social security system must embrace all the working population of the country; it must be comprehensive and include not only pensions for old people but also a system of disability benefits, mother and child protection and free medical aid.

Another crucial aspect of this progressive social policy is the assurance by the state of a system of full, comprehensive and free education based on uniform, free, and secular schools which are easily accessible. The state must assure the right to health protection through an extensive network of hospitals and polyclinics, dispensaries and a large contingent of doctors and other medical workers. The state must provide the necessary material conditions for enjoying the right to leisure, housing, as well as the right to enjoy cultural benefits, and freedom of scientific, technical and artistic work. Finally, civil, land and labour laws should be used to consolidate and expand the individual's civil rights, including the right to work the land.

Since part of the problem of the low productivity of the African worker is the result of alienation from the labour process, it is necessary to overcome this alienation and, therefore, increase production by workers' participation in management, worker's supervision of management, and eventually workers' self-management of production enterprises. Such a democratic participation at the production level will stimulate the workers to great creativity. It will also awaken their latent energy and desire to work harder and better, exploit resources and working time and generally improve the production process. The worker's consequent loyalty to the production enterprise will serve not only to improve his own labour input; the worker will also be deeply concerned that colleagues work well too. Together with them a worker will search for unexplored and unexploited ways to raise productivity and improve the results of common labour.

Similarly, at the political level, the people as a whole must take the initiative in politics. They must control the decision-making processes and decide what is produced, how and why and how the products are to be distributed. Only in this way will the economic and political dimensions of economic progress complement and mutually support each other. Only the pressure of the vast number of the toiling masses applied through their mobilization and active participation in the supervision of agricultural, commercial and industrial enterprises and supported by their organized political power is capable of tilting the balance of power between poverty and economic liberation in favour of the latter.

If the people's direct involvement in politics is thus inescapable, it must be politics of a fundamentally different kind than that practised by the present African leaders. The new African leaders must see the new politics no longer as a way of bamboozling the people or lulling them to sleep but as the only method of preparing them to undertake the governing of their country and the production of their means of livelihood. They must rid themselves of the false colonial notion that the masses are incapable of governing themselves. Experience has shown that the masses understand perfectly the most complicated problems of government and production if explained to them in everyday language and that the leaders have a lot to learn from the people. Thus, in the new politics, the masses should be able to meet together often with their leaders, discuss with them and propose as well as receive directions. At all times the people must know where they are going, how and why. Such a continuous programme of explanation is necessary because the people's struggle for economic progress and social justice is a long one. It is not the taking of one bold giant step. One of the tasks of the masses is to hold the fort against any attempt by the leaders to shrink from achieving the goals.

Under the new political dispensation, the unorganized efforts of the masses can only be a temporary dynamic. Neither stubborn courage nor fine slogans can be a substitute for organization. The masses must form themselves into viable organizations that unite in one political movement. Such a movement uniting the various organizations of the masses must be motivated and directed by their interests, dominated and guided by these organizations, devoted to the implementation of progressive policies and protected by an army that would have been transformed from an inherited colonial institution to a veritable people's defence force committed to progressive change.

Finally, this movement of the people can only succeed in maintaining peace, bringing about development and ensuring regional security in Africa if it is built around a programme with clear objectives and a definite methodology. There must be an economic programme. And there must be a doctrine on the division of wealth and associated social relations. Indeed, there must be an idea of people and of the future of humanity. A social programme concerning the division of national wealth is particularly important although the masses are usually willing to sacrifice everything for the nation, they have to be encouraged, especially in the sphere of the distribution of material welfare. A fair system of the distribution of this welfare will stimulate an upsurge in the people's patriotic zeal as well as in their labour enthusiasm and creative powers. Until the African masses are put squarely back into history, the search for peace, development and regional security in Africa can not even begin. Until the problems on their path to unity and organization are resolved that search can only lead up a blind alley. And until their victory is achieved the struggle for peace with justice in Africa will continue to be waged. Meanwhile, poverty, political repression, external intervention, South African racism and aggression persist.

Agenda for Action II: Tactical Recommendations

The Demilitarization of African States

Apart from the special case of apartheid South Africa which will be discussed later, the military in Africa should be weakened in two fundamental ways: by attacking it directly through serious proposals to limit arms flow into the African states and through legal frameworks that challenge state prerogatives to resort to violence. The arming of African states is an increasingly important factor in conflict. They are now acquiring the kinds of weapons that make war against one another a feasible proposition. For most of the African states this competitive militarization is senseless and wasteful of resources; and it deepens their dependence on international arms suppliers. An African summit meeting on disarmament to limit the armaments of the various countries of Africa and give practical and effective priority to the political mechanisms for resolving conflicts in Africa should be convened by the OAU.

The military system should be attacked indirectly by seeking to weaken its underlying causes, particularly the acute deprivation throughout Africa which is sustained by structures of domination designed to legitimate and perpetuate existing patterns of inequality within and across the states of the world. These conditions can be changed through the creation of a new socioeconomic order which facilitates equality and redistribution among states; and permits wider participation in decision-making processes within the Africa state, protects basic human rights and promotes social justice.

In order to implement this programme at the inter-state level the following recommendations are put forward: 1) the creation of a conscious policy of reducing imbalances in the terms of trade of the African states. African countries export their raw materials and primary products to the advanced capitalist states at increasingly lower prices relative to rising costs of their manufactured imports. This unfavourable balance combined with the exploitation of the supply of cheap labour in poor African countries produces a net transfer of resources from the continent to the outside world; 2) concerted action by raw materials producers in Africa and the Third World to obtain higher prices for their products in the world market; 3) limiting receipts of external loans and grants to funds which are clearly beneficial to the African country, do not distort domestic priorities and are not tied to purchases from the donor countries; 4) curtailing, monitoring and supervising the activities of the foreign multinational corporations operating in Africa with a view to ensuring that they operate on the basis of the interest of the African country, particularly with respect to the development of local research capacity to utilize local resources in the service of local needs and traditional consumption habits.

At the domestic level, the following recommendations are suggested: 1) the establishment of the right to food in all African states. In the light of the famine and hunger which have been ravaging Africa for some years now this policy should be given the highest priority. While long-term remedies are sought in structural solutions, the right of every African to adequate food must not be left to the charitable impulses of nations fortunate enough to have a food surplus. A food-first programme is the best place to start the struggle for peace, development and security in Africa. 2) A programme of income redistribution which favours low income groups. This may be implemented by a progressive taxation system, progressive limitation of the fringe benefits and perquisites enjoyed by the high income groups, progressive abolition of the earning of more than one salary by the same person, limitation of increases in wages and salaries at high incomes, increasing control over sources of income with a view to eliminating ill-gotten wealth, reduction in the rural-urban income gap by controlled location of industries in the rural areas, reduction in the differential between profits on the one hand and the income available for distribution as wages and salaries on the other, maintenance of relative price stability and in general the reduction of the real purchasing power of the high income groups. 3) Distribution of social services and the benefits of development on a broad basis. Of interest here is a popular mass-oriented programme of education, health, employment, housing, transport, drinking water supply and social security benefits. 4) Measures that would assure every citizen universal, equal and direct suffrage with secret ballot; inviolability of the individual and the home; freedom of conscience, speech, the press, meetings, strikes and association; freedom of movement and crafts; the elimination of social inequality based on sex, religion, race or nationality; the right of every individual to bring action against any civil servant in the usual manner before a court of law; the separation of the church from the state, and the school from the church; and the elimination of torture and cruelty against political prisoners.

Any programme for the demilitarization of Africa must include a clear cut policy for combating external intervention in African conflicts. The following recommendations are suggested in connection with this policy: 1) a network of regional non-aggression and defence pacts of the type agreed on in principle by the Economic Community of West African States (ECOWAS), with specific provisions against external intervention in African conflicts; 2) denial of bases, military facilities, or military overflying rights to foreign powers; 3) agreement among the African states under the auspices of the OAU to deny or threaten to deny strategic raw material supplies to the intervening powers; 4) an OAU-supervised dismantling of neo-colonial military arrangements by certain African states which were designed to prevent the overthrow of their regimes; 5) strict political controls over the political activities of the external linkage groups in Africa such as the foreign companies through which external intervention is facilitated.

Combating South African Aggression

At the global level, no moral issue commands such widespread assent as the campaign to compel the elimination of apartheid from the life of South Africa. There is no support any longer in the world for the notion that an ethnically alien and numerically small white population is entitled to monopolize power, prestige and wealth in South Africa. Changing the situation in South Africa will require tough action, as well as tough rhetoric. The liberation successes against Portuguese colonialism were a big step; but more needs to be done particularly because the United States and the other Western powers have strong vested economic and strategic interests that commit them to upholding the essential status quo.

The following actions against South Africa are recommended:

1) Concerted action to support the continuing armed liberation struggles in Namibia and South Africa in order to weaken still further South Africa's position in the sub-system of Southern Africa and eventually to overthrow the apartheid system in South Africa itself. The South African problem is the one instance in Africa where there seems to be a clear case for dealing with a military threat by military means. And the armed guerrilla struggle is the best form that this military action can take.

2) Concerted action to support the frontline states of Mozambique and Angola with arms and financial resources with which to continue to play their roles of tactical rear-base areas for the guerrilla movements fighting South Africa. In this regard every effort should be made to reverse the trend which has led to the Nkomati Accords; and Zimbabwe should be encouraged to assume its historical role of a tactical base area in the struggle against South Africa.

3) Concerted African action to reconcile the rival liberation movements and thus increase their effectiveness. Such effectiveness may also be increased by concerted diplomatic action for a worldwide recognition of these movements that will help to provide them with international respectability and easy access to external resources.

4) The use of diplomacy and propaganda to increase the isolation of South Africa and strengthen international sanctions designed to weaken it.

5) To increase the solidarity of the Southern African liberation movements with others similarly engaged in just struggles to eliminate oppression. This will enable them to share experiences and benefit from each others' experiences.

6) Concerted African and, indeed, world effort to encourage action in the United Kingdom, France and the United States to expose, weaken and break the economic and arms supply links to the present South African government.

7) Concerted African and worldwide action to delegitimize the racist government's claim to represent South African society in international institutions or elsewhere.

8) Concerted African and worldwide action to identify apartheid as a crime against humanity and to hold its perpetrators accountable as potential war criminals.

Conclusion

In conclusion, whether or not peace with justice will be realized in Africa, and when, will depend on the balance of forces between those committed to a progressive change of the social order in Africa and those whose vested interests compel them to defend the status quo that is fraught with direct and structural violence. The existence of these latter social forces and the difficulties which they create point to the fact that peace, development, and regional security in Africa must be seen essentially as political values which are opposed to the interests of powerful social forces that are internal and external to Africa and which seek to perpetuate the socio-political and economic order inherited from the colonial period.

Peace with justice must be defined not in terms of any abstract identification of what is necessary and sufficient to bring it about but by the pattern and progress of this struggle against reactionary forces. In other words, peace is essentially a value which hangs on the balance of forces between patriotism and foreign domination with the patriotic forces attempting to close the barriers against foreign control of African development and to create conditions in which foreign intervention in African affairs would be controlled, if not totally eliminated.

However, although the struggle for peace with justice at this historical period must address itself first and foremost to the political struggle, it cannot succeed unless the political struggle is also coupled with the economic struggle, the technological struggle and the struggle in general for the transformation of the productive forces. Unless this is done the tendency will be to win the political struggle but not to have the economic capability to sustain that victory. Inevitably, such a fragile success will collapse, setting back the cause of peace with justice.

As a historical phenomenon the struggle for peace, development and security in Africa must advance in stages. As a historical struggle it must be determined, and can only be determined, by the character of progress within it. This means that at a certain point the patriotic forces may retreat. At other times they may advance. But the times when they retreat and when they advance can only be dictated by the conditions of the struggle. In other words, there cannot be a blueprint created or producced by academics or politicians on the basis of which a once-and-for-all solution to the problems of peace may be found. There cannot be a blueprint designed and, on the basis of good will or patriotism, implemented in such a way as to solve all the problems in the path of the search for justice in Africa. A useful first step in approaching the task would be to build an Africa-wide social movement around support for peace with justice in Africa, develop strategies for such a movement and use it to connect short-term issues and policy recommendations with a long-term strategy of global reform.

Index

OLF	Oromo Liberation Front
OPEC	Organization of Petroleum Exporting Countries
PAC	Pan-Africanist Congress of Azania
PTA	Preferential Trade Area for Eastern and Southern Africa
RDA	*Rassemblement Démocratique Africain*
SACU	Southern African Customs Union
SADCC	Southern African Development Coordination Conference
SADR	Sahrawi Arab Democratic Republic
SPLM	Sudanese People's Liberation Movement
SWAPO	South West African People's Organisation
TPLF	Tigrayan People's Liberation Front
UDEAC	Customs and Economic Union of Central Africa
UDF	United Democratic Front
UNCTAD	United Nations Conference on Trade and Development
UNIDO	United Nations Industrial Development Organization
UNITA	Union for the Total Independence of Angola
WSLF	Western Somali Liberation Front

civil war 46, 47
Tshombe, Moise 68, 72
Tutu, Desmond 49, 104, 114

Uccialli, Treaty of 89
UDEAC 130, 135
Uganda: conflict with Baganda 67-8;
    military coups 44, 71, 79; Soviet
    military assistance 13; & war with
    Tanzania 12, 14, 127, 223
UNITA 46, 221, 222
United Kingdom: involvement in South
    Africa 231
United Nations: 145, 146, 147, 148, 149,
    150, 151; & ECA 131. 132. 138, 144; &
    role in Congo 41, 73
UNCTAD 11, 132
USA: & American Rapid Deployment
    Force 94; & arms to South Africa 231;
    & bombing of Libya 223; &
    'constructive engagement' 110; &
    investment in South Africa 107;
    military aid/assistance/agreements/
    bases in Africa 13, 90, 94; mercenaries
    221; objectives in Southern Africa 102,
    107-13; & Somalia 223

Western Sahara: & conflict 10, 12, 13, 14,
    127; & Morocco 79, 223; & OAU 55, 80
WSLF 91, 92
World Bank 8, 9, 11, 18, 35-6, 42, 95

Zaire 12, 13, 18, 222
Zambia 109
Zimbabwe 103, 105, 108, 231